CLASS ANALYSIS *and* SOCIAL TRANSFORMATION

SOCIOLOGY *and* SOCIAL CHANGE

Series Editor: *Alan* **Warde, University of Manchester**

Published titles

Gail **Hawkes** – *A* **Sociology** *of* **Sex** *and* **Sexuality**

Colin **Hay** – **Re-stating Social** *and* **Political Change**

Andy **Furlong** *and Fred* **Cartmel** – **Young People** *and* **Social Change**

Máirtín **Mac an Ghaill** – **Contemporary Racisms** *and* **Ethnicities**

Mike **Savage** – **Class Analysis** *and* **Social Transformation**

CLASS ANALYSIS *and* SOCIAL TRANSFORMATION

Mike **Savage**

Open University Press
Buckingham · Philadelphia

Open University Press
Celtic Court
22 Ballmoor
Buckingham
MK18 1XW

email: enquiries@openup.co.uk
world wide web: www.openup.co.uk

and
325 Chestnut Street
Philadelphia, PA 19106, USA

First Published 2000

A catalogue record of this book is available from the British Library

ISBN   0 335 19327 7 (pb)   0 335 19328 5 (hb)

Library of Congress Cataloging-in-Publication Data
Savage, Mike, 1959–
    Class analysis and social transformation / Mike Savage.
      p. cm. – (Sociology and social change)
    Includes bibliographical references and index.
    ISBN 0-335-19328-5 – ISBN 0-335-19327-7 (pbk.)
    1. Social classes. 2. Social change. 3. Equality. 4. Class consciousness. 5. Social mobility. I. Title. II. Series.
    HT609.S28 2000
    05.5–dc21   00-037510

Typeset by Graphicraft Limited, Hong Kong
Printed in Great Britain by St Edmundsbury Press Ltd, Bury St Edmunds, Suffolk

Contents

Series editor's preface

In response to perceived major transformations, social theorists have offered forceful, appealing, but contrasting accounts of the predicament of contemporary Western societies. Key themes emerging have been frequently condensed into terms like postmodernism, postmodernity, risk society, disorganized capitalism, the information society. These have important and widespread ramifications for the analysis of all areas of social life and personal well-being. The speculative and general theses proposed by social theorists must be subjected to evaluation in the light of the best available evidence if they are to serve as guides to understanding and modifying social arrangments. One purpose of sociology, among other social sciences, is to marshal the information necessary to estimate the extent and direction of social change. This series is designed to make such information, and debates about social change, accessible.

The focus of the series is the critical appraisal of general, substantive theories through examination of their applicability to different institutional areas of contemporary societies. Each book introduces key current debates and surveys of existing sociological argument and research about institutional complexes in advanced societies. The integrating theme of the series is the evaluation of the extent of social change, particularly in the last twenty years. Each author offers explicit and extended evaluation of the pace and direction of social change in a chosen area.

In this volume, Mike Savage offers an authoritative and incisive review and critique of recent work on social class. The sociological tradition made the working class the main point of reference, a serious handicap in the face of the dissolution of working-class culture and politics. An alternative approach to class analysis is envisaged, one which is neither a form of grand narrative nor a narrow technical specialism. Instead, class, in its lived complexity, can be used as a lens for viewing institutional change. At the centre of recent transformations is the recasting of the ideal of individual autonomy by the middle classes, most prominently in the form of projects of the self, which, although presented in populist form, is alien to and exclusive of people in less privileged positions. Cultural aspects of class relations are revolutionized. *Class Analysis and Social Transformation* develops a highly distinctive and extremely interesting argument about contemporary social change which is pursued with empirical reference to patterns of inequality, social mobility, change in industrial organization and careers, etc. This book is a fine contribution to the sociological analysis of contemporary social and institutional change.

Alan Warde

Preface *and* acknowledgements

Over the past decade the relevance of social class has been the subject of serious dispute. For some writers, the idea of class harks back to a now departed 'modern' age, and the development of new kinds of social relationships encompassed by a post-industrial, post-modern, consumer society spells the end of class (e.g. Pahl 1989; Beck 1992; Clark *et al.* 1993; Pakulski and Waters 1996). Others insist on the persistence of social class and point to the power of entrenched social class inequalities to shape life chances (e.g. Goldthorpe and Marshall 1992; Breen and Rottman 1995). This dispute involves academic sociologists, as well as journalists and politicians. It touches a nerve. This book is an attempt to take stock of this dispute and to rethink class analysis as a means of understanding contemporary social change.

My argument in this book is that class analysis can be detached from its 'modern' origins and recast in ways that demonstrate its continued relevance. But this is no easy task. Such is the embeddedness of class analysis within modernist intellectual frames that a major rethinking of the scope and nature of class analysis is necessary. After all, class analysis did develop as one of the principal tools in the legislative armoury of the 'modern' intellectual. Governments of all political persuasions passed laws in the name of class. Social movements have mobilized around the banner of class. Social scientists incorporated theories of class into their accounts of the nature of modern social relationships. The idea of social class became inextricably tied up with moral claims about right and wrong. Today, in so far as there are reasons to suppose that this legislative project has breached its own limits (see, notably, Bauman 1988, 1991), it is necessary to tease out how the scope of class analysis needs to be changed. If the ambivalence that Bauman sees at the heart of social life cannot be eliminated, but only funnelled and contained to burst back in unanticipated ways, then the very idea of class is questioned. Since the ordering which lies at the heart of the modern legislative project – and to which the concept of class has been attached – has been exposed to thorough critique, it remains necessary to reflect on whether class analysis can be thought through in different ways.

In developing my account, I draw on recent arguments of writers such as Rosemary Crompton, David Lockwood and John Scott who note the real problems in current research and call for the reformulation of class analysis around different methodological and theoretical axes (e.g. Crompton 1998). I emphasize the deep intellectual problems that class analysis in any of its current forms faces. I stress that we have learned a great deal from recent research in class analysis, and in this respect my book has a very different tone to some of the writings in sociology which trumpet the 'end of class'. Nonetheless, it is only when we fully understand the deep problems of all modes of contemporary class analysis that it becomes possible to face up to the inadequacy of hanging onto outdated intellectual tools. This is a necessary precondition to allowing us to develop a critical, *interpretative* analysis of class and stratification.

While this book seeks theoretical engagement with currents in class analysis, I also seek to conduct my argument empirically. Recent debates in class analysis tend to have been pitched at an abstract level which rarely engages directly with empirical debates about contemporary social or cultural change. Strategies for empirical research in class analysis are encased within carefully architectured deductive frameworks that have insulated class analysis research from other branches of empirically focused sociology which work from different premises. As Crompton (1998) points out, it is a striking feature of recent work in class analysis that only specific kinds of empirical evidence are deemed to be relevant to the class analysis project. This book seeks out a fuller engagement with the wide range of empirical research carried out on diverse areas of social and cultural life (particularly using British data). If class analysis is to be relevant not only to the relatively small number of people who specialize in it, but to a broader church of sociologists and social scientists, there need to be more effective ways of drawing out the implications of different kinds of empirical research for class analysis.

A subsidiary aim is to encourage a fuller critical dialogue between class analysis and a broader range of contemporary social theory. Those emphasizing the power of class tend to stress continuity and persistence, and are sceptical of the idea that dramatic social change has occurred – certainly not on a scale to seriously disrupt entrenched processes of class inequality.[1] Much contemporary social theory, by contrast, has highlighted the scope and scale of contemporary social change, and a series of conceptual approaches have been proposed to model epochal social change.[2] It is no easy matter to stage a debate between class analysts on the one hand and theorists of social change on the other because of the very different methodological and theoretical frameworks on which they draw, with the consequent danger that the different camps talk past each other.[3] Nonetheless, it is imperative that some attempt to engage in dialogue is developed so that a balanced account which explores continuity and change can be developed which allows a more nuanced perspective on contemporary social and cultural change than is currently on offer.

The ultimate test for the future of class analysis is to see whether it can renew itself, not by defensive action from entrenched positions, but by being able to go out and speak to diverse currents of social inquiry. There are submerged traditions of class analysis, concerned with examining the interplay between diverse facets of social and cultural life, which define an intellectual space that class analysis can usefully inhabit in the future. Because the concept of class was historically defined in legislative ways, it tried to impose order across diverse domains of intellectual inquiry. This process inevitably involved cross-disciplinary modes of analysis. Much of the merit of class analysis, in its traditional form, lay less in the analysis of social class itself, but more in the intellectual space it opened up which acted as a counter to academic specialization, and which offered the potential for empirically informed critical analysis. It was therefore possible to synthesize and integrate understandings of diverse aspects of social life by using the idea of class as a bridge. The concept of class was not unique to a particular academic discipline: sociologists, political scientists, geographers, specialists in social policy, philosophers, historians, art historians, literary critics, linguistic theorists and so on could all use it. The concept also allowed some kind of intellectual exchange between academic and non-academic bodies, and could successfully link debates around policy and political issues to broader academic concerns. There is a potential within the class analysis tradition to switch attention away from class itself as the kind of organizing 'master category', towards the diverse contextual fields on which the concept operates. This allows us to champion older elements of class analysis as a critical buffer against recent, more narrowly defined approaches to class.[4]

The tradition of social research which nourished class analysis remains an invaluable critical resource. If this tradition is lost with the concept of social class, one of the main intellectual spaces for critical social inquiry also disappears. I define this space as one of critical empirical research, closely allied to a hermeneutic concern with the interplay between social meanings and values and the everyday contexts of work, place and environment. A central component is to interpret contexts relationally – that is to say, by showing how cultures and meanings are linked to power and inequality. The concept of class need not, itself, play any crucial role in this intellectual endeavour – indeed, sidelining the concept of class may help to re-energize and renew it. However, the broader perspective is one that needs to be kept alive.

I advance three major claims about how class analysis can be re-energized. First, I argue that an adequate approach to class needs to confront the role of culture in class analysis. I champion a cultural mode of class analysis that draws inspiration from Bourdieu's account of *habitus*, distinction and cultural capital. Bourdieu's work is of course already well-known, though there continues to be hostility to it from some champions of class analysis (e.g. Goldthorpe 1996). In this book I defend Bourdieu's broad approach but claim that he does not adequately address the resources that have historically been attached to working-class and popular culture, at least in Britain. In developing this argument I seek to reassert E.P. Thompson's famous refrain about the need to recognize the formative role working-class culture has played in the creation of British culture.[5]

Second, I draw upon the idea of individualization developed by Beck (1992) and Giddens (1991) to examine how class relations operate through individualizing processes, and in order to consider the nature of contemporary changes in relationships between working-class and middle-class culture.

Whereas Beck and Giddens see individualization as breaking from collective class cultures, my argument will be that class cultures are powerful through being individualized in various, historically specific, ways. I emphasize that we need to fully eradicate the lingering view that classes are inherently collective agents. The strength of working-class culture in Britain lay in large part in the way it appropriated a particular understanding of the autonomous, male, individual. The last three decades has seen a subtle reworking of the relationship between class, masculinity and the individual so that a form of 'self-developmental' individualization, premised on particular kinds of middle-class employment relations, has come to define a new mode of individual identity. What Giddens and Beck read as the decline of class cultures and the rise of individualization should better be understood as the shift from working-class to middle-class modes of individualization.

Third, I argue that class analysis can do much, at the middle range, by considering the role of organization. Class analysis has tended to focus on the occupational and property basis of class. However, changing organizational processes lie at the heart of the reworking of class relations. My starting point here is Erik Olin Wright's (1985) emphasis on the role of organization assets in class stratification. In earlier work (Savage *et al.* 1992) I argued that the restructuring of organizations was of vital importance in the remaking of the contemporary middle class. In this book I retreat somewhat from the formalism in Wright's arguments, and develop a more fluid approach to organizational process and class, in order to show how organizational restructuring has involved the redefinition of boundaries between working and middle classes.

In developing these arguments, I seek to offer a way of understanding contemporary economic, social and cultural change that recognizes the extent of social transformation but does not exaggerate it.[6] Class analysis has the potential to offer much more nuanced and sophisticated accounts of social change than do many contemporary accounts. For instance, despite Giddens' claims about the reflexive feedback (the 'double hermeneutic') between academic research and 'lay' conceptions, as well as the claims of post-modernists concerning the limits of 'enlightenment' knowledge, such arguments have been largely developed and nourished by academics, rather than as ideas which develop more dialogically out of debates and concerns from both academic *and* non-academic worlds.[7] The kinds of empirical research programmes that flow from these general claims are also highly underspecified. Sceptics might claim that these ideas are indeed designed to be unfalsifiable. A mode of class analysis can be developed that takes seriously arguments about social change but empirically grounds them.

The structure of this book

I have structured this book in a way that allows those with an interest in the broader intellectual agenda I have sketched above, as well as those with more specific interests in the particular topics I examine, to make use of the book. The chapters are each designed to be relatively self-contained discussions of specific theoretical or empirical issues in class analysis. The chapters are organized into two different parts. The chapters in Part 1 lay out what I see as the impasse of class analysis and review theoretical and empirical issues in the broad tradition of stratification research in order to demonstrate some of the limitations of existing work. The chapters in Part 2 are more speculative. They take forward the claims about cultural distinction, individualization, and organization that I see as being central to the renewal of class analysis. Part 1 is therefore critical in tone and covers established areas of research, while Part 2 tries to be more constructive and explores new and emerging domains of inquiry. In all chapters except the first I develop an account of changing class relationships (focusing on Britain, but with various other examples to aid comparative reflection) which attempts to show how my arguments make sense of contemporary social transformation.

In Chapter 1 I examine the contemporary difficulties of the classical class theory of Marx and Weber. I show how the concept of class has been prominent in British social research since the nineteenth century, and that the adoption of explicit Marxist and Weberian sociological theories of class in the post-war years seemed to allow the potential for a more rigorous and exact approach to class. Most of the chapter is devoted to exploring the recent problems in both Marxist and Weberian approaches to class. I argue that the intellectual resources which these two currents have offered class analysis have now been exhausted and that it is only possible to continue to rely exclusively on them by restricting the focus of class analysis ever more narrowly.

While Chapter 1 explains why I think deductive class analysis has fallen into difficulties, the next three chapters change tack and consider in more inductive fashion whether the salience of class can be established by considering its diverse empirical manifestations. These three chapters take further my account of the impasse of class analysis. Chapter 2 criticizes arguments pointing to the existence of cohesive and collective class cultures. I show that such arguments are both theoretically inadequate and empirically unsubstantiated. There is very little evidence that class is an important, robust source of collective identity in Britain today. For this reason, it is not enough simply to say that if those interested in class focus on culture rather than structural social relationships, then class analysis can be placed on firmer ground.

Chapter 3, however, shows that structurally, in terms of the impact on people's life chances, class appears to be as important as it ever was, indeed possibly more important than 30 years ago. There is ample evidence to show not only that patterns of economic and social inequality are marked, but also that it makes good sense to see them in terms of class, albeit a form of class that is 'individualized'. In general, this is the 'paradox of class'. The structural importance of class to people's lives appears not to be recognized by people themselves. Culturally, class does not appear to be a self-conscious principle of social identity. Structurally, however, it appears to be highly pertinent. This conundrum offers a highly fruitful way of rethinking the project of critical class analysis. It creates an intellectual space to examine the complex and ambivalent relationship between cultural identity and power.

Chapter 4 rehearses this paradox further by turning to the heart of the camp occupied by the defenders of class. This is the class structural approach to social mobility developed at Oxford by John Goldthorpe and his associates. Goldthorpe's work is easily the most important and most well worked through defence of the concept of class since it fully recognizes the paradox of class analysis that I have mentioned above and offers a possible way out through the use of rational action theory. However Goldthorpe's defence of rational action theory ultimately depends on cultural foundations which are exogenous to rational action theory itself, and is therefore ultimately unable to ground itself. In empirically examining social inequality and social mobility I emphasize how classes are instantiated in people's life histories. This therefore relates to my arguments in earlier chapters where I claim that the focus on class as a collective process has neglected how class identities and class processes are bound up with individualized processes.

In Part 2 I seek to renew class analysis by drawing eclectically on theoretical and empirical debates arising out of contemporary social theory. I also develop the substantive argument about the changing character of class relations in Britain which is prefigured in Part 1. I focus on the cultural and political defeat of the male, manual working class as a central reference point in British culture and as a major axis in the remaking of contemporary class relations. Chapter 5 explores the individualization theories of Beck and Giddens. These two writers are particularly at fault in assuming that the emergence of individualized identities involves breaking from collective class identities. I draw upon the writings of Bourdieu to offer a more relational account of individual class identities, and argue that while collective class identities are indeed weak, people continue to define their own individual identities in ways which inevitably involve relational comparisons with members of various social classes. This formulation can explain many of the puzzling features of class awareness that I discussed in Chapter 2.

Chapter 6 explores recent issues in organizational theory. The lack of dialogue between class analysis and organization theory is one of the major caesurae in class analysis itself, and a greater dialogue between class theory and organizational theory allows us to gain new insights in understanding the contemporary restructuring of class identities. Organizational theory provides a way of connecting the structural inequalities discussed in Chapters 3 and 4 with the kinds of individualized modes of class awareness discussed in Chapters 2 and 5. I sketch out how we can gain a fuller understanding of the erosion of working-class identities by focusing on organizational restructuring, and examine the emergence of new technologies which enhance the development of individualized modes of working and lead to the development of 'invisible' hierarchies.

My conclusion rounds off the arguments in this book and draws upon a variety of other material to present a historically modulated interpretation of how we can understand social change in Britain as an example of the reforming of class cultures around individualized axes. This argument serves to exemplify what a form of renewed class analysis might involve.

Acknowledgements

This book has been a long time in the making and I would like to thank all those who have contributed to it and helped me develop my thoughts on the state of class analysis. My reflections began while I was working in North Carolina in the mid-1990s and I have found it very helpful to understand the 'Britishness' of debates around class from a vantage point across the Atlantic. This allowed me to step outside of the British tradition and to reflect on it more critically than I would otherwise have been able. I would particularly like to thank Peter Bearman, Joe Gerteis, Steve Pfaff, Kate Stovel and Dave Anderson for discussing these and related questions. I would like also to thank Arne Kalleberg and Judith Blau for facilitating my visits to Chapel Hill.

Since arriving at Manchester University I have gained a great deal from my many colleagues who study social inequality and stratification and who together make Manchester one of the major centres for studying the issues which I explore in this book. I would like to thank Fiona Devine, Muriel Egerton, Angela Dale and Huw Beynon (and more recently) Bev Skeggs and Alan Warde.

More generally, I have learned a great deal from discussions with various friends, especially Tim Butler, Sarah Cant, Katie Deverell, Gordon Fyfe, Susan Halford, Colin Mills, John Scott, Tim Strangleman and Frederic Vandenberghe, though I suspect not all of them were aware of this! I would particularly like to thank Simon Duncan, Muriel Egerton, Helen Hills, Talja Blokland, Paul Watt, Judy Wajcman and Rosemary Crompton, who have made helpful comments on various chapters, which were not always consistent with each other! Bev Skeggs, Alan Warde and Steve Edgell have read the entire manuscript and provided me with encouragement as well as insight into how the themes of the book might be drawn together.

This book draws in passing on three ESRC-funded research projects I have been involved with in the past decade. These three projects have all been different in historical sweep. *'Pathways and prospects: the development of the modern bureaucratic career'* (with Andrew Miles and David Vincent), has studied the emergence of the bureaucratic career in different case study organizations since the 1850s.[8] *'Gender, careers and organisations: recent developments in banking, local government and nursing'* (with Susan Halford and Anne Witz) has examined more recent changes in the gendering of organizational careers.[9] I am also currently working on an ESRC project with Brian Longhurst and Gaynor Bagnall, *'Lifestyles and social integration: a study of middle class culture in Manchester'*.[10] This book does not report the results of any of these projects (with the partial exception of Chapter 5, which explains the joint authorship of this chapter). However, I have taken the opportunity to step back from the detailed results of these projects and to consider what light they bring to bear on class analysis. I therefore refer to relevant findings from these projects at various points in the book.

Versions of chapters in this book have been presented (often in very different formats) to the following universities:

- University of Cambridge (October 1997)
- University of Southampton (November 1997)
- University of Sussex (December 1997)
- Nuffield College, Oxford (December 1997)
- Manchester Metropolitan University (February 1998)
- University of Durham (November 1998)
- University of Liverpool (November 1998)
- University of Edinburgh (December 1998)
- University of Lancaster (March 1999)

I have also presented versions of these chapters to the following conferences:

- 'Does Class Still Unite', Leuven, Belgium, January 1998
- 'Professional and Gentlemanly Cultures Amongst the British Middle Classes', Paris, January 1998
- 'The Ambivalences of Class Identities' (with Gaynor Bagnall and Brian Longhurst), British Sociological Association, Glasgow, April 1999

Finally, on a personal note I might add that it is possible to see my own ambivalence about the state of class analysis related to my own feelings about living in both Britain and the USA in recent years. If, as I argue in Chapter 1, there is something distinctively British about debates around class, it is perhaps testimony to my own complex feelings about trends in British society which are registered here. I have found it difficult to live in the USA, even while Britain (or at least, England) appears to be lacking any clear political direction. No doubt these feelings colour much of what I say. In any event I would like to thank my partner Helen Hills for sharing these journeys and ambivalences with me.

Mike Savage

Notes

1 Goldthorpe's work is a particularly pronounced instance of this trend. See Goldthorpe (1995) for one characteristic contribution along these lines.
2 The main schools are *post-industrial society* theory (Bell 1973); *post-modernism* (taken to be a theorization of social change, as instanced in Harvey (1989) rather than as a series of philosophical arguments); *post-Fordism* (see Amin 1994); disorganized capitalism (Lash and Urry 1987, 1994); *reflexive modernization* (Beck 1992); and *late modernity* (Giddens 1990, 1991). The best review of some of these different perspectives is Kumar (1995), but see also Smart (1990). Castells (1996, 1997) offers the most empirically grounded account of contemporary global change. These different arguments are taken up in succeeding parts of this book.
3 The only existing attempt to debate these themes is parts of Crompton (1998).
4 As I go on to explore in later chapters, the work of Bourdieu offers currently the most developed theoretical formulation of this kind of argument.
5 In developing this argument I attempt to reflect on, and synthesize, my earlier, rather different, work on working-class formation (Savage 1987, 1996a) and on middle-class formation (Savage *et al.* 1992; Butler and Savage 1995).

6 In this respect I share common ground with the argument of John Scott (1996).

7 This is indeed one of Bauman's (1988) claims about the increasing self-referentiality of academic knowledge as advanced capitalism finds newer ways of securing social order which rely less on the role of intellectuals and more on the ability of consumer capitalism to 'seduce' the population. Bauman's arguments are taken up in later chapters.

8 Ref. R000232803. Results have appeared in Savage (1993), Stovel *et al.* (1996), Savage (1998) and Savage *et al.* (forthcoming).

9 Ref. R00023277301. Results have appeared in Halford and Savage (1995a, 1995b), Halford *et al.* (1997) and Halford and Savage (1997).

10 Ref. R0002236929.

Part I
ISSUES *in* CLASS ANALYSIS

1 *The* travails *of* class theory

The sociological debate on class and stratification has, since at least the Second World War, been organized around arguments between Marxist and Weberian approaches (e.g. Giddens 1973; Abercrombie and Urry 1983; Edgell 1992). In recent years, however, both perspectives have in different ways encountered serious intellectual difficulties and the status of class within their conceptual frameworks has become distinctly less secure. The challenge to the labour theory of value, traditionally a cornerstone of Marxist class theory, has spawned considerable uncertainty as to the conceptual place of class analysis within Marxism. Superficially the state of Weberian stratification analysis looks healthier, since there continue to be significant numbers of sociologists who champion Weberian approaches to class analysis. However, Weberian deductive class analysis has become more distant from broader intellectual currents within the social sciences. It has presided over the marginalization of the study of the cultural and subjective dimensions of class at the same time that issues of identity and culture have taken on a higher profile in the social sciences as a whole.

Before expanding on these arguments, I place the issue of class within a broader intellectual frame. For, at least within Britain, a distinctively sociological approach to class, drawing on Marx and Weber, developed relatively late, really only after 1945. There is a much longer intellectual prehistory to class analysis. The peculiar historical identification in Britain of class analysis with social scientific study in general means that debates about the status of class analysis invoke fundamental questions about the status of the social sciences. The debate on class is therefore relevant even to those who feel they have no direct stake in it. The first section of this chapter briefly examines how and why class analysis became tied up with the self-definition of the British social sciences, and explains why challenges to its intellectual credibility led to a serious identity crisis concerning the nature and purpose of critical social science.

The 'Britishness' of class analysis

An interest in social class sometimes appears to be the private hobby of British academics. To be sure, the interest in social class is not confined to

British circles: it is possible to find recent discussions about social class in the USA (e.g. Clark *et al*. 1993), other parts of Europe (e.g. Eder 1993), and elsewhere (e.g. Martin 1998). Nonetheless, the debate seems to have particular resonance in the United Kingdom (UK) (and especially in England). Most recent books devoted to considering the contemporary state of class analysis have been written, or edited, by British academics.[1] Studies of class in Britain continue to be the linchpin for debate, even where comparative analysis is used. Indeed, one of the reasons for the intractability of the debate on class concerns the way that the idea of social class is wrapped up with the historical identity of the British social sciences – its 'canon' and its traditions. The debate on class is tied to a particularly British debate about the nature of the social sciences in general and sociology in particular.

The reasons for this 'Britishness' of class analysis are complex. Class proved important as a means by which British social scientists identified their distinctive expertise *vis-à-vis* other national traditions (notably, that of the USA). It allowed them a way of measuring the progress of their chosen techniques of analysis, as well as a way of securing a public hearing for their findings. As the British social sciences developed their legislative programme during the nineteenth century by carving out a distinct realm of the 'social' that was theirs to study, their definitions and understanding of the 'social' tended to be conflated with 'social class'. Attempts to 'order' the social so that it was amenable both to intellectual inquiry and political intervention (to allow ordering through 'gardening', to use Bauman's (1988 metaphor) used the idea of class as a core device for classifying and placing boundaries. Social groups within the social body (Poovey 1995) became conterminous with social classes. Four specific points bear this out.

First, the elaboration of the 'political arithmetic tradition' (Halsey *et al*. 1980) (which involved the development of survey methods to classify and measure social inequalities) became bound up with finding techniques for defining and distinguishing social classes (Bulmer *et al*. 1994b; Szreter 1996; Yeo 1996). Since survey methods involved 'class-ifying' people in various ways, their elaboration went hand in hand with the construction of class classifications. Thus the Victorian social reformers Booth and Rowntree saw one of their main contributions as differentiating social classes according to their wealth (see Hennock 1976, 1987; Vincent 1990; Bales 1994).[2] From the late nineteenth century, more explicit uses of measures of 'social class' were developed, in dialogue with the development of the registrar general's class schema, first encoded in the 1911 census. The registrar general's class schema drew upon medical eugenics to define a distinctive five-class model of British society, and this model of class persisted in a recognizable form into the 1980s and even beyond (see Szreter 1996; Crompton 1998; Marshall *et al*. 1988). In the twentieth century this body of work matured as national random sample surveys allowed the examination of the relationship between social class and social mobility, educational attainment and health outcomes (Glass 1954; Goldthorpe *et al*. 1980; Halsey *et al*. 1980; Crouch and Heath 1992). Certainly until the period after the Second World War, all the major innovations in British survey techniques involved the use of class-based measures[3] and improvements in the measurement of class became identified with the progress of social science itself.

Second, as the social sciences in Britain grew in the twentieth century, new and developing branches devoted to studying British society drew on the established discourse of class as a means of anchoring themselves in a recognizable tradition of social scientific inquiry, thereby giving themselves intellectual credibility and legitimacy.[4] The discipline of social policy had direct roots in the 'political arithmetic' tradition, and became codified in the middle years of the twentieth century as the welfare state expanded and as writers such as Beveridge, Titmuss and Marshall defined its intellectual remit. The idea of class played a key role in defining the subject matter of this new social science. Marshall (1950) in particular developed an influential model of citizenship linked to class. Later still, in the 1950s and 1960s, the nascent discipline of social history placed class centrally, as historians such as Harold Perkin (1968) and Edward Thompson (1963) developed a distinctive class-centred approach to history. At the same time, the expansion of sociology also saw the elaboration of class analysis as one of its core concerns. Within all these new social sciences, the definition of the 'social' invoked 'class'.[5] Taking this point further, it is interesting that early attempts to institutionalize British sociology which did not appeal to the idea of class failed. Thus the efforts associated with the Sociological Society, which attempted to develop a non-class type of urban ecology/sociology under the leadership of Geddes, failed to get backing and led to them being labelled as cranks (see Yeo 1996). Only when sociologists took up and ran with the baton of 'class' did they begin to enjoy a certain measure of intellectual respect.

British sociology was a late developer compared to the situation in the USA or France, and it was only in the 1960s that it became established as a discipline taught in most British universities. In this formative period for British sociology the study of class, and especially the working class, provided one of the main 'topics' for the nascent discipline. Sociology could demonstrate its distinctive expertise by providing methodologically rigorous studies of an intellectual topic that had been opened up by other branches of the social sciences.[6] In the same period, class analysis could also be seen as the handmaiden to the development of a specifically British approach to social theory, based around various kinds of 'conflict theory' which offered an alternative to dominant American functionalist currents of the day (e.g. Lockwood 1964; Rex 1968). Class thereby offered a valuable device for establishing the legitimacy of British sociology, and although subsequent years saw newer axes emerge as foci for sociological thinking,[7] they all had to jostle with the initial defining role of the class analysis tradition. It was thus that Marx and Weber – rather than Durkheim or Simmel – played a key role in defining the intellectual space in which British sociology matured in the 1970s. The key British social theorists of the 1960s and early 1970s without exception looked to these two figures for intellectual sustenance. John Rex, David Lockwood and Anthony Giddens all helped to make the social theories of Marx and Weber, both of which placed class at their core, central to their theoretical reflections.

Third, the concept of class played a crucial role in linking academic debates to political programmes. The concept of class is unusual in the social sciences in that it meant something to social actors as well as to academics. The result was that debates on class were not purely academic ones. As the 'political arithmetic' tradition became rooted in Fabian political discourse, an association between the Labour movement and what might be termed 'progressive' social scientific thinking took place. This led to a pronounced feature of twentieth-century intellectual life, in which the subject of 'class' played a key mobilizing role in defining intellectual camps and in giving purpose to intellectual inquiry. The idea of class was a rallying cry as much as a concept.

Finally, it is striking how, especially since the Second World War, British concerns with social change have been couched as arguments about how social classes are changing. It is difficult to find any sustained interpretation of social change in Britain from 1950 to 1990 that was not expressed in these terms. In the 1950s Williams and Hoggart were interested in how 'commercialization' (Hoggart 1956) was eroding working-class cultures. In the 1960s Zweig (1961), Abrams and Rose (1960), and Goldthorpe and Lockwood 1968a, 1968b, 1969 debated the significance of affluence for class relations. Later still, speculation took place on how the rise of youth culture related to class cultures (Hall *et al.* 1975), and on the significance of new forms of ethnic and racial relations (Hall *et al.* 1975; Gilroy 1987; Small 1994). Even as late as the 1980s, arguments about the impact of Thatcherism on British political culture (Crewe and Sarlvik 1983; Jessop *et al.* 1988) tended to be related to debates about the waning impact of class. Similar themes arise in recent arguments about disorganized capitalism, post-Fordism, and post-industrialism, all of which couch their theses in terms of arguments about the declining salience of class. The idea of class serves in all these kinds of account as a rhetorical device that provides writers with a 'benchmark' to measure how far social relations have changed.

The idea of social class became central to the British social scientific tradition. This explains why challenges to the centrality of social class as the key analytical tool for understanding the mainsprings of British society have caused emotional soul-searching as well as intellectual scrutiny among social scientists. To admit that class is not the central feature of British society is to cast doubt on the relevance of the intellectual heritage of British social science itself. It also has direct implications for the professional project of the social sciences, especially sociology. If class is dispensed with, then the value of the tradition of British social science is much restricted, and ideas need to be drawn from elsewhere to develop a more persuasive and useful intellectual enterprise.

This point explains the fascination with the state of class analysis that is to be found in recent sociology. It is noteworthy that during the heyday of class analysis there were few general overviews of the state of class analysis in British social science as a whole (see Savage 1994). In part this reflected the ongoing controversial state of the field, given the existence of chronic disputes between Marxists, Weberians, feminists and others (e.g. Crompton and Gubbay 1977). It also reflected the difficulty of defining class analysis as a discrete research programme that could be manageably detached from a programme of study about Britain, or 'society', as a whole.

It is precisely this situation that has changed markedly in recent years. Since the late 1980s there has been a proliferation of books reviewing the general state of class analysis in the British social sciences (Saunders 1990a; Edgell 1992; Scase 1992; Crompton 1998; Breen and Rottman 1995; Butler and Savage 1995; Bradley 1996; Lee and Turner 1996; Marshall 1997; Devine 1998b). There have also been numerous heated exchanges in scholarly journals about the state of class analysis.[8] More important than the specific arguments about class which are developed in these books, and which will be discussed as appropriate below, is the fact that their appearance marks the possibility of writing books about class in ways that are 'boundaried' and thereby delimited from other branches of sociology. Only from the mid-1980s was class analysis written as if it were a sub-field of sociology, rather than as the core of British sociology *tout court*. This itself is testimony to the waning relevance of class analysis to many areas of sociological inquiry. From the 1960s the centrality of class within stratification research was challenged as the significance of gender, race and ethnicity was signalled, leading to class analysis having to stage a defensive, holding action with respect to these other processes.[9]

Furthermore, as Bauman (1988) has argued, as academic expertise and knowledge has become less central to capitalist reproduction, this has allowed a greater detachment of academic concerns from political debate (see also Rose 1993). The result is that there is less need to anchor sociology in 'lay' concerns, and thereby more esoteric, specialized and self-referential branches of sociology have proliferated. There is also evidence that the intellectual core of sociology has shifted away from class to the 'individual'. Arguments about individualization (Beck 1992), about the intersection between individuality, structure and agency (Giddens 1990), and about the construction of individual subjectivity (Rose 1989; Lury 1998) now command a much more central place in sociological reflection. This framework for thinking about social change offers an alternative to the traditional class-based emphasis that formed the centre of the British canon.

The study of class is no longer central to British sociological analysis, and the debate on class is largely about whether this should be celebrated or lamented. There are three possibilities here. One school, associated with Goldthorpe and his colleagues continues to defend the class analysis tradition, and makes no concessions to current intellectual trends that have gone in other directions. Strikingly, Goldthorpe's recent work has made it clear that if one has to chose between the 'class analysis programme' and the newer concerns of sociology, then it is the latter which should be dispensed with. Goldthorpe's call is for a fundamentalist defence of the British social sciences which seeks no dialogue with recent preoccupations. His work shows much more interest in debates in economics than in sociology, and he clearly differentiates his concerns from qualitative sociology and history (see Goldthorpe 1991, 1998). It will be clear that whatever the intellectual merits of these arguments are (and I shall show in various points in the book that they are considerable), this view offers no way of popularizing class analysis to a wider audience.

A second position is the mirror image to that of Goldthorpe. This is to accept, even celebrate, the demise of class analysis, as a sign that the social sciences have moved on to more fertile pastures. This position, associated with writers such as Giddens (1990), sees class as a throwback to a now outdated tradition of sociological study. This current of thought is in fact shot through with contradictions since the idea of class reappears in hidden and indirect ways. Also, as I demonstrate in this book, discarding established traditions of scholarship is counterproductive and prevents us from constructing an adequate historical account of current changes.

This book explores the third possibility. This is to reposition class analysis within sociology by undertaking a critical review both of class analysis and of the preoccupations of contemporary sociology. Rosemary Crompton (1998) has gone furthest in this endeavour. She argues that what has come to be called the 'class analysis programme', based around the focus on 'employment aggregates' is only one, rather restricted, way of understanding class. She argues that life can be breathed into class analysis tradition by resuscitating other, now overlooked or discarded, approaches to the study of class – for instance, those concerned with historical change and with culture. I am sympathetic to this line of argument. Nonetheless, while at one level Crompton's advocacy of a pluralist approach to class is welcome, there is a danger that central conceptual difficulties are not faced up to. Rather than acknowledge the deep conceptual, methodological and empirical uncertainties around the conception of class, the possibility is held open that simply broadening out class from its 'employment aggregate' focus may be enough to restore its vitality. This formulation understates the very real problems that face a class analysis paradigm of any sort. Only by fully exposing and acknowledging these problems can the prospects for some kind of revival really be addressed, and it is hoped that this book might be some small contribution to this project.

A first stage of this exercise is to consider the contemporary relevance of the classical foundations of sociological class theory. I have argued that the centrality of class in the British social sciences was a result of the particular way it was configured in the history of social science disciplines. Part of this association lay in the way that Weber and Marx were enshrined in the canon of sociological theory. It is therefore essential to show how these two thinkers, whose ideas continue to offer vital insights for understanding contemporary social relations, can no longer be appealed to to shore up class analysis. The basic problem faced by contemporary class analysis is that the classical 'class theory' of Marx and Weber can offer no good reason to see class as a particularly important concept to understand the dynamics of social life. I now examine underlying problems in both Marxist and Weberian modes of class analysis and show how they have become more marked in recent work. Only by recognizing the real weaknesses of the classical traditions of class analysis is it possible to take stock and move on. The last part of this chapter explains how the issues raised in this introduction are taken up in later chapters of the book.

The labour theory of value and the crisis in Marxist class theory

The central reason for the hegemony of the concept of class during the twentieth century lies in the intellectual and political influence of Marxism.

This is not to say that most writers on class are or were Marxists. Indeed in Britain (as in the USA and elsewhere) the dominant approach (notably that associated with the political arithmetic tradition) disavowed any direct Marxist heritage. Nonetheless, especially in the years after 1917, following the Russian Revolution and the creation of the Soviet Union, even non-Marxist writers on class felt it necessary to settle their account with Marxism as a preliminary to presenting their own formulations. Arguments over Marxism therefore played a crucial role in the development of the British class analysis tradition. They can, for instance, be seen in the writings of T.H. Marshall (1950), the early Raymond Williams (1956), Ralf Dahrendorf (1959), David Lockwood (1958, 1992), Gordon Marshall and his associates (1988), and John Scott (e.g. 1996). In particular, the work of John Goldthorpe exemplifies this point. All his major statements on the scope of class analysis proceed by rhetorically distancing himself from Marxism (e.g. Goldthorpe *et al.* 1980, Ch. 1, 1982, 1988; Goldthorpe and Marshall 1992). For this reason the appeal of class theory can only be understood as ultimately linked to the power of Marxism both as a body of thought and as political practice.

For classical Marxism the idea of class linked political practice with social theory. It explained how the dynamics of capitalism, based on class inequality, led to a practical politics of class struggle. Of course, in reality, class struggle was often defined in terms of national or party interest, but even so, its ability to act as a rallying cry was crucial. The challenge to Marxism as a viable political project linked to the fall of communist regimes since the late 1980s ultimately had a profound impact on class analysis. Marxism as an intellectual force has held up well and continues to be a live influence in the social sciences after these political changes, and there have been important attempts to reformulate Marxism in ways that renew its intellectual appeal. However, this reconstruction of Marxism has gone hand in hand with the downplaying of class as a fundamental feature of Marxist analysis. The result is to lead to a kind of 'new academic Marxism' in which class analysis has no central part to play.[10]

Marx's great insight was to show how exploitation was the main principle structuring social relations, and thereby that class could be seen as *the* fundamental social contradiction. For Marx the idea that some social groups wrested a 'surplus' from other social groups, and that the character of this surplus extraction was historically specific, allowed class to be seen as the fundamental, axial, feature of any society. Of course, this idea could be taken up in numerous ways, some of which tended not to emphasize class. The well-known tensions between Marxism's scientific and its humanistic wings involved rather different understandings of the class concept. Its scientific champions, from the time of Bernstein onwards, espoused a Marxism that detected objective laws of social development, based in the ability of productive forces to lead to evolutionary social change. They therefore did not leave much space for class struggle to have much independent power in shaping historical developments (e.g. Cohen 1978). Nonetheless, even for writers of this 'scientific' persuasion, social classes were still important as the 'bearers' of progressive social change. Even though the members of the proletariat had little choice but to represent the role allotted to them by historical destiny, they were still the agents who ushered in social change, and their actual empirical existence was not in doubt. In the alternative humanistic Marxist tradition, class played a significantly more important conceptual role. This tradition, especially important in Britain, emphasized the role of agency, and the contextuality of struggle and conflict in determining social change. This was linked to a concern with how classes develop, how they could come to exhibit shared meanings and values, and how they could shape historical developments.

During the 1960s and 1970s defining and conceptualizing class became the central feature of Marxist debates. Unlocking the 'true' nature of class seemed to lie at the heart of the Marxist project. Analysing the extraction of surplus value was seen as central to the project of Marxist economists to understand the cyclical tendencies of capitalism (Baran and Sweezy 1966), and understanding how changes in capitalism were leading to a redefinition of class relationships energized Marxist academics. Poulantzas (1975), Carchedi (1977), and Abercrombie and Urry (1983) provided new class maps of late capitalism that interpreted the rise of new white-collar middle classes in the context of the changing nature of capitalist production processes, and showed how class divisions could be defined in terms of the underyling antagonism between capital and labour. Similarly, the debate between structuralist and humanistic Marxists reached particular bitterness in this period. Those influenced by Althusserian structuralism, such as Hindess and Hirst (1975) and Richard Johnson (1978) locked horns with defenders of E.P. Thompson's humanistic and culturalist Marxism (see Thompson 1978). At the same time a series of major historical works, such as Barrington Moore's (1966) study of *The Social Origins of Dicatorship and Democracy* and Robert Brenner's (1976) studies of the transition from feudalism to capitalism developed powerful class centred accounts of social change. In the 1970s the analysis of class seemed pivotal to most Marxist-inspired analytical questions in history and the social sciences.

The situation now looks very different. Much of the work cited above looks dated and of doubtful intellectual relevance to contemporary intellectual concerns. Some writers argue that this simply reflects the turn against Marxism in academic circles as sociologists 'sell out' (Wood 1986). Marxists have, however, shown remarkable intellectual vitality in regrouping in face of the challenge to Marxist politics. The interesting point, however, is that this regrouping has distanced Marxism from claims about the centrality of class. New academic Marxists have adopted modes of analysis which focus on the dynamics of capitalist development, and are not directly concerned with making links to political movements, or they have searched for 're-demptive' forces which might still be agents for anti-capitalist political change, but which are not the working class. Such redemptive hopes tend either to be marginal figures from the past, as in the appropriation of Benjamin's writings (e.g. 1973), or forward looking, utopian ideas, as in Habermas' (1984) communicative ethics associated with the ideal speech situation. In neither case do actually existing social classes play an important role.

Diverse currents of 'new academic Marxism' can be detected, only one of which (that associated with analytical Marxism) shows any interest in class analysis. The problem of Marxist class analysis revolves around the labour theory of value. In classical Marxist theory, the labour theory of value simultaneously provided a theory of capitalism and a theory of class. By distinguishing productive from unproductive labour, it was possible to analyse both the dynamics of capital accumulation as well as the class relations inherent within capitalism. It therefore played a fundamental role in showing how class and capitalism were interrelated. The last major class theorists to use the labour theory of value were Poulantzas (1975), and Carchedi (1977). But since this time few Marxists have drawn on the labour theory of value in their reflections on class. Part of the reason lies in the difficulty in analysing the position of non-manual workers. Much white-collar work is concerned with the distribution and circulation of information, commodities and capital. Therefore, if such workers are deemed to be 'productive', then it becomes difficult to distinguish production from other aspects of capitalist society. If, by contrast, they are seen as non-productive, then the conclusion follows both that the working class is declining in numbers, and also that the activities of non-productive workers may be of great economic significance. If this is true the relevance of the labour theory of value for analysing capitalism seems limited. It furthermore becomes difficult to define non-arbitrary boundaries between 'productive' and 'unproductive' workers. Similar intellectual problems surfaced in the 'domestic labour debate', whereby the problems entailed in defining women's housework as non-productive were illuminated by feminists (e.g. Barrett 1980).

Additionally, analytical Marxists, notably Cohen (1988) have brilliantly exposed the logical problems entailed in using the labour theory of value. Cohen notes that a commodity produced at a particular time (and embodying a certain amount of socially necessary labour) may actually be exchanged at a later date for much more or less than it might have been exchanged for at the time it was produced. Given that this is so, the labour theory of value must be wrong. A herb, for instance, which is found to be the cure for an illness may suddenly increase in exchange value despite the fact that no more labour is embodied in producing it (picking or growing it) than before. One Marxist response is to recognize the 'transformation problem' which emphasizes the distinction between price and value, and accepts that the price (though not the value) may change according to contingencies such as these. However, in this case the point of distinguishing the 'value' of a product becomes unclear.

It is therefore not surprising that most recent Marxist analyses of capitalism downplay the labour theory of value. Postone's (1993) reworking of Marx's theory of capitalism is an interesting example. His critique proceeds by differentiating 'traditional Marxism' from 'categorial Marxism': 'The social critique from the standpoint of "labour" understands that form of domination especially in terms of class domination, rooted in private ownership of the means of production: the social critique of labour in capitalism [i.e. Postone's categorial approach], however, characterizes the most fundamental form of domination in that society as an abstract form of domination underlying the historical dynamic of capitalism' (Postone 1993: 68). Postone therefore sees capitalism not primarily as a class society, but as a society with generic powers, notably the instrumental character of labour in general. Postone's account of Marx tallies with Foucault's (1966) claim that Marx did not break with the neoclassical assumptions of his day, but in fact consolidated them. Just as Foucault claims that Marx's work embodies an implicitly bourgeois conception of the human subject, so Postone argues that the 'labour theory of value' is simply taken over from Ricardo and other bourgeois writers (see also Cohen 1995, Ch. 7, on the relationship between Marx and Locke). The more fundamental critical step, Postone claims, is to move away from the idea that one group of people 'exploit' another, in favour of the recognition that the capitalist system as a whole exerts particular systemic powers over all its members. Postone's critique therefore questions traditional Marxism's reliance on 'surplus value' as the device by which the working class is exploited by the capitalist class, in favour of a systemic approach which sees all labour, including presumably that of senior managers and employers, as being based on instrumental abstract labour. Within this perspective, there is no room at all for any developed or elaborated class theory (see especially Postone 1993: 314ff.).

Given problems such as these, it is striking that many reformulations of Marxist economic theory do not depend on the labour theory of value for their conceptual distinctiveness. One example is the emergence of the Regulation School, associated with writers such as Aglietta (1987), Lipietz (1987), and more recently with writers such as Boyer (1990), Jessop (e.g. 1990) and Harvey (1989). Regulation School writers have developed the intellectual bridgehead between Marxist analyses of capitalism and currents in structuralist thought deriving from Althusser and Poulantzas. They explore the historically specific constitution of different 'regimes of accumulation', the societal forces which serve to stabilize (at least temporarily) the inevitably unsteady capitalist system. This enterprise does not require any more than a rhetorical role for a labour theory of value, but instead examines the different means by which capitalism is regulated at the societal level (Fordism, post-Fordism, etc.), and the kinds of conditions which either secure capitalist reproduction or threaten it. Within this framework, class is itself of little analytical importance compared to the macro-processes, usually associated with the powers of nation states and other large-scale institutional forces, to secure conditions of reproduction. Classes are largely the effect of structural processes and have little independent force.[11] An example is that in his celebrated account of the rise of post-modern cultures, Harvey (1989) does not directly relate cultural change to new forms of class relation.

It is doubtful that these writers would deny the existence of surplus value extraction. Rather, it becomes a kind of background condition, of such universal persistence in capitalism that it plays no fundamental role in explaining the specificities of particular capitalist systems. Some Marxists have taken this argument even further. Arrighi's (1994) account of *The Long Twentieth Century* argues that the dynamics of capitalism are organized much more around financial cycles than around any obviously class-related tensions. Arrighi argues that since the fourteenth century there have been clear cyclical patterns, in which phases of production tend to give way to 'monetized' and financially driven modes of capital accumulation (see also

Ingham 2000). The dynamic, driving force of capitalism does not lie with class relationships, but with the interplay between different modes of capital accumulation and their intersection with forms of territorial regulation.

Although critical theory works within rather different intellectual fields than Marxist economic theory, there are some interesting parallels between it and regulationist Marxism. As Anderson (1976) has emphasized, the emergence of critical theory during the mid-twentieth century marked a distinct turn away from economically centred accounts. Writers such as Adorno, Benjamin, Marcuse and Habermas emphasized the structural character of capitalism (see Jay 1973; Wiggershaus 1994). Because they argue that social classes are produced by capitalism, they see the working class as absorbed within capitalist social relations. These writers therefore search for redemptive and 'progressive' political forces outside the capital–labour relationship. The working classes are too powerfully structured by capitalism to be able to effectively criticize or redeem it. Walter Benjamin's work, which has proved highly influential in recent years (e.g. Gilloch 1996; Caygill 1998) has concerned itself with rescuing marginal, fleeting and forgotten figures such as rag-pickers, flâneurs and idlers in order to uncover their critical potential. Other critical theorists have looked towards young people (Marcuse 1964), or towards utopian kinds of social interaction (in the case of Habermas' ideal speech situation) to find some kind of critical space from which to confront capitalism. In order to find the potential for critical change these authors focus on non-class groups whose existence lies altogether outside the capital–labour relationship.

Another important post-Marxist current is the neo-Gramscian turn associated particularly with Stuart Hall (1980) and Ernesto Laclau and Chantal Mouffe (1985). Here the critique of social reductionism is explicit. These writers interpret Gramsci as criticizing economically determinist, class-centred explanations of cultures and ideology and emphasize that discourses construct the social field. Laclau and Mouffe stage an alliance between Gramsci and elements of post-structuralist theory to claim that meanings are produced by the play of difference in discursive formations and therefore that they cannot be seen as the product of any clear social base. The most manifest example of the kind of challenge this offers to class theory comes in the social history of Patrick Joyce (1990, 1993, 1995) whose challenge to the primacy of class has led to vituperative exchanges with eminent social historians (e.g. Kirk 1994; Savage and Miles 1994). This body of writing has moved with relatively little difficulty from post-Marxism to non-Marxism, and increasingly sees no need to identify with any Marxist heritage (e.g. du Gay 1996).

All these diverse Marxist currents have therefore turned their attention away from class. They would not deny that contemporary capitalism is a society divided by class, but they do not see the processes driving contemporary social change as class processes. The only exception to this general trend in new academic Marxism is that associated with analytical, or rational choice Marxism, found in the work of Elster (1985), Roemer (1982), Wright (1985), Cohen (1988, 1995) and Carling (1990). These theorists have attempted to place Marxist class theory on secure 'micro-foundations' by formally considering how exploitative relationships can be defined in ways that are not dependent on the labour theory of value. The main analytical issue here, discussed by Cohen (1988, 1995) concerns the definition of exploitation. Cohen claims that to define the relationship between capital and labour as inherently exploitative entails drawing on a theory of 'self-ownership', whereby all individuals are deemed to properly control themselves[12] (and hence the capital–labour relationship involves workers losing such control). Cohen argues that this notion is actually one which is drawn on by right-wing libertarians in their defence of individual freedoms – that there is no way of distinguishing in principle the capital–labour relationship from that between a state and its taxpaying citizens. Taxpaying citizens have no choice in deciding whether or not to pay tax, in the same way that workers might be deemed to have no choice in whether to seek a job.

Recent attempts to define exploitation prove equally problematic. Erik Wright (1996) claims that exploitation is anchored in the employment relationship, though not in the labour theory of value. Wright argues that in exploitation the exploiters need the exploited (for instance, by making them work to produce profit for them), whereas in other forms of oppression (for instance, based around gender and ethnicity) the oppressed could be completely eliminated. However, this seems a difficult contrast to draw, since it can be argued that misogynist men, for instance, still need women, albeit in appropriately subordinate modes. The same argument could also be made with respect to ethnicity (Said 1978).

Where this leads to, as Weberians of various kinds have (sometimes smugly) pointed out, is the impossibility of defining the capital–labour relationship as *the* fundamental social divide, of a different order to the injustices of race, ethnicity, gender, and so on. And indeed, a number of analytical Marxists have tried to develop a pluralist approach to stratification in recognition of this point. Wright's work represents the best known example. In his early work (1978), building on Carchedi and Poulantzas, Wright rooted class divisions in terms of the functions of different occupational groups in the employment structure and argued that some groups occupied 'contradictory class locations'. However, in the early 1980s Wright reformulated his class theory on a 'game-theoretical' basis. This involved defining class not on the basis of a person's relationship to the extraction of surplus value, but according to whether they were in relationships that they would be better off by being out of (Wright 1985).[13] Following the arguments of Roemer (1982), this led Wright to identify three different axes around which exploitative relationships form. The most important of these is property, around which the distinction between employers and employees is generated. Employees are also divided according to their relationship to authority and skill assets. In the former case those with power at work can be said to exploit those without it, while in the latter case, those with socially scarce expertise can be said to exploit those without such expertise.

Wright's approach has been the subject of much scrutiny (Marshall *et al.* 1988; Wright 1989; Savage *et al.* 1992; Gubbay 1997), and a number of telling criticisms have been made. Wright's account of skill assets does not explain how the fact that one person has skills disadvantages another person without such skills. Answering this question means going outside Marxist explanations, for instance by drawing on Weber's account of social closure (whereby those with skills restrict teaching them to others, so enhancing their market position), or by relating skill assets to Bourdieu's arguments about cultural capital (Savage *et al.* 1992). The problem with the idea of organizational assets is that it tends to depend (in ways I discuss in Chapter 6) on the idea of rigid organizational hierarchy, with a clear zero-sum relationship between organizational superiors and subordinates.

Recognizing these problems, Wright's more recent work continues to distinguish property, organization and skill as assets in class formation, but on rather different grounds, whereby those relying on managerial authority and skill draw additional 'rents' from their employer. While this is an interesting reformulation of class analysis (see Sorensen 2000), it is clear that the Marxist underpinnings of the argument are tenuous indeed. It would appear that while Marxism continues to be a live intellectual force, it no longer has the interacting conceptions of the mutual constitution of class and capitalism at its core. Indeed, it seems that Marxists have travelled down one of two roads, either choosing capitalism or class as their focus. They have either developed their arguments around the systemic properties of capitalism, or they have sought to find new foundations for the definition of class, but they have not linked the two in a theoretically coherent way. Therefore, we must conclude that the idea that exploitation between capital and labour is the key dynamic feature of capitalism no longer plays a particularly important part in the conceptual framework of Marxist analysis – though it undoubtedly continues to play a major rhetorical role. With this intellectual departure Marxist class theory loses its major anchor. If it cannot be said that one class exploits another, and that this exploitation colours all aspects of that society, then the relevance of class is cast into doubt. What we are left with, in Wright's work, is a recognition that organizational power, property and skills 'matter', but no very clear account of how and why they do so. This sets the stage for us to see whether Weberian stratification theory can do better.

Weber and the limits of deductive class analysis

In recent years there has been a notable revival of neo-Weberian stratification theory, especially but not exclusively in the UK (Goldthorpe and Marshall 1992; Witz 1992; Pakulski and Waters 1996; Scott 1996). It is possible to detect a triumphalist tone in this writing.[14] Some Weberians revel in the intellectual problems that have confronted Marxism, and argue that a Weberian class analysis can provide an altogether more robust base for contemporary class analysis. It is certainly true that this neo-Weberian tradition constitutes the most internally coherent approach to class analysis currently on offer, and I will take up many of the themes and ideas emerging from it in later chapters. Nonetheless, neo-Weberian theory ultimately fails to provide a robust *foundation* for class analysis.

Before I develop this argument, I should note that neo-Weberian class theory is itself internally divided. There are disagreements about how the relationship between class, status and party (or command, as Scott 1996 prefers to define it) should be theorized. Some neo-Weberians, such as Goldthorpe and Marshall, emphasize the importance of class over status and party, while others such as Scott (1996) or Lockwood (1995) make considerably more of these dimensions of stratification. As Goldthorpe and Erikson (1992) indicate, there are also points of convergence with elements of Marxist class theory, especially the recognition that classes are located in employment relations.[15] What marks out a distinctively Weberian mode of class analysis is the attachment to a deductive mode of analysis which makes no substantive claims about the ontological reality of class. Neo-Weberians make no *a priori* claims about the importance of class. Rather, the existence or non-existence of classes is seen as an empirical question. Weberian research therefore focuses on examining the conditions under which classes do or do not become social collectivities (see for instance Giddens 1973; Goldthorpe *et al.* 1980; Scott 1996), by focusing on the diverse processes of 'structuration',[16] and 'class formation'.[17] Scott, for instance, is quite open to the idea that the working class no longer exists as a coherent social grouping (see Scott 1996, Ch. 8). This point explains why Goldthorpe insists that his form of class analysis does not depend on a theory of history or a theory of exploitation (see Goldthorpe 1991, 1995; Goldthorpe and Marshall 1992).

This perspective can certainly be effective as a critique of other perspectives on stratification, to which Weberian accounts are often presented as foils. This rhetorical strategy allows neo-Weberians to present themselves as occupying the sensible 'middle ground'. However, it tends to make any virtues of neo-Weberian analysis rather dependent on the weaknesses of other perspectives. Or, more strongly put, if no one believes in the other positions, who cares about the proposed mediation Weberians offer?

The use of a deductive mode of class analysis has its roots in Weber's 'ideal type' methodology that was his response to the problem of the 'fact–value' distinction (see Brubaker 1984; Hennis 1988). Weber recognized the inherently value-laden quality of social observation. People's interests were bound to affect their choice of research topic. Weber claimed that the 'ideal type' allowed researchers the best chance to avoid projecting their own values onto their research findings. By heuristically highlighting certain features of a given phenomena it became possible to see how certain implications for action might follow. Thus, much of Weber's work was concerned to show the unintended consequences of particular value systems, in ways which allowed him to sociologically demonstrate how values could change things in ways which did not rely on the explicit moral frameworks which were embedded in them.[18]

The major intellectual issue that Weber wrestled with concerned the reflexive implications of the ideal type methodology itself. Ideal type methodology does not explain why a particular topic – for instance, that of social class – is interesting or important to study. The choice of topic is ultimately arbitrary, and cannot be justified internally. Given this arbitrariness, one strategy is to consider a culturally 'live' topic that is widely discussed and has considerable social prominence as a starting point and then to subject this to critical analysis. This explains why Weberian class analysis was ultimately dependent on the vitality of Marxism and on the general topical interest in questions of class and class politics. Because the issue of class was hotly debated inside and outside academia, this seemed good grounds for Weberians to explore it. In this process the kinds of intellectual challenges posed by Marxism also serve as the questions which galvanize Weberians. In what circumstances does economic and social inequality lead to protest and revolt? How does economic inequality colour various aspects of social life? Rhetorically, Weberian arguments depended on claiming that they offered 'sensible' answers to these sorts of questions compared to the reckless formulations offered by hot-headed Marxists.

However, if interest in class fades from public view, this argument for sociologically scrutinizing it becomes markedly weaker. In this situation, an alternative reason to choose a research topic emerges. Here the values leading to an interest in a given research project come not from broader social and cultural debate, but from academic tradition, more narrowly defined. This is the step which Goldthorpe and Marshall (1992) take in their recent defence of the class analysis programme. They claim that the class analysis 'programme is attractive because it represents a specific way of investigating interconnections of the kind that have always engaged the sociological imagination, that is to say between historically formed macro-structures on the one hand, and on the other, the everyday experience of people within their social milieus, together with the patterns of action that follow from this experience' (1992: 382). This formulation sounds innocuous but its implications are significant since class analysis is justified internally in terms of its relationship to an older tradition of the sociological imagination. Goldthorpe and Marshall's arguments draw on the philosophy of science associated with Popper and Lakatos, who deem a topic worthy of study when a particular research tradition (in this case, that deemed to be associated with the 'sociological imagination') regards it as significant. It is not too difficult to see the tautological dangers of this mode of argument. Class analysis is worth pursuing because the tradition from which it emerged sees it as useful. Even if is true that class analysis is useful in pursuing the sociological imagination,[19] the danger is that there are no reasons why anyone outside this tradition should see the topic as being of interest, since the appeal is to the scientific community rather than a broader constituency.

There is a view that suggests that recent defences of class analysis have been empiricist in tone (Pahl 1993). If this were true, then one could prove 'objectively' whether one should be or should not be interested in class simply by inspecting the results of various research inquiries, and no prior value commitment would be involved. In fact, Goldthorpe and his colleagues have always emphasized that class can only be shown to be significant if a prior decision is made to analyse things from the appropriate 'class structural' perspective.[20] They do not deny that in some areas predictors other than class may 'explain' more.[21] Class analysis does not stand or fall on whether it is the major predictor of life chances. It is not possible to compare rival perspectives in a purely empiricist way. Contemporary neo-Weberian stratification theory gives no good reason to study class, but only a series of propositions about how to study class if one decides to embark on that particular project.

The best known problem associated with this increasingly self-referential tradition of class analysis, examined more fully by Crompton (1998), concerns the way that, during the 1980s, debates on class became focused around measurement issues. The 'point' of class analysis was rarely discussed: rather, attention focused on how best to define class in occupational terms. In this debate, three major contending measurement schemes were discussed in British research. The registrar general's class schema, which had been developed by government statisticians at the start of this century and which distinguished five major classes according to the 'standing' of different groups in society, and later according to the skill required of different groups, was the common target. The Marxist class schema of Erik Wright, which itself changed radically between the late 1970s (Wright 1978) and the mid-1980s (Wright 1985, 1996) was also scrutinized. This also tended to be found wanting compared to the class schema developed by Goldthorpe *et al.* (1980).[22] Goldthorpe's class schema, which distinguishes seven main classes according to their distinctive employment relations, and whose main analytical distinctions are between employers, employees and the self-employed, and between those on 'labour' and 'service' contracts, has generally been found to be the most internally rigorous and useful, even though its *theoretical* basis remains a matter of dispute (Savage *et al.* 1992).

The main way that neo-Weberians test the validity of different measures of class is by using 'criterion validity', which considers whether class schemas accurately measures what they are meant to measure. Evans (1992a: 213) argues that the best test of validity 'is to assess whether the schema divides the occupational structure in such a way as to identify important cleavages in the job characteristics which are considered theoretically important by Goldthorpe and his colleagues'. The focus here is not on considering the relevance of class for any given outcome, but on the consistency of the way that a given measure represents accurately what it claims to represent. This approach is undoubtedly useful operationally, but its effect is to divert attention from the broader conceptual issues that are taken almost as 'given'. The effect is to further isolate class analysis from the interests of those who are not confirmed members of the tradition.[23]

Of course, it should be noted that both the theoretical specification of different measures of class and the use of criterion validity are only seen by the champions of class analysis as a preliminary step to their intention of examining the impact of class on specified dependent variables. However, it should also be noted that the types of outcomes regarded as appropriate objects for study are narrowly defined. Political change, collective action, cultural representations, etc. have been seen as outside the purview of prediction.

Weber himself was aware of the tension between the hermeneutic and scientific elements in his thinking, and late in his life became concerned about the way in which his commitment to ideal type methodology could undercut his recognition of the value-laden quality of social life. Ideal types depend on 'hollowing out' the substantive meanings of particular social actions in ways which can be seen as part of the same rationalizing process that Weber tried to understand in ideal typical ways. Weber's pessimism came from his recognition that his own chosen ideal typical method was consistent with the whole drive towards rationalization which he saw as one of the defining features of modernity. In one of his most celebrated essays, 'Science as a Vocation' Weber (1948) shows how the scientific method was unable to provide a foundation for itself, and how it always threatened thereby to undercut itself.[24] Weber's response was to appeal to the 'heroic' university professor to discriminate as much as possible between fact and value, but he recognized the limitations of this response. In his later work he became increasingly interested in Neitzchian currents, in recognizing that the values, which had been kept out of play by scientific methods, cannot but burst back into social life. This also forms part of the arguments taken up by Bauman in his emphasis on the inability of the ordering principles of modernity ever to finally resolve the ambiguities inherent in social life. Goldthorpe, who is fully aware of the methodological issues at stake in his advocacy of a deductive approach to class analysis, argues that because no ultimate resolution of value issues can be hoped for, it is best not to talk about them at all – a sort of gentleman's agreement not to air one's dirty linen in public. Weber's view, however, is somewhat different. Although he accepts the irresolvable nature of value disputes, not addressing these values has real costs too – it contributes to the 'disenchantment of the world'.

By taking the route of deductive social theory, the class analysis of Goldthorpe and his followers has gained consistency at a cost. The cost, in this case, is the inability to engage with other research traditions or to take cues from matters of concern or interest outside the specific tradition from which class analysis is derived. It is striking that whereas the Marxist tradition has shown considerable verve in self-criticism (notably in the analytical Marxist school), and in engaging with ideas from outside its own canon, Weberian scholarship has not done this, even where this might not prove difficult. Thus, despite the potential of Weber's theory of bureaucracy as a means of reflecting on the relationship between organizational processes and class analysis, there are rather few contemporary Weberians who have shown much interest in considering the role of organization in class analysis (a partial exception is Scott 1996). Similarly, Weber's theory of status seems to allow intellectual space for reflecting on cultural processes and class formation. However, there has been very little interest from within the Weberian camp in empirically examining the nature of status and its interrelationship to class. For all the considerable sophistication of neo-Weberian stratification theory, it has been unable to ultimately ground class itself. Triumphalist neo-Weberians who celebrate the problems of Marxist class theory have perhaps rejoiced prematurely. Who is interested in the Weberian answers to Marxist questions, if Marxist questions are no longer being asked?

Whither class analysis?

The impasse of class theory refers first and foremost to the exhaustion of the classical tradition of class theory. I have argued in this chapter that the conceptual cupboard of classical class theory looks dusty. To those not so-cialized into its particular interests, the problem is not that the cupboard is bare, but rather that the items inside seem out of date. What both Marxist and Weberian perspectives on class lack is any clear theoretical explanation as to why and how class matters. Marxist writers, we have seen, have shown how capitalist dynamics are crucial to understanding contemporary social life. What they have failed to do is to show why this necessitates theorizing class (rather than capitalism). Neo-Weberian writers have run up against the limits of Weber's own ideal type methods. They are able to give an elaborate account of how class might be defined, conceptualized and measured if an observer is prepared to take the intellectual gamble that it is important. Neither Marxists nor Weberians are able to provide a convincing explanation to anyone sceptical of the importance of class that class is a fundamental feature of social life. Marxists are more likely to persuade the observer to examine the systemic dynamics of contemporary capitalism.

Yet, despite the theoretical problems of class analysis, there is wide-spread recognition from both Marxists and Weberians that property, organ-ization/authority and skill/expertise are significant structuring devices in producing social division. Given the problems of Marxist and Weberian class theories, one response is *not* to find a new foundation for class theory, like taking a rabbit out of a hat (though there are some interesting recent attempts to do precisely this).[25] Perhaps a little more time messing around, in more empirical vein, by examining the processes by which property, organ-ization and culture are related to class formation may be a useful strategic venture. In this book I seek to draw out some of the empirical and theoret-ical issues raised in various fields of research which have been influenced by class analysis over recent decades, in order to gradually excavate ground on which to develop my arguments about property, cultural capital, organiza-tional processes and individualization. However, this exercise involves strip-ping away redundant ideas about class as much as it does developing new perspectives, and in the following three chapters I will take further my reflec-tions on the impasse of class analysis. I will show that three topics, all taken to be central to traditional class analysis (class consciousness and identity, economic inequality, and social mobility) do not readily support easy claims about the centrality of class. The next three chapters can therefore be read both as a review of research in three leading fields in class analysis, and as reflections on the difficulties (and some virtues) in empirically grounding class analysis.

Notes

1 See for instance Edgell (1992), Crompton (1998), Lee and Turner (1996), Butler and Savage (1995). The exceptions are Wright (1989) and Pakulski and Waters (1996).
2 Booth (1903) distinguished eight classes and Rowntree (1902) seven. These class definitions were not based on occupational criteria but were according to the wealth and general prosperity of households. One indication of Booth's intentions is revealed in a letter written to Alfred Marshall: 'I am engaged on an attempt to

describe analytically the industrial and social status of the population of London; that is to state the proportions in which different classes exist, with the actual present condition of each' (Bales 1994: 105).

3 For instance, Glass' (1954) study of social mobility was the first national random sample survey.

4 Social anthropology, being devoted to 'other' countries, did not need to elaborate a class-based approach. Economics, much of which was concerned with international economic issues linked to empire, also tended not to rely on a class-based perspective, though traces of this can be found, for instance in the writings of Toynbee.

5 See Joyce (1994).

6 The prime example of this, of course, was in the affluent worker studies of Goldthorpe and Lockwood (1968a, 1968b, 1969), which promised a sociological study of issues – i.e. the culture and politics of affluent manual workers – which had been opened up in the previous decade by political commentators such as Abrams and Rose (1960).

7 For instance, the emergence of ethnomethodology in the late 1960s, feminism and the renewal of Marxist theory in the 1970s, etc.

8 The most important of these have been in the *International Journal of Urban and Regional Research*, sparked off by Pahl (1989); in *Sociology*, sparked off by Goldthorpe and Marshall (1992); and in *International Sociology*, sparked off by Clark *et al.* (1993).

9 On gender, see (for instance) Barrett (1980), Walby (1986); on race see Rex and Moore (1967).

10 In this respect it is the final playing out of the trend diagnosed by Anderson (1976) whereby the western Marxist tradition has steadily distanced itself from economic issues and become more involved with cultural questions as the twentieth century has advanced.

11 Which is not to say that Regulation School concepts cannot help to illuminate certain issues pertaining to class. One example is the way that their interest in consumption may lead to a concern with patterns of class-based consumption behaviours.

12 To be exact, 'according to the thesis of self-ownership, each person possesses over himself, as a matter of moral right, all those rights that a slaveholder has over a complete chattel as a matter of legal right, and he is entitled, morally speaking, to dispose over himself in the way such a slaveholder is entitled, legally speaking, to dispose over his slave' (Cohen 1995: 68).

13 There are serious philosophical problems in identifying states such as these. Wright's conception tends to depend on a zero-sum conception of power, whereby the furtherance of one person's interests involves the denigration of another, but there are situations where both parties can benefit and yet it can still be said that exploitation occurs. In addition, it does not follow that, if one person does suffer, they are necessarily unjustly treated (and hence exploited). See Cohen (1995).

14 For instance Goldthorpe and Marshall (1992), and in more gentle tones, Scott (1996).

15 This issue of the possible reconciliation between Marxist and Weberian class theory is discussed in Abercrombie and Urry (1983), Savage (1994) and Crompton (1998). The recent work of Tilly (1998) might be seen as an attempt to marry the two traditions.

16 This is Giddens' (1973) term which was first coined to examine the relationship between economic and social class and was subsequently given more general application in his broader social theory (see Giddens 1984).

17 The emphasis on class formation is pronounced, especially in Lockwood (1958), Goldthorpe (e.g. 1983) and Marshall *et al.* (1988).

18 The classic example, of course, is *The Protestant Ethic and the Spirit of Capitalism* (Weber 1905).

19 There are no prima facie reasons why class analysis is better placed than say, political sociology, urban sociology, the sociology of science and technology, the sociology of the life course, or indeed any other sub-field of sociology, to explore the interaction between 'historically formed macro-structures' and the 'everyday experience of people'.

20 Consider the following quote from Goldthorpe and Marshall's (1992) paper: 'to study social mobility within the context of a class structure, rather than, say, that of a status hierarchy, is a conceptual choice that must be made a priori' (p. 387).

21 See for instance, their discussion of the 'immediate causes' of 'low educational attainment, voting labour, and suffering from chronic bronchitis' which are not necessarily directly due to class (Goldthorpe and Marshall 1992: 386).

22 The best discussions of these issues is Marshall *et al.* (1988), and more recently Crompton (1998).

23 A good example can be found in the difficulties Evans has in engaging with ways of reflecting on social stratification other than his own. See the debate between Evans (1997, 1999a) and Blackburn and Prandy (1997). Another example of this general point is Morris and Scott's (1994) critique of the account by Marshall *et al.* (1994) of the underclass for not operating with an appropriately Weberian concept of the class structure.

24 In this respect, Weber presages the post-modern critique of Enlightenment reason which has become powerful in recent years (see Lyotard 1979; Bauman 1988).

25 Notably Aage Sorenson's (2000) attempt to draw out of neoclassical economics a way of deriving classes by the rents from which they derive their income, and Charles Tilly's (1998) attempt to define classes according to different forms of categorical relationships. It might be noted here however, that Tilly does continue to draw strongly on the Marxist and Weberian heritage of class analysis.

2 *The* **limits** *to* **class consciousness**

This chapter examines whether, and how, people are aware of class. For, if class identities matter to people, then this is a powerful reason to defend class analysis, whatever the theoretical problems of class analysis may be. I therefore sidestep – albeit only strategically,[1] – the conceptual problems delineated in Chapter 1. And indeed, it can be argued that the attempt to place class analysis on a deductive footing – in the neo-Weberian style discussed in Chapter 1 – is to retreat from one of the enduring sources of appeal of the British class analysis tradition. Many of the most celebrated British writers on class have been less concerned with the theoretical logic of class analysis than with the enduring cultural centrality of class. Consider Edward Thompson, who argued in *The Making of the English Working Class* (1963) that it was the subjective awareness of class and injustice which was central to the processes of class formation which developed in industrializing Britain. Consider also British cultural studies, especially as articulated through the Centre for Contemporary Cultural Studies (CCCS), which emerged from debates about class cultures (Hoggart 1956). Even in sociology, writers such as Gordon Marshall make the popular salience of social class a major part of their defence of class analysis. In *Social Class in Modern Britain*, Marshall *et al.* (1988: 155) note that 'our data suggest that contemporary Britain is still widely perceived among its population as being class structured, and . . . class is readily available as a source of social identity to most people'. Class matters because people think it matters. So long as it is salient, class should be a matter of interest, whatever problems there may be in providing a satisfactory deductive concept of class.

This chapter will consider first the kinds of claims made by those arguing for an inductive, culturalist theory of class, and second the relevant evidence which bears on the extent to which Britain can be seen as a class conscious society. I detail three separate, though at times interrelated, currents of academic work that have stressed the importance of class cultures. These three traditions are, first, neo-Weberian industrial sociology (associated particularly with David Lockwood); second, social history (associated with Edward Thompson); and finally cultural studies (associated with Richard Hoggart and Raymond Williams). These three currents of work all promised, in the 1960s, to offer a way of rejecting functionalist theories of cultural integration by showing how British culture was stratified by class. However, all three intellectual currents came up against serious conceptual problems in the following decades, and found it impossible to find a non-reductionist way of handling culture, with the result that there is no satisfactory way of understanding the relationship between class and class consciousness.

The difficulties faced by the culturalist writers of these three traditions are not simply problems of conceptualization, but are related to sustained empirical difficulties in showing that class is a major source of social identity in Britain. In the second section I show that Britain is not a class-conscious society, at least not in the sense that people have well-developed and articulate views about membership of collective class groupings and a clear sense of their place in the class system. The conclusions of this chapter are therefore stark. Despite the calls of sociologists such as Crompton (1998) for a renewal of cultural approaches to class, the conceptual resources and empirical evidence does not offer any ready hope for this venture.

Culturalist approaches to class analysis in British social research

Industrial and stratification sociology

As I discussed in Chapter 1, the emergence of academic sociology in Britain from the 1950s involved a sustained attempt to draw on the theoretical heritage of Marx and Weber to provide a rigorous theorization of class. This mode of sociological analysis actually arrived late on the British intellectual scene. Earlier approaches, notably that associated with the 'political arithmetic' tradition, drew on culturalist conceptions of class. Of course these researchers were concerned to draw up 'objective' measures of class. Nonetheless, even Booth and Rowntree insisted that social classes were defined culturally, and thereby that the salience of social class was linked to the popular recognition of class. Class was hence a measure of status. This can be seen in late Victorian attempts to develop an official class 'map' of the British population. Szreter (1996) has shown how the registrar general's class schema, first used in 1911, encoded cultural assumptions about the standing of different social groups. It placed professionals at the top, managers and administrators next, and the manual working class, divided into three levels, at the bottom. This class schema continued to be officially used until the 1970s, and its rationale continued to be defined in status terms: 'The unit groups included in each of these [class] categories . . . have been selected so as to ensure that, so far as possible, each category is homogenous in relation to the basic criterion of the *general standing within the community* of the occupations concerned' (derived from Reid 1989: 53, emphasis added).

The registrar general's class schema never validated its claim that its class model accurately reflected popular perceptions of the status order. This weakness threw down the gauntlet to sociologists, using new survey techniques, to examine whether its categories did indeed reflect popular assumptions.[2]

During the middle years of the twentieth century the main sociological alternative was the Hall–Jones scale, developed in Merseyside in the 1930s and used by Glass (1954) in the first major British social mobility study. The same procedure of devising a class schema whose validity was dependent on its ability to tap popular views about the social standing of occupations was continued by Goldthorpe and Hope (1974). They asked respondents to rank occupations on four dimensions,[3] which led to the 36 categories which were to form the Hope–Goldthorpe scale, and which were in turn to be the building blocks of the Nuffield class schema (Goldthorpe *et al.* 1980).

The legitimacy of this intellectual project rested upon the claim that the class schema acceptably measured the way people *perceived* the social hierarchy. Subjective class awareness was fundamental to anchoring the meaning of class, and the study of class awareness and class consciousness was thereby an essential feature of the tradition. Glass' book *Social Mobility in Britain* (1954) therefore contained extensive discussions of the extent of class awareness in Britain, and his research effort also led, in the late 1950s and early 1960s, to a string of case studies examining, in unprecedented detail, the nature of class consciousness in Britain.

Undoubtedly the key figure in elaborating the sociological interest in class consciousness was David Lockwood, whose study of *The Blackcoated Worker* (1958) was subtitled *A Study in Class Consciousness*. He used a detailed case study of a specific occupation (clerical workers) to underscore how manual and non-manual workers inhabited different cultural worlds with very different sets of attitudes and values.[4] Theoretically, Lockwood wrestled with the implications of class awareness for analysing norms and values, where he engaged with American structural functionalism. Here, a paradox unravelled. The main conceptual warrant for suggesting that there were commonly held beliefs about social class was actually a functionalist one. For functionalists, beliefs about the different standings of social groups reflected the different social worth which these groups were supposed to have. However, as class analysis developed in British sociology, its leading exponents, notably Goldthorpe (1964) and Lockwood (1964) disputed this functionalist premise and insisted that power conflicts shaped social relations and cultural frameworks. However, if these critiques of functionalism were true, then how could they point to the existence of general norms and assumptions about social class divisions which they simultaneously invoked in order to justify class analysis and to find a way of measuring class? This was an emerging logical flaw in the British class analysis tradition. If class was as important as they suggested, then there should be no consensus about what constitutes the ranking of occupations. But if there is no consensus, then how could class be measured culturally?

This intellectual problem led to the dissolution of the cultural tradition within sociological class analysis. It set in train an intellectual reformulation of class analysis which was to lead, over a decade later, to the deductive Nuffield approach to class analysis in which Goldthorpe staked out a non-culturalist approach to class which did not rely on the existence of shared popular views about class. However, for much of the 1960s, it seemed possible to defend a culturalist perspective that did not demand a functionalist foundation. Lockwood's work was crucially important here. He recognized that while there may indeed be no overarching social norms defining social rankings and values about class, it may be possible to show how particular kinds of values and norms arose out of different kinds of social location. He helped to theoretically elaborate an approach to class analysis (later labelled the 'Structure–Consciousness–Action' (S–C–A) model (see Pahl 1989) which argued that different modes of class consciousness were the key mediating factor in explaining how social position gave rise to class action. His most important arguments were developed in the mid-1960s (especially Lockwood 1966) as part of his involvement in the 'affluent worker project' which he undertook with Goldthorpe (Goldthorpe and Lockwood 1968a, 1968b, 1969). Lockwood argued that three distinctive kinds of working-class images of society could be distinguished. First, there was a 'them and us' mentality based on the recognition of power inequalities between classes; second, there was a deferential outlook in which loyal workers followed true leaders; and third, there was an instrumental attitude in which people recognized many differences according to how much money people earned. Lockwood argued that each of these had a distinctive social location (mining communities, farming villages, and new industrial towns being the 'ideal typical' cases).

Lockwood's work in the late 1950s and early 1960s, with its rare combination of theoretical sophistication and empirical range, can be seen as the culmination, the high point, yet also the breaking point, of the entire British class analysis tradition as it had developed over the previous century. The intellectual problem Lockwood faced was how to root 'images of society' in specific social milieus without *reducing* such values to social structures. Lockwood's own intellectual trajectory shows how seriously he recognized the difficulty of defending his own arguments. For much of the 1970s and 1980s he wrote little, yet his few writings of the period indicate growing unease with the S–C–A model he had helped to develop. His paper 'The weakest link in the chain?' (Lockwood 1988) offered a devastating critique of the reductionism inherent in Marxist approaches to class (but which also had implications for his own earlier formulations). In his sophisticated analysis of the social theory of Durkheim and Marx (Lockwood 1992) he distanced himself from class analysis. He argued that neither Marx nor Durkheim provided a theoretical resolution to the structure–action dualism, and although he held out the prospect of Weber offering a more satisfactory perspective, the Weber he drew on was one who emphasized the irreducibility of social norms to any kind of social base. In his most recent analyses, Lockwood has endorsed a model of 'civic stratification' which disputes the extent to which class is a key factor in the stratification process (Lockwood 1996).

Lockwood's own intellectual course is therefore indicative of broader problems in the sociological study of class consciousness. At a more practical level, the critique of functionalism also had implications for the kinds of ranking exercises that placed occupations in classes. It was difficult to find an adequate methodology to defend the ranking exercise by which early class classifications were drawn up. Goldthorpe and Hope (1974) offered the last major attempt in Britain to defend the ranking exercise, by allowing respondents to rank occupations using several criteria and then assessing their consistency across different headings. However, a series of withering critiques of ranking surveys were developed by Coxon and Jones (1978, 1979), who claimed that people's responses to such surveys did not distinguish between their own views and those which they were *supposed* to give. Pawson (1989) showed that Hope and Goldthorpe failed to address the problem of 'interviewing as a social occasion' (see also Coxon and Jones 1978, 1979). The responses given by respondents might either be a reflection of what they felt the social ranking of occupations to be, or their own personal valuation of those occupations. Although reasonably consistent rankings could be obtained, it was not clear that these reflected anything more than intelligent people replying in a way which they thought would win them social approval.

Since the 1970s there have been no sustained inquiries into the ranking of occupations, a striking fact in its own terms. It is noteworthy that official attempts to root class measures in status categories ended in the 1970s.[5] The justification for the registrar general's class schema was changed in this decade so that in 1980 it was claimed that the classes were not meant to reflect different levels of social standing, but rather different levels of skill (although in fact the actual classes distinguished changed very little). Perhaps the most striking development was that as Goldthorpe began to report the results of the Nuffield mobility studies, he subtly changed the criteria for measuring class. He no longer linked his class schema to the ranking of occupations, but instead to the *objective* work and market situation which they were felt to exemplify.[6]

Research in the 1970s demonstrated that many people simply did not have consistent or clear class images (see the debate following Lockwood's formulations of different 'working-class images of society' (Bulmer 1975)). Researchers struggled to find workers who were consistently proletarian, deferential or instrumental. More usually, attitudes from all three of these perspectives (and others) were articulated by the same people. This added to the feeling that no clear patterns of class consciousness existed, but rather that different kinds of views were 'wheeled on' in different situations. Thus Westergaard (1970) pointed out that allegedly instrumental workers could sing revolutionary songs when there was a strike, and Newby (1975) showed that deference was situationally specific.

These points were given particular force by Michael Mann (1970, 1973) who argued that survey evidence disputed the existence of radical working-class consciousness. He instead 'noted that the radical elements of workers' consciousness in Britain and the U.S. were of the "populist" kind . . . rather than of a class or political kind . . . the compliance of the working class with the authority structure of liberal democracy rested largely on the "pragmatic acceptance" of its lowly position in society' (Mann 1973: 30). Mann's arguments concerning the way that powerless classes developed 'dualistic consciousness' became echoed in other work of the time, for instance Lukes' (1971) emphasis on the third face of power, in which power is so pervasive that those subject to it are not able to question its presuppositions.

Leading writers nurtured within the British culturalist tradition increasingly distanced themselves from it. While Lockwood chose to emphasize the irreducibility of values to any direct social base, Goldthorpe moved in the other direction. He embraced instrumentalism, in which he argued that rational actors, from different class positions, would act in different ways because of the different constraints and opportunities that faced them.[7] This intellectual move allowed Goldthorpe to explain why class affected people's actions, even in the absence of class consciousness. People from different social classes, and with the same general outlook, can, by virtue of their social position, engage in different kinds of actions. Thus, he argued that class conflict in the 1970s:

> reflect[ed] a heightened dissent over distributional, and in turn industrial relations issues – *which presupposed ultimate goals that were largely held in common*: for example those listed by Crosland of 'choice, leisure, comfort, privacy and a more spacious family life', plus, I would want to say, greater control over one's destiny in working life.
>
> (Goldthorpe 1988: 47, emphasis added)

Goldthorpe sees 'rational action theory' as a preferable way of conceptualizing the salience of class rather than the S–C–A model that Lockwood elaborated. Certainly, it is striking that even in his most robust defence of class analysis, written with Gordon Marshall (Goldthorpe and Marshall 1992), he makes no claims concerning the cultural salience of class.

We have seen how sociological emphases on class consciousness proved theoretically problematic. Sociologists were unable to simultaneously offer a critique of functionalism, a valid class schema, and a non-reductive analysis of class identity. In this respect the sociological tradition, which promised so much, ultimately came unstuck. While it is possible to lament the sidelining of 'culture' within the Nuffield tradition (Crompton 1998), it needs to be understood that this move was in response to a major intellectual problem. It is not adequate simply to call for a reinstatement of a cultural perspective within class analysis without recognizing how the deep intellectual problems that became apparent in the 1960s might be overcome. This is the moment to consider whether writers in social and labour history offered any kind of way out of this impasse.

Social and labour history

Despite the remarkable flowering of industrial sociology in the 1960s, it was the Marxist labour historians who became the most celebrated exponents of culturalist perspectives on class. Undoubtedly the main influence was E.P. Thompson, whose *The Making of the English Working Class* (1963) exercised a profound impact on subsequent historical, and too a lesser extent sociological, scholarship. Like Lockwood and the British sociologists, Thompson's ire was directed against American functionalist sociologists. The main target was Neil Smelser (1962), who argued that industrialization brought about the modernization of social relations almost mechanically, and did not recognize the role played by historical actors themselves in bringing about social change. Thompson, by contrast, emphasized that the 'working class had been present at its own making', and that the cultural idioms and values of the emerging working class itself played a crucial role in defining the course of British history, and in particular in development of modern democratic freedoms. For Thompson (1978: 85) class consciousness was a crucial defining feature of class itself:

> when we speak of a class we are thinking of a very loosely defined body of people who share the same categories of interests, social experiences, traditions and value systems, who have a disposition to behave as a class, to define themselves in their own actions and in relation to other groups of people in class ways.

For Thompson, the English working class came into being during the early nineteenth century, by drawing upon old cultural motifs of the 'Freeborn Englishman' which had existed for several centuries. Through championing a democratic, radical politics that challenged the Establishment and celebrated working-class culture as an embodiment and practical expression of a democratic and populist culture, the working class was established at the centre of British society and politics. Thompson (e.g. 1965) claimed that this cultural presence persisted, in part through the influence of the labour movement, into the late twentieth century and remained an enduring force defining the best, most progressive features of British social and political life.

Thompson established the idea that class should be seen as a cultural process that was dynamic and historically mutating. Although his focus on the relationship between class structure and class awareness was similar to that which Lockwood was exploring at the same time, his historical sensibilities allowed him greater flexibility in handling it. Lockwood's ideal type (of three types of working class image of society) was a-historical, and did not explore how interplay between consciousness and structure over time might affect these images.[8] Yet Thompson exposed himself to attack from two sides, which raised rather similar issues to those which confronted Lockwood in his attempt to develop a non-reductive account of class cultures. Some Marxists claimed Thompson did not anchor class consciousness sufficiently in the social relations of capitalism (see Johnson 1978; Anderson 1980) and therefore conceded too much to the autonomy of culture. On the other hand, conservative historians disputed empirically whether the evidence was sufficient to allow Thompson to claim that working-class culture existed in the form that he identified (e.g. Currie and Hartwell 1965). Thompson skilfully, if not always convincingly, defended his middle course between these two lines of attack for much of the 1960s and 1970s. His case was made less by the clarity of his methodological arguments about class consciousness, and more by the extent to which his work offered a persuasive narrative of British social history which retained some of the distinctive emphases of traditional historiography (for instance, the idea of there being a British democratic tradition), but which inverted some of the usual emphases (so that the working class became the key democratic force).

Thompson's work was thoroughly ambivalent methodologically. He publicly hid these ambiguities behind rhetorical flourishes that emphasized the way that the 'historical method' could (in some mysterious way) resolve enduring theoretical problems such as the relationship between structure and agency (e.g. Thompson 1978). Ultimately, these problems could not be evaded. The question Thompson ducked was how can one legitimately derive claims about working-class cultural values from the atypical historical materials which happen to survive the passage of time. In *The Making of the English Working Class* (1963) Thompson's strategy was to extrapolate the existence of class cultures from the writings of radical leaders and from specific social and political movements, notably reform campaigns and trade union action. Given that such movements hardly exhausted the kinds of collective actions carried out by popular groups at the time, he did not make it clear how he could generalize from these in a satisfactory way.

There were two possible ways of resolving this issue. One of them drew upon anthropological endeavours to show how popular actions embodied particular cultural frames, and thereby to show how specific kinds of material culture, ritual customs, and political repertoires could be 'decoded' to reveal the class cultures which lay behind them. In his later work Thompson pursued this project with a series of illuminating studies of popular movements such as food riots and customs such as wife selling (Thompson 1995). During the 1970s this body of work gained emphasis as the history of 'material culture' and the focus on everyday life, especially strongly developed in German research (Ludtke 1982), seemed to offer a robust way of generalizing about class cultures from particular examples of micro-history. The study of popular culture, and in particular the examination of leisure (Stedman Jones 1974), as well as working practices (e.g. Joyce 1987) were all grist to this mill. However, as this body of work developed, it became increasingly difficult to identify class as being the main determinant of such cultural frameworks. Gender, ethnicity, age, national identity, religion and a myriad of other processes all seemed equally, or more, salient in the structuring of these kinds of popular activities, and class retreated into the background.

A second, alternative way of filling out Thompson's approach to class was developed at a slightly later date. This proceeded in the opposite direction from that of the anthropological movement, and placed greater emphasis on analysing textual documents. As I have emphasized, the use of these sources formed part of Thompson's own approach, but his reading of the documents stressed that class cultures could be discerned by placing these documents in their historical context. Stedman Jones (1984), in his account of Chartist political writing, conducted a closer textual reading of these accounts in order to show how the explicit narratives rarely made reference to an economically grounded theory of class, but rather relied on political discourse. This line of argument was taken further by Joyce (1990) who drew more explicitly on post-structuralist writing to show how routine texts arising out of popular culture in the late nineteenth century exhibited a populist rather than class-based frame of reference.

Joyce's arguments have been the subject of acrimonious debate, the details of which we can pass over here.[9] Although Joyce's rather catholic fusion of diverse, and by no means compatible, intellectual currents[10] has readily exposed him to flanking intellectual charges demonstrating the lack of intellectual coherence in his arguments, he is right to point out that his critics have no robust and adequate theory of class and culture to fall back on. This is manifest by the fact that his critics have also embraced a linguistic approach to culture (see Belchem and Kirk 1997a), even if they prefer to place this within a socially contextualized, realist perspective (see Belchem and Kirk 1997b: 2–3). This critical response to the 'linguistic turn' has depended on reviving a traditional view of history as complex and multivalent, which is thereby incompatible with any kind of reductionist move,[11] and which is not conducive to retaining a coherent theory of class consciousness in its wake. Some historians have continued to explore ramifications of British class cultures by completely eschewing thorny questions of theory (see notably McKibbin 1998). Perhaps the most compelling recent historical work that faces up to this issue is that by Lawrence (1998), which, while distancing itself from post-modernist textual emphases, recognizes the inherent impossibility of any mode of political representation fully absorbing that which it claims to stand for.[12] Lawrence's arguments could be used as much for cultural as for political representation and clearly point to the lack of a coherent theory of class consciousness within contemporary social history.

Cultural studies

In many respects cultural studies offers the most intriguing case to reflect on the intellectual trajectory of the concept of class consciousness. It is remarkable that a discipline which emerged in the 1960s primarily as a set of intellectual reflections on class cultures has, in less than 30 years, shifted its intellectual foundations so much that the study of class has almost entirely disappeared from its agenda.[13] More than either sociology or social history it has embraced post-structuralist currents that have proved highly critical of class-based accounts of cultural forms. Its intellectual shifts therefore elucidate some of the problems in developing a satisfactory account of the relationship between class and culture.

The origins of cultural studies in Britain lie with the influence of Richard Hoggart and Raymond Williams, whose work provided influential models for the discipline. These writers had links with the same intellectual current as the social historians discussed above, largely due to their common involvement in New Left political debate of the time. They forged a distinctively British understanding of the relationship between class and capitalism. Whereas intellectuals in comparable capitalist nations emphasized the extent to which the working classes were especially prone to be absorbed into the 'mass society' brought about by the expansion of commercial capitalism, writers such as Hoggart and Williams (drawing partly on the same intellectual move as was being made at a similar time by Edward Thompson) emphasized that 'traditional' working-class values might constitute some kind of critical bulwark against 'massification'. Whereas writers in other nations focused their cultural anxieties on the ability of the middle classes to sustain 'treasured' national values, in the British case it was the working class whose cultural calibre was the subject of 'worry'. There were no British sociologists to compare with the Americans C. Wright Mills (1951) and W. Whyte (1957) in lamenting the declining ability of the American middle and white collar classes to resist the creeping forces of bureaucratic conformity. In the British case the focus was on whether the working class were able to resist such pressures and whether they were able to retain their role as the 'progressive' force in British society.

This intellectual move needed to construct the working class both as potential victim of mass commercialism, *and* its potential saviour. Both Williams and Hoggart found a way of reconciling this tension by presenting a nostalgic historical picture of the working class, in which old, traditional working-class values were contrasted with the contemporary difficulties facing working-class culture posed by the spread of commercial forces. This argument drew strongly on autobiographical material. Having both been brought up in working-class families between the two world wars, their writings looked back autobiographically at the lost world of their childhood, and drew attention to the close bonds and ties characteristic of what they saw as 'working-class communities'. They focused less on the precise content of class beliefs and more on the values they saw as embedded in distinctive working-class forms of sociability, in the everyday fabric of life, or what Williams calls 'the structure of feeling'. This perspective is different from that of Lockwood's 'images of society'. Whereas the latter focused on the actual contents of popular beliefs (for instance concerning how people understood power relations), the former emphasized the emotional and intuitive dimensions of social solidarity. Williams and Hoggart saw working class culture as embodying a kind of working class collectivism which was a welcome counter to the competitive and individualistic culture characteristic of dominant capitalist, middle-class, society. For Hoggart (1956: 68, 70):

> In any discussions of working-class attitudes much is said of the group sense, the feeling of being not so much an individual with a 'way to make' as one of a group whose members are all roughly level and likely to remain so ... [this feeling] arises from a knowledge, born of close living together, that one is inescapably part of a group.

The same idea is perhaps found more clearly and directly in the writings of Raymond Williams. For Williams (1958: 327), working-class culture:

> is not proletarian art, or council houses, or a particular use of languages; it is rather, the basic collective idea, and the institutions, manners, habits of thought and intentions which proceed from this. Bourgeois culture, similarly is the basic individualist idea ... the culture which it [the working class] has produced ... is the collective democratic institution, whether in trade unions, the co-operative movement or political party.

Both writers articulated a vision of the essential collectivism of working-class culture. This was seen as opposing the individualism of middle-class culture and thereby provided them with a lever for drawing on working-class culture to mount a cultural critique of commercializing capitalism. This sense of the close relationship between communal ties and working-class culture proved enormously influential in affecting the terms of debate about the nature of contemporary cultural change.

There have been many recent critiques of Williams' and Hoggart's work. Neither are dispassionate or 'objective' accounts. Their work can be criticized as sentimental, as exaggerating the cohesiveness and solidarity of working-class life (see Bourke 1994), and as not recognizing the dynamic, changing qualities of working-class culture (e.g. White 1983). These empirical objections are, however, not the fundamental issues at stake here. What is striking about the intellectual legacy of early cultural studies is the formulation of class cultures as historical residues, as nostalgic figures whose lingering presence could help explain current concerns. The great advantage of such a formulation is that it did not depend on a 'real', or at least 'empirically demonstrable' working-class culture to make its powerful intellectual case. It was possible to see class cultures as memories, as ghostly figures whose decline helped to place contemporary cultural forms in relief. Undoubtedly the most celebrated examples of this mode of analysis come from the CCCS, whose work in the 1970s used this nostalgic mode of explanation to examine all manner of cultural forms as diverse as football hooliganism, youth culture, and racism (e.g. Hall and Jefferson 1975). In all cases the mode of explanation was the same. The break up of the nostalgic 'working-class community' led to attempts to symbolically reclaim the integrity of these old, imagined spaces, but in displaced, even 'debased' forms.

This mode of explanation was not to survive the late 1970s. The impact of feminism (CCCS 1978), and a growing awareness of issues around race and ethnicity (CCCS 1982) led to a critical re-evaluation of the nostalgic working-class community. Intellectual currents associated with the structuralist turn, influenced initially by the rediscovery of the writings of Antonio Gramsci, and the French Marxist philosopher Louis Althusser, stressed the autonomy of cultural values – the extent to which they were 'relatively autonomous' from economic determinants (e.g. Hall 1980). These currents were taken much further during the 1980s as the post-modern critique of social science developed and challenged representational models of truth and knowledge – i.e. that beliefs, narratives or accounts could be seen as either true or false accounts of an objectively existing 'reality' (see for instance Lyotard 1984). More significantly still, because the early traditions of cultural studies defined class cultures as inherently collective cultures, they had nothing to say about the forms of individualized cultures which writers such as Giddens (1990) and Beck (1992) came to see as being of major significance. It was social theorists such as Foucault (1974, and see Rose 1989) and Strathern (1991) who appeared to offer more help in reflecting on these issues.

Ultimately, Hoggart and Williams undercut the value of a class perspective by defining it in both historical and collective terms. By taking this analytical step, the warrant for which was not anchored empirically, the idea of class was cast into a mould which made it difficult to use as a source of investigation for new cultural phenomena. It was not until the 1980s saw the popularization of Bourdieu's arguments, with their rather different emphases on the relationship between class and culture, that a perspective more able to examine the limited cultural salience of class appeared.[14]

In this section I have argued that the British inductive tradition reached its height in the 1960s. During this period, a series of major works put the study of class consciousness centre stage and promised to offer a powerful interpretative tool in the study of social class. Thirty years later, this potential has not only failed to redeem itself, but it seems that the intellectual foundations for this project have been shot to pieces. It is important to recognize the full gravity of this situation. It marks the 'dead end' of the British inductive class analysis tradition. Arguably, the only British researchers who have fully recognized this point are Goldthorpe and his colleagues. Their response has been to place class analysis on an entirely different footing.

The problems faced by the writers within this tradition are not just conceptual, however. There is an undercurrent flowing beneath these debates, which surfaces in the writings of Mann, Joyce and others, and recognizes that British society is actually not characterized by strong class awareness or class identities. The starting point for studies of class and culture should be the weakness of class consciousness, as I now go on to argue.

Is Britain a class conscious society?

Class identity

There is precious little evidence which indicates the existence of strong collective and articulated class cultures in contemporary Britain. Admittedly, most British people, when asked by survey researchers, have no difficulty in placing themselves in a social class. Young (1992) notes that only around 2 per cent of respondents interviewed by the annual British Social Attitudes Survey 'don't know' what class they are in. Reid (1989, 1998) shows that there has been no tendency over time for people to be less likely to allocate themselves to a class. From the 1950s to the 1980s surveys indicate that well over 90 per cent of people identified themselves as members of one class or another. Reid himself notes that 'a reasonable conclusion from this type of research would be that the term "social class" has a good deal of currency among the population at large and that people are prepared to use it themselves' (Reid 1989: 34).[15]

In general, British people tend to identify themselves as working class. Marshall *et al.* (1988) found that (when pressed) 3 per cent of people identified themselves as upper or upper middle class, 24 per cent claimed that they were middle class, 12 per cent that they were lower middle class, 11 per cent that they were upper working class, 38 per cent that they were working class, and 4 per cent that they were lower working class. It is striking that although the majority of the British labour force are in non-manual occupations, more people defined themselves as 'working class' (58 per cent of the responses of those placing themselves in a class) than middle class (42 per cent). This general picture is confirmed by other sources. The annual British Social Attitudes Survey indicates a remarkable consistency over time in the kinds of class identifications people chose. In the seven years between 1983 and 1991 the number of middle-class identifiers varied from only 24 to 27 per cent;

and the number of working-class identifiers varied from only 44 per cent to 48 per cent. As Young (1992) also indicates, if the 'upper working class' identifiers are included among the working class, no less than two thirds of the population regard themselves as working class.

This pattern is comparatively unusual. In other countries middle-class identification runs at much higher levels. In the USA, the comparable survey to that carried out by Marshall *et al.* (1988) found that only 27 per cent of Americans regarded themselves as 'working class' (see Gerteis and Savage 1998). In Japan, around 90 per cent of people think of themselves as 'middle class', and virtually no one identifies as being 'working class'. These figures have changed hardly at all since the 1960s (see Imada 1998). What can we make of these findings? Marshall *et al.* (1988) claim that they indicate the robust nature of class identification in Britain, since few people articulate alternative identities to that of class. However, this has been disputed by Saunders (1989) who claims that Marshall *et al.* (1988) bombarded respondents with a series of questions about class before asking them about their actual class identity, a procedure which is likely to lead respondents to identify in class terms.[16] If people are offered a series of social categories, then they may be able to place themselves within them, but it does not follow that they are salient to them. For instance, when people are asked to place themselves not in social classes but in ranked groups (with 1 at the top and 10 at the bottom), only 1 per cent 'did not know' which group they were in (see Brook 1992: 6, 15). Yet sociologists have rarely used this evidence to argue for the idea that people actually think in ranked hierarchical terms rather than in terms of class (though see Prandy 1997). The American case is interesting because (unlike the British case) there are widely fluctuating responses about class identification in different surveys (see Devine 1998b). The most likely reason for this fluctuation is simply the different question wordings used in different surveys (see Vanneman and Canon 1987).

People's responses to questions about class identification may also be an indirect way of 'refusing' class identity. The American and Japanese cases point to the tendency of people to claim to be middle class because this seems the least 'loaded' of various class definitions, and hence might be an indirect way of repudiating the entire 'class' discourse altogether. Kelly (1998) has argued that Japanese people claiming to be 'middle class' are just supporting the altogether more diffuse idea that they are part of the 'mainstream' or are 'ordinary' people. The British case is also interesting. It is striking that in the British Social Attitudes Survey people tend to avoid the 'extreme' classes, notably the 'upper middle' class at the top (around 2 per cent of respondents) and the 'poor' class at the bottom (3–4 per cent of respondents). The same evidence can be found in Marshall *et al.* (1988). In other words, the reason why working-class self-identification is strong in Britain may be that it also is seen as being the 'mainstream' category, which lies above the 'poor' or 'lower working class', but below the middle and upper middle class.

Support for this argument comes also from qualitative research. Devine's (1992a, 1992b) study of the social identities of affluent manual workers in Luton emphasized that the identities of nation, region and ethnicity were all strong, and need not override notions of class but could sit alongside them. Devine emphasized that most of her respondents saw themselves as 'ordinary', sometimes linked to phrases such as being 'ordinary working people'. These terms did not lead people to distinguish between middle and working class, but they can be seen as reflections of a 'mainstream' consciousness. Devine also discusses the salience of class, and in particular the way that the concept of class was used more willingly in some contexts (for instance, discussing politics) than others.

My own current research with Gaynor Bagnall and Brian Longhurst also points to the ambivalences of class identities. Our in-depth interviews with 200 people living in four sites in Manchester indicate that around two thirds of people can define themselves in terms of class. However, class identification is usually ambivalent, defensive and hesitant, prefaced by phrases such as 'I suppose I'm . . .' or 'probably I'm . . .' (see Savage *et al.* 2000). It is also striking how significant numbers of respondents made it clear that they had never thought about class before, while others switched between a working-class and middle-class definition of themselves in the course of the interview. This hardly suggests that they had thought through or reflected on their class identity with any precision.[17] However, in general, although respondents were hesitant in assigning themselves to classes, they were able to articulate a sense of class as a political issue, as a topic which was relevant to the social and political structure of British society (see the further discussion of this research in Chapter 5). Bradley (1999) comes to very similar conclusions from a very different sample. Using a workplace sample of 198 employees in the North of England she found that no less than 47 per cent refused to identify themselves as members of a class. Even those who did often talked ambivalently about their class membership. Bradley also shows that working-class identification continued to be more popular than middle class identification.

Other survey evidence suggests that much of the apparent salience of class is linked less to a strong sense of class belonging, and more to a sense of class as a major anchor for social inequalities.[18] People certainly have a strong sense that British society is riven by class conflict. Around 75 per cent of people in 1991 thought that social class mattered either 'a great deal' or 'quite a lot' in affecting people's opportunities (though Young (1992) also suggests that there is a slow but steady decline in the numbers of people assenting to this proposition). During the Thatcher years of the 1980s, the proportion of people feeling that class conflict was strong increased somewhat (see Abercrombie and Warde 1994). However, these findings may not be what they seem. The language of 'class' is one of the few public discourses which openly acknowledges the existence of social conflict (in contrast to languages of citizenship, welfare, nationality etc. which appear to be inclusive). Thus people may use the language of class to talk about their sense of social division, but in this process they may be more concerned with class *conflict* than *class* conflict. The term 'class' may simply be a secondary term on which to hang their main claim. Devine (1992a, 1992b) notes that the term 'class' is also used with most willingness and precision in discussions of

Table 2.1 How much conflict is there between the following social groups?

Is there conflict between	Strong/very strong	Not very strong/none	Don't know
Poor and rich	49.8	44.2	5.0
Working and middle class	19.1	75.5	5.5
Unemployed and those with jobs	37.6	55.4	6.9
Management and workers	52.7	41.4	5.8
Farmers and city people	25.5	66.3	8.1
Young people and older people	35.9	57.7	6.3

Source: Brook (1992: 6).

politics. When people talk of class conflict they may really be emphasizing their sense that the political arena is characterized by disagreement and conflict.

To pursue this point, Table 2.1 reports people's perceptions about which groups they think there is conflict between. It is striking that most people *do not* think that there is conflict between the middle class and working class (the terms they are most likely to use to characterize *their own* class membership). They are much more likely to state that there are conflicts between management and workers, the poor and rich, the unemployed and people with jobs, and even farmers and city people. Of course, it is quite possible, analytically, to see any of these (especially management and workers) as class conflicts: however, it does not follow that people themselves see such conflicts in terms of class. People seem to see social conflict around them but do not see themselves as engaged directly in such conflict. They chose self-assigned class labels which tend not to be seen as in conflict, while recognizing that conflict takes place in society, and that the idea of class has some generic link to this.

To conclude, the term 'class' has considerable popular currency, and it seems that people use it both to identify themselves in class terms and also to make sense of political conflict. However, class does not seem to be a deeply held personal identity, nor does 'class belonging' appear to invoke strong senses of group or collective allegiance. In so far as class is significant, it is largely with respect to politics.

Class consciousness

Studying class consciousness involves going beyond studying how someone identifies as a member of a class, and examines the extent to which a person's view about class forms part of a coherent social outlook which can be said to be consistent and organized in terms of class. Within Marxist theory it is possible to distinguish between a strong and a weak sense of class consciousness. The strong sense, drawing on Marxist and Leninist arguments, sees 'true' class consciousness as existing when members of classes are aware that class is the critical axis of social life. For the working class, class consciousness is a mode of critical awareness, which can be used to generate a political critique of capitalist society and a radical transformation of the social structure. By contrast a weaker sense of class consciousness might be what Lenin refers to as 'trade union consciousness'. Here people's sense of social and political awareness may be strongly linked to class, but there may be no recognition that revolutionary, or even more gradual, change is necessary.

Let me start with a few words concerning the strong sense of class consciousness. Even in the classic Marxist tradition this was recognized as a utopian ideal, produced in exceptional circumstances (for instance in the presence of a powerful revolutionary party, or particular contingent political conditions), rather than the routine or expected product of capitalist society. Sociologists have therefore normally been interested in the latent possibilities of revolutionary class consciousness, which is usually seen as evidence for the lack of ideological incorporation of workers into the prevailing belief system or 'dominant ideology'. There is evidence that workers have historically not endorsed the prevailing social order (e.g. Westergaard and Resler 1975), but have rather developed a sense of 'pragmatic acceptance' (see also Marshall *et al.* 1988). There continues to be consistent evidence that people tend to feel society is unjust, that inequalities are more marked than can readily be justified, and that people do not, in a sense, get what they deserve. Be this as it may, there is very little evidence that these popular feelings turn into a radical class conscious critique of contemporary society in which people feel that revolutionary changes in class relationships would alleviate these problems. Marshall *et al.* (1988: 190) emphasize that there is no evidence from their 1988 study which can 'be said to reflect a mature or developed class consciousness comprising class identity, class opposition, class totality and the conception of an alternative society'.[19]

This therefore leads us to consider class consciousness in a weaker sense, where there is no claim that it has any revolutionary potential, but simply that it is a major organizing feature of social life. I have already indicated the problems which Lockwood ran up against in his attempt to develop a model of different 'working-class images of society': subsequent research showed no clear consistency of social and political attitudes, as might be expected. The rather different efforts of Erik Wright (1996) to examine the nature of class consciousness are also problematic. Wright constructed an 'anti-capitalism' scale from a variety of different attitude questions and examined whether people from different class positions tend to have systematically divergent views on capitalism. However, Wright's 'anti-capitalism' scale combines the responses to five different questions to form a composite scale (see Wright 1996, Ch. 14). The problem is that this assumes a priori what should be demonstrated empirically. It is assumed that if people adopt one 'anti-capitalist' value (for instance that employers should not be allowed to hire scab labour during strikes) this will tend to go along with other 'anti-capitalist' attitudes (for instance that some people receive less income than they deserve). There is the problem that by calling his scale an 'anti-capitalist' scale Wright is smuggling his own values into the analysis rather than asking people directly what they think about capitalism. It would seem possible to agree that 'large corporations have too much power in

American/Swedish/Japanese society' without necessarily being intrinsically anti-capitalist, for instance. There is also the problem of the multidimensionality of people's responses to attitude questions. It is possible for people to have the same score on the attitude scale (and hence to be assumed to be similarly anti-capitalist) while actually answering all five questions which go to make it up in very different ways. Indeed Gerteis and Savage (1998) have re-analysed Wright's survey to show that American workers tend to be anti-capitalist with respect to strikes, but not with respect to management and corporate rights.

Using his rather problematic procedures, Wright argues that members of the working class in America, Sweden and Japan are somewhat more likely to have 'anti-capitalist' attitudes than members of the bourgeoisie. However Wright also finds that there is considerable national diversity in the extent to which this relationship holds up. In the remarkable Japanese case, not only are there quite limited differences between the classes, the bourgeoisie are actually somewhat anti-capitalist in their orientation (Wright 1996, Figure 14.2). The relationship between class consciousness and class location is highly mediated by national context. This confirms Marshall's (1988) critique of Wright's approach to class consciousness. Marshall emphasizes that class consciousness is not an individual or 'micro' phenomenon as Wright supposes, but that it is a collective product.

Recent British research on political attitudes emphasizes, however, the complexity of popular attitudes and the difficulty of reading off such attitudes from class. Interestingly, some of the most insistent defenders of this point are actually defenders of class analysis. Heath *et al.* (1985) argued that popular attitudes towards politics in the 1983 general election could not be understood in terms of a simple left-right (pro and anti capitalist) scale in the way that Wright would suggest. Instead, Heath *et al.* emphasize that popular attitudes are arrayed along two different axes. Attitudes towards the economy can, they claim, be seen as class based, with a left-right axis in which those supporting the working class tend to favour a role for the public sector in the economy – for instance by supporting nationalization. On the other hand, Heath *et al.* note that there is also an axis of libertarianism– conservatism, concerned for instance with the environment and personal freedom, which does not map neatly on to the class axis. In 1983 46 per cent of electors chose 'consistent' options for both liberal and class issues (i.e. they thought that (a) companies should be nationalized and that nuclear weapons should be reduced; (b) that there should be no change for either or (c) that nationalized industries should be sold off and nuclear weapons increased). The majority held divergent views.

Heath's work emphasizes that class does not appear to organize people's attitudes in any consistent way and that there are some issues – around personal freedom and liberties (the kinds of issues which have been termed 'post-materialist' by Ingleheart 1990) which are only very indirectly related to class. Indeed, the 1980s and 1990s saw a shift towards more 'right wing', market-oriented views towards the economy at the same time that liberal views concerning personal freedoms became more popular. This theme is also taken up by Evans (1992b) in his partial critique of Marshall *et al.* (1988).

Examining six different questions used by Marshall to construct a composite index of class-consciousness, he shows that there is remarkably little consistency between any of the particular questions. Evans (1992b, Table 5) also shows that very few attitudes have any clear link to particular class locations. He emphasizes also that attitudes towards inequality and towards the 'worse off' (for instance the unemployed or low paid) are not related to class: 'The class structuring of class consciousness . . . does not imply class structuring of concern for those on welfare, or opposition to the free market' (Evans 1992b: 249). And he finishes by noting that 'for those beliefs and values that do not involve obvious class related costs and benefits – even when they involve egalitarian concerns – class appears to be relatively unimportant' (p. 254).

Conclusion

The main lessons from this chapter are clear. The British tradition of class analysis, which defined the importance of class as linked to its wide social and cultural currency, has failed, both conceptually and empirically. I have shown that once the assumption that there are shared perceptions about class values is dropped, a Pandora's box of intellectual problems is opened. Conceptually, class theorists have been unable to find an adequate theorization of class consciousness which avoids, on the one hand, normative functionalist claims that class is based in shared social values about the social standing of particular occupations, and on the other hand, economic reductionism, where values are simply seen as a reflex of social location.

I have explored the failure of three different paradigms. Lockwood tried to develop a non-reductive typology of images of society, but this account exaggerated the consistency of people's world views, and depended on an ultimately deterministic perspective if it was to become anything more than illustrative. Historians such as Edward Thompson championed historical accounts of class consciousness, but failed to ground their arguments methodologically, and provided no clues as to how the class character of different cultures was to be empirically established. Finally, accounts arising from cultural studies provided a series of brilliant ideas about social and cultural change in Britain, but invoked a nostalgic mode of defining class culture inquiry that could not withstand more rigorous questioning.

These conceptual problems were linked to empirical research showing that class-consciousness is not developed and that class identities are not particularly strong in British society. Admittedly, class is a widely understood term, and people do use the term to make sense of some aspects of British society. However, Britain is not a deeply class conscious society, where class is seen embodying membership of collective groups. Although people can identify themselves as members of classes, this identification seems contextual and of limited significance, rather than being a major source of their identity and group belonging. Furthermore, people's social attitudes and views are too ambivalent to be seen as part of a consistent class-related world view. Finally, people's own class location shapes only some of their views, and even then, in highly mediated and complex ways.[20]

There are only a few signs that contemporary commentators on class have fully recognized the importance of these findings. To be sure, there are some writers such as Scase (1992) and Eder (1993) who have emphasized the absence of class awareness. Crompton (1998) has emphasized the need to interrelate status with class in order to show how modes of action are linked to economic relations. Although this argument is undeniably powerful, she does not fully discuss one of the major problems inherent in this exercise, which is the lack of a clear intellectual basis for grounding culture and class. Because of these problems, one cannot fail to be impressed by Goldthorpe's brilliant reformulation of class analysis on a non-inductive, non-culturalist base. Goldthorpe has appreciated more readily than most the need to situate class analysis deductively and to repudiate its culturalist origins. Although elements of the culturalist perspective are still present in his work, he has energetically recast it around deductive procedures, and his work constitutes the most intellectually rigorous form of class analysis currently on offer.

In this chapter we have seen a further aspect of the impasse of class analysis. At this point the reader may well wonder why the concept of class should not be completely thrown out. My argument, to be developed in later chapters, is that it is possible to reclaim a culturalist approach to class analysis, though this has to be developed in the full knowledge of the limitations of existing approaches to this question. My next chapter begins this task by showing how class continues to be implicated in the organization of economic inequality.

Notes

1 I should note that I do not endorse a fully-fledged inductive methodology. Rather, my argument here is that given the limitations of existing class theory, there is value in embracing a kind of 'strategic inductivism'. Given the impasse in class theory, there is merit in re-energizing the 'sociological imagination' by turning to consider what other branches of social research might indicate the salience of class to be in their specific areas of interest, as a prelude to working up a more developed theoretical approach to class analysis. Although I do not seek to defend this claim here, I would see this approach as compatible with the critical realist argument that it necessary for theory to be addressed to ideas about social relations as much as to social relations themselves. See Collier (1994, Ch. 6).

2 Hall and Jones (1950), Young and Willmott (1956), Goldthorpe and Hope (1974).

3 The four dimensions were standard of living, power and influence over other people, level of qualifications and value to society.

4 Lockwood's was only the best known of a major wave of comparable studies, many of them published by Routledge in the *'International Library of Sociology'* series. Other examples are Tropp's *The Schoolteachers* (1957), Kelsall's *Higher Civil Servants* (1955), Tunstall's *The Fishermen* (1962) and Hollowell's *The Lorry Driver* (1968).

5 The one partial exception to this point is the development of the Cambridge Scale (e.g. Prandy *et al.* 1980). This adopted the idea that inequality was continuous in nature (not based around bounded classes). However, rather than use attitude questions from surveys to measure such hierarchies, it extrapolated these from friendship structures. For a recent restatement, see Blackburn and Prandy (1997).

6 This was the first move towards Goldthorpe's advocacy of deductive class theory which has led to the elaboration of his more recent class schemas.

7 It should be emphasized that Goldthorpe adopts a deductive mode of rational choice theory. He thus does not claim that people necessarily do act rationally, simply that this is the easiest default assumption from which sociologists can most effectively start.

8 Though of course Lockwood's work in general shows a very strong commitment to historical issues. My point only relates to the ideal type contained in his 1966 paper.

9 The debate has generally been contained in the journal *Social History*. See Mayfield and Thorne (1992), Lawrence and Taylor (1993), Joyce (1993, 1994), Vernon (1994), Kirk (1994), Eley and Nield (1995) and Steiberg (1997). For an overview of this debate see Price (1997). I have presented an overview of some of these historical issues in Savage and Miles (1994).

10 Joyce draws upon the post-structuralist arguments of Derrida, the structuration theory of Giddens, the relational sociology of Bourdieu, Foucault's conception of 'governmentality' (Joyce 1995) and American narrative positivism without adequately showing the compatibility of their rather different approaches.

11 See for instance Richard Price (1997: 35): 'To construct history only through the arbitrary means of language and metaphor is also to deny the possibility of history as a multilayered, inter-textual set of relationships between the various spheres of social experience'.

12 'It is by . . . concentrating our critical attention on the ambiguity inherent in the claim to "speak for the people" that we can hope to understand both the role of party and the dynamics of popular politics more fully' (Lawrence 1998: 267).

13 Though in the past two years it should be pointed out that there are some signs of a trend to reassert the importance of class (see Skeggs 1997).

14 I consider the significance of Bourdieu's work in Chapter 5.

15 There are some departures from this general picture of unanimity. The most surprising in some respects is that reported by Marshall *et al.* (1988). Here the authors note that while 90 per cent of the sample could put themselves in a class when asked, a rather smaller proportion – 60 per cent – actually thought of themselves as belonging to a class.

16 It is possible that this may explain why Marshall *et al.* (1988) found a lower proportion of class identifiers than other surveys (see note 15). Perhaps it was precisely because people had been sensitized to the political issues around the question of class that they were more likely not to identify in these terms.

17 Though in some cases they clearly had, and their ambivalence reflects an awareness of their own liminal class positions, due to social mobility, for instance. These points are fully discussed in Savage *et al.* (forthcoming), and see also Chapter 5.

18 Young (1992) notes that 58 per cent of people feel 'very close' or 'fairly close' to others in the same class position as themselves, but if, as suggested above, class is seen as being a sign of being ordinary, then this simply means that people tend to be close to people they also see as being ordinary.

19 These four terms are those used by Michael Mann (1973) as constituents of class consciousness.

20 Of course I am not claiming that structural class relations do not impact on cultural forms. My argument here is more modest: that British people are not, by and large, conscious class actors with strongly, reflexively held, class-based beliefs. I develop my analysis in Chapter 5.

3 Economic inequality *and* social class

One of the most powerful defences of the concept of social class is that no other concept rivals it in exploring the sociological ramifications of economic inequality. Whatever its conceptual and empirical problems might be, if the cost of dispensing with class analysis is the complete eclipse of issues of inequality from the sociological agenda, then this may not be a price worth paying.[1] Today, leading defenders of the relevance of class, such as Scase (1992), Westergaard (1995) and Adonis and Pollard (1997) continue to see entrenched economic inequality as the bedrock of class. Yet there is a strange paradox (see also Crompton 1998; Devine and Savage 2000) that the study of economic inequality has increasingly been seen as a separate issue to the study of social class and plays little part within contemporary class analysis (see Morris and Scott 1994 for a particularly strong statement to this effect). This further contributes to the impasse in class analysis.

This chapter reclaims the study of economic inequality for class analysis by arguing against four possible objections to the idea that economic inequality – however widespread, persistent and ingrained – has much to do with class. First, as I discussed in Chapter 1, the notion of class (certainly in the Marxist tradition, but also more generally) emphasizes the centrality of the conflict between capital and labour (see for instance Crompton and Gubbay 1977; Scase 1992) as the key mechanism behind class inequality. But it could be argued that this no longer applies. In the early and mid-twentieth century, most people obtained their income either by selling their labour in the labour market and receiving wages or a salary, or by receiving a return from capital (in the form of profit, investment income, rent from property etc.). It was hence plausible to see a poor, manual working class confronting a rich capitalist class. However, or so the argument might run, today the picture is much more complex. There are sources of income which do not appear to be either returns on labour or capital in any easily classifiable way – notably income drawn from the state as benefit or welfare allowances. It has also been argued that the growing numbers of salaried, 'middle class' workers are in employment relations which are only indirectly related to the divisions between capital and labour (e.g. Goldthorpe 1982; Abercrombie and Urry 1983; Savage *et al.* 1992; Butler and Savage 1995; Crompton 1998,

Ch. 4). Furthermore, people draw income from both labour and capital. Today, around half of the adult population earns wages or salaries and also invests in capitalist markets (many of these being people with occupational pension schemes). People can also gain income from sources outside the labour market, for instance by the capital gained as houses increased in price (see Saunders 1990b). The issue here, then, is whether the capitalist labour market continues to be at the heart of economic inequality in the way that both Marx and Weber claimed.

Second, even in so far as the labour market continues to be the central source of income it does not follow automatically that the concept of class is useful. It is striking that those economists who have examined changing patterns of income and wealth rarely use the concept of class (e.g. Atkinson 1980; Hills 1996; Goodman *et al.* 1997). A frequent objection to applying the class concept is that it divides people into sharply-bounded social groups, whereas in fact economic inequality is 'graduated' in the shape of a statisticians 'curve' with few distinct cut-off points.[2] It has also been argued that classes imply a uniformity of interests among those allocated to a common class position, whereas actually there is great variety in people's economic position and it is ultimately rather arbitrary to place class boundaries around any groups.

This leads on to a third objection. It is not self-evident that inequalities between people are due to structural class divisions rather than being the result of individual factors, such as the extent to which people work hard, the extent and nature of their skills, their motivations and so forth. Some economists (e.g. Mincer 1980) have argued that just as there are returns to capital, whereby financial investment by firms in technologies, product development etc. can lead to economic rewards, so people are able to invest in their 'human capital'. They can thereby increase the returns to their labour, in the form of higher income, better job security and in other related ways.

Finally, there are social processes other than class that also structure economic inequality. Ethnicity, gender, age and geographical location are all possible candidates. For instance, one of the main factors affecting economic position is a person's household circumstances, which might be seen as largely independent of social class. During the inter-war years, the vast majority of married women with dependent children were not employed for a wage. It may have been acceptable to see the economic position of the male breadwinner as the crucial factor influencing the economic circumstances of other household members, and to argue that the male head of house was crucial for articulating the household into the class system (as Goldthorpe 1983 famously argued).[3] However, in recent years, as the conventional nuclear family has formed a minority of household types, and female income has formed a higher proportion of household income,[4] this argument has become more difficult to sustain. Since an individual's economic position rests in part upon the type of household in which he or she lives, rather than on the social class position of any one of that household's members, it is less certain that class itself is so crucial.

I have highlighted these points to emphasize that there are numerous reasons why economic class and economic inequality are not necessarily the same thing. It would be quite inappropriate to claim that because Britain is deeply economically divided it is therefore class divided. Nonetheless the argument of this chapter is that class *is* implicated in economic inequality, and that new resources within class analysis can be developed from this recognition. I pay particular attention to two themes that I develop later in this book, concerning the role of organizational processes and the individualization of class inequalities.

I begin by considering the nature of economic inequality associated with property, focusing especially on whether it is possible to pick out a distinct capitalist class from data on economic inequality. In the second section I consider the nature of inequalities within the labour market in order to demonstrate the relevance of a class perspective. The third section examines trends in income inequality over time, to show how recent patterns have accentuated processes of class polarization, and to elaborate how economic class relations have been 'individualized'.

Property and wealth in contemporary Britain

Let me begin with a broad overview of economic inequality in Britain, using evidence from the Joseph Rowntree Foundation's Report in 1995 (Joseph Rowntree Foundation 1995a, 1995b), the most recent source to hand. Table 3.1 shows how the share of the nation's income is divided between various groups.

You can see from Table 3.1 that in 1979, nearly 21 per cent of the total income earned in the UK went to the richest 10 per cent. On the other hand the poorest 10 per cent earned only 4.3 per cent of the total national income. Table 3.1 shows how these distributions changed during the 1980s. Perhaps the most striking fact is that the richest 10 per cent increased their share of the nation's income (before housing costs) to over one quarter (26 per cent), while the poorest 10 per cent saw their share of the nation's income dropping to 3 per cent. In 1991/2 the richest 10 per cent earned over eight times as much as the poorest 10 per cent, whereas in 1979 they earned

Table 3.1 Distribution of income: HBAI series 1979 to 1991/2

	Share of successive tenths of individuals by equivalized disposable income (before housing costs)									
	Poorest	*2*	*3*	*4*	*5*	*6*	*7*	*8*	*9*	*Richest*
1979	4.3	5.7	6.6	7.6	8.5	9.5	10.7	12.2	14.2	20.6
1981	4.0	5.6	6.5	7.4	8.4	9.5	10.7	12.2	14.5	21.1
1987	3.6	5.0	5.9	6.9	8.0	9.1	10.4	12.2	14.9	24.2
1988/9	3.2	4.7	5.7	6.9	7.9	9.1	10.6	12.4	15.0	24.6
1990/1	2.9	4.5	6	6	8	9	11	12	15	26
1991/2	3.0	4.4	6	6	8	9	10	13	15	26

Source: Joseph Rowntree Foundation (1995b, Table 3).

less than five times as much. The 1980s saw a marked polarization of economic fortunes as Britain became a much more unequal society. The number
who gained were significantly smaller than those who lost out, however.
Leaving aside the richest 10 per cent, every single decile group earned either
a smaller proportion of the national income (groups 1–7), or earned only
very slightly more (groups 8–9). At most, only around 30 per cent of the
population increased their share of the national income. Table 3.1 therefore
shows a marked concentration of the national share of income towards the
already wealthy. The conclusions of the Joseph Rowntree Foundation are
confirmed by every other source (e.g. Goodman *et al.* 1997).

Table 3.1 refers to relative rather than absolute shares of national income. Because Britain as a whole had become wealthier, many people who
actually saw their share of the national income decline were still better off in
absolute terms than they were in the 1970s. The exception is the poorest 10
per cent who have seen little change in their absolute income over the past
20 years. Cuts in welfare spending in the intervening period have hit this
group hard.[5] If we think about shifts in income in absolute terms the privileges of the wealthy become yet more striking. The real income of the wealthiest 10 per cent rose by over 60 per cent between 1979 and 1993/4 (Adonis
and Pollard 1997, Table 2), an astonishing increase in prosperity.

Wealth (in the form of investments in stocks and shares, housing, land
and so forth) is even more unequally divided than income. In 1998, 52 per
cent of the population had a total wealth of less than £40,000, and much of
this was the value of their home. But the very rich are different, with the top
10 per cent of the population owning 50 per cent of the nation's wealth.
Wealth can be accumulated and stored up (in the form of stocks and shares,
property etc.) whereas income cannot (it is paid at an hourly, weekly or
monthly rate, or very occasionally as annual compensation for work done).

However, significant change in wealth-holding has taken place in recent decades. The richest 1000 people in Britain in 1999 (according to *The
Sunday Times*) own £115 billion in wealth. This is only around 4 per cent of
the total wealth of the nation, but is nonetheless a huge amount. During the
1980s and 1990s the very rich enjoyed a period in which their fortunes
soared at a scale which is probably unparalleled in history. The wealthiest
200 people saw their income double in just ten years, from 1989 to 1999.[6] If
the wealthiest 1000 people were allowed to keep £1 million, but their wealth
over and above this was redistributed to the poorest sections of the population, the 12 million or so people on or below the supplementary benefit
level would each receive a windfall of almost £10,000.

There has also been a significant shift in the types of people who are
the predominant wealth-holders. As Rubinstein (1981) and Scott (1982, 1991)
have shown, traditionally the wealthy were drawn from aristocratic landed
circles and from a banking and financial élite. Rubinstein has shown how
these groups continued to dominate wealth-holding even after industrialization in the early nineteenth century led to the emergence of industrial
capital on a significant scale. Admittedly, with the agricultural depression at
the end of the nineteenth century, and more significantly as Britain's pre-
dominance in world trade and industry faded during the twentieth century,

the position of these groups deteriorated (see Cannadine 1990). Nonetheless, as late as the 1960s a traditional wealthy establishment, dominated by old financial and landed interests, could still be detected.

In recent years, however, the hold of the traditional establishment over the main sources of wealth has declined.[7] An interesting example of this trend is that the queen herself, listed as the wealthiest person in Britain as recently as 1993, was ranked as 87th in 1999. By the late 1990s only a minority of the very wealthy belonged to the traditional British establishment, at least according to its usual indicators. In 1997 only 10 per cent of the top 1000 had been to Oxford or Cambridge universities (though 7 per cent had been to Eton public school alone), and around 14 per cent had titles (not all of these being from titled backgrounds). According to *The Sunday Times*, only 29 per cent had inherited their wealth (though this is not to say that the remainder came from poor or even average backgrounds). Among the very rich one can find significant numbers who have 'worked their way up'. There is also evidence that a trend towards economic globalization has increased the number of non-British born or educated people in the ranks of the very wealthy in Britain.

There can be little doubt that those born outside the establishment 'charmed circle' can become wealthy. Nevertheless, we should not deduce from this that we live in a meritocracy. What is striking about the list of the very wealthy is that they tend not to have acquired their fortunes by earning high salaries (though they not infrequently do earn high salaries),[8] or by climbing promotion ladders to the top of corporate hierarchies, or by pure entrepreneurial graft in building up enterprises and ploughing back profits. In the *rentier* style discussed by Scott they have earned their fortunes by acquiring property of diverse kinds and benefiting from the increasing value of such property in land and stock markets. This property may take the form of companies (or parts of companies) which they have formed, bought or inherited, or it might be through trading on the stock exchange or other financial markets. Intellectual property is increasingly significant, evidenced by the wealth of musicians such as Paul McCartney or Elton John whose musical copyright carries great financial rewards, or, more unusually, of 'blockbusting' authors such as Jeffrey Archer. In general, much of the vast fortunes the wealthy have acquired are based on their ability to derive *rentier* income by taking advantage of market fluctuations in the price of their assets.[9] The 'very wealthy' are a polyglot group, whose fortunes are derived from *rentier* activities.

The very rich, those who depend on property for their income, tend to be socially invisible. Even in the recent past the ownership of property made the wealthy visible, as wealth, especially in its landed forms, was displayed in modes of conspicuous consumption, notably through ownership of country and town houses, participation in élite social circles, activity in local voluntary activities and so forth. Even those *nouveau riches* who made their fortunes during the nineteenth and early twentieth centuries participated in this process. Today, this situation has changed dramatically. In its new, fluid forms, 'property' is largely invisible because its accumulation does not depend on visible display. As an example, the wealthiest man in Britain, Hans

Rausung, is little known. To be sure, many of the rich continue to have a considerable public profile, but such a profile is not dependent on their wealth.

It has been suggested that recent trends in capital ownership have diffused capitalist sources of income down the social hierarchy, and that the percolation of such forms of income may have clouded the salience of capital–labour division (see Saunders and Harris 1994). In the early twentieth century, 90 per cent of the workforce were wage earners. Very few of these workers would earn any money from investments: most people rented their homes and if they made arrangements for their pension it would normally be through a mutually owned Friendly Society which controlled its own assets and did not invest in stock markets. Today, the situation is considerably more complex. 15 million people invest in some form in the stock market, though most of these do so indirectly, through their membership of pension plans, or through taking out life insurance policies. Direct share ownership has increased since the 1980s, partly due to the privatization programme and government policy which has created tax advantages from investing in shares (through PEPs and ISAs), and more recently due to the de-mutualization of building societies.

The question here is whether this form of 'petty *rentier*' income is significant in affecting class boundaries. Table 3.2 compares how the broad sources of income have changed between 1965 and 1995/6. It can readily be seen from the second column that the entire period was one of a considerable improvement in income levels, at least for the possibly rather spurious 'average' household. But the most striking change appears to be the changing share of income derived from wages and salaries. From 1965 to 1980 around three quarters of all income came from paid employment. However, from 1980 the proportion of income derived from this source fell to less than two thirds. There are three main reasons for this. First, the proportion of income deriving from self-employment has risen somewhat, from less than 6 per cent in 1980 to nearly 10 per cent by 1994/5. This reflects the well-known growth in self-employment in the 1980s and 1990s, which reverses a long-term trend where such employment was in decline (see Fielding 1995). Second, income from annuities and pensions has more than doubled, which reflects the rising proportion of elderly people in the population, as well as the growing numbers of people covered by pension schemes of various kinds. Finally, social security benefits account for a larger share of average income, largely due to the rise of unemployment and the growing number of households who meet government poverty thresholds.

Care needs to be taken in interpreting these trends. At least two of the headings in Table 3.2 ('self-employment' and 'annuities and pensions') are in fact very closely linked to labour market rewards. Income from self-employment does not present any substantial problems for class analysts: both Weber and Marx recognized the existence of a group of self-employed, petty bourgeoisie, who stood somewhat outside the main class lines of capital and labour, but nonetheless in a distinct class position of their own. Income from investment is a little more complex. Nonetheless, it is important to place such streams of income into perspective. Outside the wealth élite, such income is likely to bear some ultimate relation to the amount of income

Table 3.2 Income and source of income 1965 to 1995/6

	Number of households	Weekly household income		Source of income					
		Disposable	Gross[1]	Wages and salaries	Self employment	Investments	Annuities and pensions[2]	Social security benefits[3]	Other sources
		£	£	Percentage of gross weekly household income					
1965	3,392	19.65	24.10	76.0	7.5	3.6	2.2	8.4	2.4
1970	6,393	28.47	34.33	76.7	6.6	4.1	2.6	8.9	1.1
1975	7,203	55.73	70.45	77.4	5.7	3.6	2.4	9.9	0.9
1980	6,944	114.76	140.44	74.6	5.8	3.2	2.7	12.5	1.2
1985	7,012	163.47	205.03	68.9	7.1	4.1	4.7	14.1	1.1
1990	7,046	257.70	317.08	67.0	9.5	6.0	4.9	11.1	1.4
1991	7,056	274.97	337.99	65.7	8.8	7.0	5.1	11.9	1.6
1992	7,418	280.04	342.93	65.0	8.6	6.1	5.7	13.1	1.5
1993	6,979	288.44	353.03	64.7	8.3	5.1	6.2	13.9	1.9
1994/5	6,853	298.43	369.25	64.4	9.5	4.4	6.4	13.5	1.8
1995/6	6,797	306.80	380.89	64.3	8.6	4.8	6.8	13.7	1.7

Notes: 1 Does not include imputed income from owner-occupied and rent-free households.
2 Other than social security benefits.
3 Excluding housing benefit and council tax benefit (rates rebate in Northern Ireland) and their predecessors in earlier years.
Source: ONS, Family Spending 1995–96, © Crown copyright 1996.

earned from wages and salaries, since those who have more disposable money from their labour market income may well be those who can afford to spend on investments. If this is true, then investment income for most people is subsidiary to, and derivative of, income from the labour market.

It is worth noting further that notwithstanding the privatization pro-gramme of the Conservative government in the 1980s, and the attempt to extend the proportion of the population holding shares, the rise in income from investment has been extremely modest. Furthermore, the most signi-ficant factor affecting this income is the interest rate (with the maximum share of 6.1 per cent in 1992 taking place at a time of high interest rates). Excluding fluctuation caused by this factor, there is only marginal evidence of a net increase in money from such sources. Petty capitalism does not appear to have become a significant source of income for the population as a whole.

Calculations from the Joseph Rowntree Foundation (1995a) suggest that in 1991/2 the bottom 50 per cent of the population earned an aver-age of £2 a year from shares; the next 40 per cent earned perhaps £60 a year. By contrast the top 1 per cent of the population earned about £20,000 on average from shares (see Scott 1997: 287). It was only when annual house-hold income rose above £25,000 that significant wealth could begin to be accumulated (Banks *et al.* 1996).

In general, involvement in labour market activity continues to be the key influence on the ability to tap other sorts of income, even if these other income streams are realized at later moments in an individual's life (pen-sions, for instance).[10] The main exception concerns income from 'social secur-ity benefits', which rose from 8.4 per cent in 1965 to around 13 per cent in the early 1990s. Here there is no direct link between labour market position and level of benefit (in the sense that the amount of benefit obtained is linked to one's former income – though the welfare systems of other coun-tries do take this factor into account – see Esping-Andersen 1990). However, since certain groups of employees within the labour market are more prone to unemployment, it can be argued that there are indirect links.

This same general point concerning the indirect – but still fundamental – significance of the labour market for the structuring of economic inequal-ity also applies to other possible elements of income. Table 3.2 excludes windfall income, such as from inheritance or other gifts, and also possible income from the housing market. During the period of house price inflation in the 1980s, when homeowners could frequently sell their houses for much more money – even in real terms – than they purchased them for, it was commonly argued that home ownership offered new opportunities for in-come generation (see notably Saunders 1990b). However, even in this boom period of house price inflation, some more sceptical voices emphasized that once the costs of home ownership were taken into account (for instance on repairs and maintenance) the net gain to be made from home owning was rather limited (Duncan 1990).

With the spectacular collapse of property prices from the late 1980s until the mid-1990s, it has become evident that capital gains from housing are fragile and dependent on particular market conditions. Rises in property prices in the late 1990s proved extremely sensitive to location and type of house, with high quality middle-class housing rising rapidly in price, but cheap, mass housing frequently continuing to lose value.[11] Hamnett (1995) shows that the extent to which homeowners can make capital gains depends critically on the period in which they bought their first house. If they bought their house directly before a period of house price inflation, then it was possible for households to accumulate up to £5000 per year. However, even this figure does not take into account moneys paid back in mortgage repayments, or in repairs, and it would appear that in general the housing market has not proved to be a significant source of income. The equity which can be built up in housing is also related to the amount of money which households from different classes can invest in it. Hamnett and Seavers (1996) show that professional and managerial households have considerably more housing equity than manual workers.[12]

Let me reiterate my basic argument. Broad patterns of wealth-holding and income in Britain point quite unambiguously to the existence of a very small class who earn their wealth from property, and a much larger class who predominantly rely on income from their labour, whether in the form of wages or salary. There is nothing to fundamentally challenge the accuracy of Marx's arguments about class relations here (see more generally on this point Scase 1992). Recent trends have seen a clear polarization, which has favoured the wealthy. Forms of *rentier* income deriving ultimately from property ownership are more unequally distributed than is income from the labour market, and the expansion of shareholding and investment income in the past 20 years has therefore accentuated, rather than reduced, economic inequality. Contemporary economic and social change does not appear to undermine the salience of this basic class divide. The labour market remains the fundamental arena for the generation of income. Around two thirds of income is attributed to wages and salaries, and labour market position is also crucial for unlocking the potential to accumulate income through pensions, housing equity, investments etc. Even for the very wealthy whose income is derived from *rentier* sources, labour market position can be vital. Senior managers of companies are often best placed to reap rich dividends in the form of share options when companies are refloated.[13] It is not just the amount of income which an individual obtains at any one moment in time which is important, but also the *potential* this might contain for the realization of future reward. The ability to acquire wealth depends on *organizational centrality*, the ability of individuals to direct organizational change from its heart and thereby reap its rewards. This suggests the need to look at individual and household trajectories and the way that these might link to class boundaries.

Labour markets, income and social class

I have argued that the broad parameters of wealth distribution in Britain can be explained in terms of a broad class division. However, there are major differences in the income levels of the large group of people who rely on income earned from their labour (see Table 3.3). How – if at all – can income

Table 3.3 Mean weekly incomes (£), by occupational group, 1998

Occupational group	Men, full time	Women, full time
Managers and administrators	625.6	435.3
Professionals	568.4	458.4
Associate professionals	515.9	375.8
Clerical and secretarial	291.9	257.6
Personal and protective services	339.5	220.1
Sales occupations	339.6	231.0
Craft workers	360.4	217.7
Plant and machine operatives	332.9	228.6
Others	280.4	193.3
Average	427.1	309.6

Note: Figures for full time weekly pay, for those whose income is not affected by absence.
Source: New Earnings Survey (1998, Section A).

differences between those relying primarily on the labour market be theorized in terms of class?

Table 3.3 reveals clear occupational differences in pay. Among both men and women, the highest paid occupational groups (managers and administrators in the case of men, professionals in the case of women), earn well over twice the weekly pay of the worst paid group, the 'other' occupations (for instance, postal workers and kitchen workers). Even more marked pay differentials can be found by comparing the best paid men and the lowest paid women: male managers, for instance, earn well over three times the income of 'other' women workers.

Pay differences become even more marked if one examines specific occupations. The highest paid specified male occupation in Britain in 1998 was 'treasurers and company financial managers', who on average earned £1070 a week. The lowest paid men were kitchen porters, earning just £171 a week. The equivalent extremes for women were doctors (earning £680.10) and bar staff (earning £156.50). Table 3.3 shows that the major occupational divide, for both men and women, is between professional and managerial occupations and the rest. For men there is a large gap between the £516 earned each week by associate professionals (the worst paid of the three most affluent groups), and the £360 earned by craft workers, the best paid of the manual and routine white-collar groups. There is relatively little difference among manual workers and routine white-collar workers: indeed if anything manual workers are paid rather more than routine white-collar employees. The picture is very similar for women. Managers, administrators and professionals are all substantially better off than even the best paid white-collar or manual workers. Some kind of a broad class division between managers, professionals and administrators on the one hand and manual and routine white-collar workers on the other is evident, which suggests that income inequality can be related to categorical differences between the middle and working class (see Tilly 1998). Furthermore, this division is more marked than other possible categorical divisions (between ethnic groups, for instance).[14]

Table 3.4 Income and source of income by occupational grouping of head of house, 1995/6

	Number of households	Weekly household income		Source of income					
		Disposable	Gross	Wages and salaries	Self employment	Investments	Annuities and pensions[1]	Social security benefits[2]	Other sources
		£	£	Percentage of gross weekly household income					
Occupational groupings of head of house									
Professional	294	532.52	714.86	90.1	2.2	3.2	1.1	2.1	1.2
Employers and managers	781	509.76	699.59	90.4	1.2	3.4	1.5	2.5	1.0
Intermediate non-manual	470	409.13	533.94	88.5	1.8	2.6	2.1	3.5	1.5
Junior non-manual	397	288.36	356.72	82.1	0.9	2.8	3.4	7.9	2.9
Manual	1,498	300.54	374.69	86.6	0.8	1.1	1.5	8.4	1.6
Skilled	849	330.91	418.39	89.6	1.0	1.1	1.0	6.5	1.0
Semi-skilled	512	272.60	333.70	82.3	0.7	1.1	2.5	10.4	2.9
Unskilled	137	216.76	257.60	78.1	0.1	0.9	1.6	17.3	2.0

Note: 1 Other than social security benefits.
2 Excluding housing benefit and council tax benefit (rates rebates in Northern Ireland).
Source: Social Trends (1996, Table 8.6)

It is possible that differences between households might be less than between individuals, if highly paid men live with poorly paid women, and vice versa. Table 3.4 shows the weekly income of households grouped according to the occupational group of the 'head of house' (the household member in the highest occupational category). If Table 3.4 indicates less inequality than was the case for individuals, we would be entitled to think that household processes tend to 'equalize' individual inequalities. But in fact, this is not the case. The most affluent households are 'headed' by professionals, where household disposable income in 1995/6 was around £533 per week. This is in contrast to the earnings of households headed by unskilled manual workers, where earnings were only around 40 per cent of this level, at £217 per week. Between these two extremes lie the other groups. Skilled manual households earn 50 per cent more than the unskilled, but still rather less than households headed by intermediate non-manual workers, while households headed by employers and managers earn nearly as much as those headed by professionals. There is slightly more inequality between households than there is between individuals, because relatively affluent men tend to live with relatively affluent women and vice versa (see Savage *et al.* 1992; Crompton 1995). Goodman *et al.* (1997) show that although household dynamics have a complex impact on income and poverty levels, it is wrong to say that certain types of household (e.g. nuclear families) are better or worse off than any other (e.g. single parents). Among pensioners, there has been a growing polarization which reflects the distinction between those able to draw on pension arrangements and savings, and those reliant on the state pension.

There is distinct 'lumpiness' in the distribution of income at both household and individual level. This is compatible with ideas of a broad class division within the workforce. I now explore this possibility further by examining two alternative possible explanations of inequality, based on status and skill, before returning to consider the relationship between class and income more fully.

Status

One explanation of labour market differentials might be that those people in jobs which have the highest public esteem are rewarded most while those who work in jobs with low status earn the lowest. Thus the reason why professionals such as doctors and lawyers have the highest levels of income is because these groups are held in the highest public regard. This approach is compatible with functionalist approaches to stratification, as championed in the USA in the 1940s and 1950s (e.g. Davis and Moore 1945), where it was claimed that the distribution of income reflects a general social consensus about the social value of different jobs. However, as I have shown in Chapter 2, there are problems in demonstrating that there is a social consensus concerning the ranking of occupations, and in recent years few have tried to 'test' whether this might be a plausible explanation of pay differences.

In fact popular opinion tends towards the idea that pay differentials should be narrowed. In 1987 the *British Social Attitudes Survey* asked their respondents to estimate the earnings of 11 occupational groups, and also to

Table 3.5 Earnings and status in Britain, 1987

Title	How much do they earn (median)?	How much should they earn (median)?	Actual earnings, men	Actual earnings, women
Bricklayer	£9,000	£10,000	£8,580	–
Doctor (general practitioner-GP)	£20,000	£20,000	£24,000	–
Bank clerk	£8,000	£8,500	£10,400	£6,708
Owner of small shop	£10,000	£11,000	n/a	n/a
Chairman of large company	£60,000	£35,000	–	–
Skilled factory worker	£10,000	£10,000	£9,932	£7,072
Farm worker	£6,000	£8,000	£6,396	–
Secretary	£7,000	£8,000	£9,100	£8,008
City bus driver	£8,000	£8,500	£9,100	–
Unskilled factory worker	£6,000	£7,000	£8,424	£5,876
Cabinet minister	£30,000	£25,000		

Source: Brook (1992, Tables F-22 and F-23; New Earnings Survey (1987).

indicate what they 'should' earn. Table 3.5 lists the findings, together with the actual earnings of these groups, where such figures are available.

Table 3.5 indicates that for many jobs there is a remarkable congruence between what people in different occupations earn, what people think they earn, and what people think they should earn. However, in general the public tends to think that high earners should get somewhat less, and low earners should get somewhat more. The pay of both company directors and cabinet ministers in particular was regarded as much too generous. The pay of GPs was regarded as acceptable at £20,000, though this was in fact something of an underestimate of their actual pay. At the other end of the spectrum, there was a belief that the pay of secretaries, bus drivers, unskilled factory workers, bank clerks, and bricklayers should all be raised. Indeed in recent years there has been a steady increase in the number of people who think that pay differentials are too large. In 1983 72 per cent of respondents to the British Social Attitudes Survey thought this, a figure which increased to 87 per cent in 1995 (Spencer 1996: 87). The evidence from Table 3.5 indicates that the public does not believe that large pay differentials are justified: it therefore seems difficult to see wage inequalities as linked to those status perceptions.

Human capital theory

Another explanation for occupational pay differentials is offered by 'human capital theory' which argues that pay reflects the financial premiums that skills can attract in the labour market. Better paying jobs exist to give people an incentive to learn the appropriate skills – equally, even among people in the same occupations, those who invest in their own labour (for instance by improving their skills, working hard and so forth) can expect to earn more money. It is noteworthy that the idea of skill as a justifiable reason for pay inequality commands considerable popular support: it is indeed one of the very few ideas generally viewed as an acceptable reason for pay inequality. An indication of the legitimacy which this idea commands is that official classifications of class, which we saw in Chapter 2 traditionally used status as their criteria for ranking occupations, have recently turned to using the criteria of skill as a means of grouping occupations. In 1980 the preamble to the registrar general's class schema noted that: 'these [class] categories have been selected in such a way as to bring together, so far as possible, people with similar levels of occupational skill' (quoted in Reid 1989: 54).

However, research does not suggest that skill, at least as measured by qualifications obtained, is a prime factor in explaining pay inequality. Dale and Egerton (1997) found that they could explain 34 per cent of young men's pay variance and 47 per cent of young women's pay variance (using data from the National Child Development Study), when they included occupational, educational and demographic variables. Only 7 per cent of variance in men's pay (measured in terms of their weekly income) is caused by qualification level, around 2 per cent by their aspirations, and 5 per cent by their ability. Variations in women's pay are affected more by their qualifications (13 per cent), but the basic finding is not much different: less than one fifth of the variation in pay appears to be due to (measurable) human capital.[15] Women who have only ever worked full-time tend to have systematically increased levels of pay compared to those who have worked part-time or have interrupted their working lives, for instance to have children.

Interestingly, for women as for men, 'aspiration' and 'ability' are relatively insignificant. The former finding is particularly interesting in view of Catherine Hakim's (1995) arguments that the preferences of different types of women for careers or domestic life are a major factor in affecting their work destinations. However, the kinds of preferences appear to have developed later once women have entered the labour market and may be an adaptive response to structural constraints and opportunities facing them (see Ginn *et al.* 1996).

There is little here which offers much solace to human capital theorists (and see also Leslie and Pu 1996). It can be argued in defence of human capital theory that attitude and ability measures are not measured very well since, in the National Child Development Study (NCDS), they are measured when the respondent is aged 11 and 16 respectively, with the result that there is no recognition that attitudes and abilities may change over time. Nonetheless the weak performance of these variables is still worthy of comment. Questions can also be posed as to how the impact of qualifications on earnings (which is in any respect rather small) can be interpreted. Lissenburgh and Bryson (1996) demonstrate that graduates earn more than non-graduates because graduates work in relatively well paid occupations for which graduate qualifications are essential. Getting good qualifications allows entry to high paying jobs. This is different from the idea that a high level of qualifications in itself is a cause of high pay. Rather, as social closure theorists such as Randall Collins (1975) emphasize, qualifications allow barriers to be placed around particular occupations, thereby forcing up the incomes of those workers in those occupations (see also Brown 1994). Skill cannot be seen as a straightforward measure of human capital. As Phillips and Taylor (1980) have argued, conceptions of skill have historically been associated with dominant social groups. Men's jobs have tended to be regarded as more skilled than women's jobs, even when by any objective criteria they appear to be no more difficult. Male compositors were able to define their work, based around keyboard skills, as 'skilled', while women keyboard workers with very similar skills were not able to command skilled status (see Cockburn 1983). Similarly, Witz (1992) has shown how male professional groups, such as doctors, were able to gain greater privileges than female professional groups, such as nurses. Skill can therefore not be divorced from power: the ability to define one's work as skilled, as well as to gain the resources and support to acquire the kinds of skills necessary to carry out particular jobs.

In the light of these, and other arguments, it is helpful to turn to the arguments of Doeringer and Piore (1971) who do not think that human capital theory can provide an adequate account of income inequality. Dual labour market theorists claim that employees work in two or more types of labour market with differing kinds of returns for skill. In secondary labour markets, characteristic of much manual employment and unskilled service sector employment, there is little need for skilled workers. In this sector there is little extra advantage in having human capital: even if workers are well qualified and work hard, they will not be able to increase their earnings significantly. By contrast, in the primary sector, composed of various skilled jobs, such as among professionals and managers, there is a need for more skilled and hard-working employees, and hence investment in human capital can be expected to lead to financial rewards, as well as promotion and career advancement. Theodossiou (1996) has tested this argument by distinguishing workers according to whether they work in the primary or secondary labour market. He finds that by doing this he can explain around 41 per cent of the variance in earnings, and, interestingly, different factors explain the variance in the two sectors. In the primary labour market the longer you have stayed in a job the higher your income is, whereas in the secondary labour market your length of service has no impact on your pay levels. In the secondary labour market pay is linked to the market conditions in which firms work (pay is lower when demand for products falls off) whereas there is no such relationship in the primary labour market.

These findings are striking. They suggest that the differences between well off and less well off employees cannot be seen as only due to the kinds of skills and talents which the well off possess. To be sure, more skilled and talented workers tend to be better rewarded. But it is quite wrong to see human capital as an individual attribute, which individuals can choose to either invest in or neglect. Skills can only lead to rewards within occupational and organizational contexts which 'value' skills. Different kinds of occupational and organizational contexts provide different kinds of incentives and cultures that can encourage or discourage people from improving their skills. The logic of the primary labour market is that mere tenure in a job should be credited with increasing levels of pay, whereas those in secondary labour markets do not have such expectations built into their jobs.

Class, human capital and earnings

Perhaps class theory offers an alternative to the rather benign views of both status theory and human capital theory? It is, however, an interesting point that class analysis has in recent years directed relatively little attention to social polarization and economic inequality (though see Martin 1994). This is partly because class theorists themselves were ambivalent about the relationship between class and income.

Because Weber defined classes in terms of the labour market position of different groups of workers, writers within the Weberian tradition define classes in part through the kinds of income levels they can command. Marxists, by contrast, focus on employment relationships (notably the division between capital and labour) as being the crucial defining feature of class, and the *source* of income, rather than its *amount*, is held to be crucial. Marxists thereby think that members of the same class may have very different income levels, but because they are enmeshed in similar employment relationships they can still be said to have a commonality of position (in relation to members of other social classes, for instance). However, like Weberians, Marxists also see class as ultimately tied up with social inequality, and would normally anticipate a clear relationship between the two.

Certainly, there seem good prima facie reasons to suppose that economic inequality takes a class form. Tables 3.3 and 3.4 show that there is a major gap in the incomes of professionals and managers, on the one hand, and routine white-collar and manual workers on the other. This division has considerable theoretical warrant in the arguments of John Goldthorpe concerning the distinction between those employed on a 'service contract' and those on a 'labour contract':

> Employment relationships regulated by a labour contract entail a relatively short term and specific exchange of money for effort. Employees supply more or less discrete amounts of labour, under the supervision of the employer or of the employer's agents, in return for wages which are calculated on a 'piece' basis. In contrast, employment relationships within a bureaucratic context involve a longer term and generally more diffuse exchange. Employees render service to their employing organisation in return for 'compensation', which takes the form not only of reward for work done, through a salary and various perquisites, but also comprises important *prospective* elements – for example salary increments on an established scale, assurances of security, and through pension rights, after retirement, and above all, well defined career opportunities.
>
> (Erikson and Goldthorpe 1992: 41–2)

Professionals and managers are advantaged, compared to those on a labour contract, because the indeterminate nature of their work means that they can strike a harder bargain with their employer. Manual workers, on the other hand, whose labour can be more precisely codified, can be paid on a piece rate, as a direct reward for labour done, and their weaker market position is reflected in their lower earnings. It should be noted that the occupational categories used in Table 3.3 do not directly map onto Goldthorpe's class schema, but Evans (1992a) shows that there is indeed a clear relationship between a person's income and their location in the Goldthorpe class schema. Drawing on data from 1984, Evans (1992a) argues that around 31 per cent of the variance in pay is attributable to class location.

However, some writers, such as Gershuny (2000) prefer to draw on modified forms of human capital theory to relate income to the different kinds of resources individuals accumulate over the course of their lives. Gershuny claims that an index of a person's resources – which include sex, age, current or most recent occupational status, highest educational qualification, number and age of children and parent's occupations – can explain 42 per cent of the variance in their income in 1991 which compares favourably with the 36 per cent that can be explained by class categories. Gershuny also emphasizes that one virtue of his approach is that the index of resources tends to be a better predictor of someone's economic situation over the longer term. The index of resources measured in 1991 still explains 32 per cent of the variance in income in 1995, whereas a person's class position in 1991 only explains 25 per cent of the variance of their income in 1995. He suggests that social processes are in some ways 'stored' in an individual's routines and abilities and that measuring these kinds of individual attributes can usefully account for their trajectories.

As Gershuny recognizes, it is not surprising that by adding numerous variables into his index of resources, he can claim a stronger correlation with income than that simply derived from occupational class alone. What is interesting about Gershuny's account is that he seeks to marry individual, resource-based explanations of pay with more social explanations. A person's location in professional and managerial jobs allows him or her greater prospect to work in an environment by which they can acquire further resources to augment their labour market position. Individual and class processes work together, rather than as alternatives.

In pursuing this argument, it is useful to show how trends in income are linked to the power resources of different income groups (see Tables 3.6a, 3.6b, 3.7a, 3.7b). Those people who exercise most power in leading and organizing change are thereby best able to reap the rewards, while those who have least power are likely to be most adversely affected. I have used two different sets of tables because the official occupational classification changed in 1990, and it is not possible to directly compare the 1980s and 1990s.

I consider first the extent to which occupational income deviates from the national average in 1975 and 1990, by comparing columns three and seven of Tables 3.6a and 3.6b (Note that age comparisons for women in Table 3.6b have not been included because women's age-wage profiles are complicated by childrearing.). The most noteworthy point is that income differentials between professionals and managers on the one hand, and manual and routine non-manual workers on the other tend to become more marked between 1975 and 1990. For men in 1975 (leaving aside general managers for whom there is no comparative data in 1990), the best paid group (professionals in education and health) earned 32 per cent more than the national average for men. The worst paid male groups (those in farming and fishing)

Table 3.6a Facets of income by occupational group, 1976–1990

MEN Occupational group	1976				1990			
	Median weekly pay (–)	% deviation from national average	40–9 as index of average	Top decile as index of median	Median weekly pay (–)	% deviation from national average	40–9 as index of average	Top decile as index of median
General managerial	296.1	42.7	114	–	–	–	–	80
Professionals in management	268.0	31.6	114	61	385.2	49.2	112	49
Professionals in education, health and welfare	272.1	32.1	109	49	322.9	25.1	108	98
Literary, artists	226.3	12.8	115	72	308.0	19.3	118	60
Professionals in technology	244.3	22.6	116	55	328.1	27.1	115	69
Other managers	226.6	12.8	109	67	317.9	23.1	111	61
Clerical	174.7	-10.3	111	46	215.9	-16.4	115	77
Selling	180.8	-9.9	113	56	231.8	-10.2	120	33
Security	200.0	6.2	110	46	299.5	16	106	62
Personal service	144.1	-21.0	105	49	169.1	-34.5	113	51
Farming, fishing	134.3	-28.0	104	40	169.5	-34.4	106	59
Processing	170.0	-4.4	108	39	226.2	-12.4	114	64
Making, repairing	174.4	-7.6	109	46	220.9	-14.4	113	53
Metals, electric	186.4	1.0	107	42	248.9	-3.6	117	50
Painting	177.3	-6.2	106	40	217.6	-15.7	112	69
Construction	176.0	-4.4	110	49	220.0	-14.8	110	55.4
Transport	161.5	-6.4	105	45	212.9	-17.5	110	
All occupations	186.8		112		258.2		112	

Notes:
Income expressed in gross earnings per week, 1976 figures are reported in 1990 prices.
1 % by which the income for specified occupational group is below or above that for all occupations.
2 An index of the amount by which median income for 40–9-year-olds exceeds that of the occupational group as a whole where 100 = identical to the occupational group.
3 % by which the income for the top decile of earners in this occupational group exceeds the average.
Source: New Earnings Survey (1975, 1990).

Table 3.6b Facets of income by occupational group, 1976–1990

WOMEN

Occupational group	1976			1990		
	Median weekly pay (–)	% deviation from national average	Top decile as index of median	Median weekly pay (–)	% deviation from national average	Top decile as index of median
Professionals in management	211.4	44.4	57	333.6	65.6	55
Professionals in education, health and welfare	207.0	41.8	53	258.5	28.3	38
Literary, artists	152.3		75	268.3	33.2	59
Professionals in technology	176.6	20.0	65	249.3	23.7	50
Other managers	146.6	0.1	67	239.8	19.0	60
Clerical	135.9	–7.0	41	182.1	–5.2	43
Selling	100.5	–31.2	43	152.8	24.7	53
Security	165.0	13.0	56	268.5	33.3	33
Personal service	120.1	–17.7	46	139.4	–30.8	47
Processing	113.4	–22.3	38	151.9	–24.6	42
Making, repairing	119.1	–18.4	43	144.7	–28.2	43
Metals, electric	137.1	–6.9	32	163.4	–18.9	42
Painting	129.9	–11.0	33	154.3	–23.4	42
Transport	135.6	–3.3	57	163.6	–18.8	46
All occupations	146.0					

Notes:
Income expressed in gross earnings per week. 1976 figures are reported in 1990 prices.
1 % by which the income for specified occupational group is below or above that for all occupations.
2 % by which the income for the top decile of earners in this occupational group exceeds the average.
Source: New Earnings Survey (1976, 1990).

Table 3.7a Facets of income by occupational group 1991–1998

MEN Occupational group	1991			1998		
	% deviation from national average	40–9 as index of average	Top decile as index of median	% deviation from national average	40–9 as index of average	Top decile as index of median
Managers	40.4	112	192	46.4	110	197
Professionals	34.1	108	159	33.0	106	166
Associate professionals	17.5	111	175	20.8	108	180
Clerical	−25.7	116	162	−31.7	111	155
Craft	−14.5	109	150	−15.6	109	164
Personal services	−14.6	117	151	−20.5	121	162
Sales	−13.8	119	173	−20.5	120	184
Plant operatives	−20.0	108	156	−22.1	107	164
Other	−31.2	109	161	−34.3	105	164

Source: New Earnings Survey (1991, 1998).

Table 3.7b Facets of income by occupational group 1991–1998

WOMEN Occupational group	1991			1998		
	% deviation from national average	40–9 as index of average	Top decile as index of median	% deviation from national average	40–9 as index of average	Top decile as index of median
Managers	32.0	100	180	40.6	102	182
Professionals	51.2	102	132	48.1	101	138
Associate professionals	24.9	109	148	21.4	105	147
Clerical	–11.8	102	153	–16.8	102	149
Craft	–28.4	103	170	–29.7	98	165
Personal services	–22.3	102	164	–28.9	102	169
Sales	–23.6	100	169	–25.4	98	186
Plant operatives	–25.6	103	150	–26.2	102	154
Other	–33.0	101	159	–37.6	101	165

Source: New Earnings Survey (1991, 1998).

earned 28 per cent less than the national average. By 1990, the differentials between the best off and worst off occupational groups had widened. Those occupations with incomes significantly above average in 1975 tended to be markedly better off in 1990. All those occupational groups with below average income levels in 1975 had poorer relative income levels in 1990. For men, Table 3.6a indicates that a clear process of polarization did take place between 1975 and 1990, *which largely amplified and accentuated pre-existing divisions*. In some cases the shifts are extremely marked. Professionals in management roles earned one third more than the national average in 1975 but one half more than the national average in 1990. Personal service workers earned one fifth less than the average in 1975 but over one third less in 1990.

There are only two exceptions to this general process of class polarization. Professionals in education, health and welfare saw a slight decline in their income relative to the national average (see Elliott and Dufus 1996), while metal and electric workers, who (unusually for manual workers) earned very slightly above the national average in 1975, earned slightly below the national average in 1990. But the broad patterns for men are clear. *All* manual workers saw deterioration in their income levels relative to the working population as a whole. Nearly all professional and managerial workers saw a relative improvement in their position, the exception being the mainly public sector professionals who work in education and welfare. Clerical workers and personal service workers also saw relative decline which placed their earnings position similar to that of manual workers.

Table 3.6b indicates that trends for women are a little less straightforward. The earnings of women in management pull away from the average in a similar way to male salaries. The relative fall in female professional income is noteworthy, however, especially as the professions are a large employer of 'middle-class' women. The earnings of women in clerical and sales work (two large employers of female labour) also rise relatively between 1975 and 1990. However, the situation of female manual workers is very similar to that of men, with a considerable deterioration in their relative pay levels. We see a similar process of polarization for women as for men, though professional women tend, in relative terms, to be losing out.

This discussion can be replicated for the 1990s by glancing at columns two and five of Tables 3.7a and 3.7b. It can readily be seen that the occupational categories have changed and that no direct comparison can be made with the earlier period. Between 1991 and 1998 male managers and associate professionals continued to earn relatively more while all manual and routine non-manual workers saw their income drift further below average. Professionals continued to see a slight decline in their relative income, probably due to the fact that most of these worked in the public sector where income levels were pegged. Women managers continued to perform relatively well, but both female professionals and associate professionals fell back somewhat. Women clerks and sales workers who (under somewhat different occupational classifications) had done relatively well between 1975 and 1990, also slipped back in the 1990s.

In general there is marked polarization, for both men and women, between 1975 and 1998. Those already advantaged in the 1970s have been best placed to reap the rewards of change. The main exception, that of professionals, is particularly interesting in view of the argument put forward by defenders of human capital theory which might suggest that those with more skills would be more highly rewarded, since if this argument were true one might expect professionals to do rather better.[16] It is true, as Gosling and Meghir (1994) show, that income polarization between occupational groups is also mirrored by that between groups with different levels of educational qualifications. However, they also point out that there has been marked wage dispersion among workers with similar levels of educational attainment. In 1978 the best paid 10 per cent of those who left school at 16 earned 2.25 times that of the worst paid 10 per cent. By 1992 this ratio had risen to nearly three times. Gosling and Meghir indicate that wage differences have risen among men with the same educational attainment and the same levels of experience.

There is no doubting that the groups which have gained most in economic terms – professionals in management roles (1975–90) and managers (1991–8) – are precisely the groups who are most likely to be intimately involved in devising and implementing restructuring of various kinds. A glance at Tables 3.6a and 3.6b indicates that in absolute terms the increase in their incomes was marked. Male professionals in management roles saw their weekly pay increase by £68 per week (controlling for inflation), while the small number of equivalent women saw their real weekly pay rocket from £211 to £334. On the other hand, workers employed on labour contracts, with limited skills and little potential for retraining faced an increasingly competitive labour market and have seen their relative (and sometimes their absolute) pay slip. This is as true for skilled manual workers (such as electrical workers or skilled construction workers) as it was for less skilled manual workers. It is misleading to identify the problem as resting with only a small group of unskilled manual workers (as do Goodman *et al.* 1997: 164–6). Skilled craft workers, as well as professionals, have lost out in relative terms.

I want now to consider other pertinent features of income trends since 1975 relevant to this discussion. Table 3.6a records the extent to which those aged between 40 and 49 earn more than the occupational average and thereby allow us to identify whether there is an age premium, and if so, how this varies by occupation. The point of ascertaining this is to allow us to see whether professionals and managers earn higher income at later ages in ways consistent with Goldthorpe's arguments about the prospective rewards associated with their class position. Rather surprisingly, the evidence reveals that managers and professionals do not have a marked age premium. There is also a tendency for their relatively small age premium to fall over time. In 1976 earnings for managers and professionals in their forties were 14 per cent higher than for the occupation as a whole, but these figures had declined to between 6 and 10 per cent higher by 1998. Other figures from the *New Earnings Survey* indicate that professionals earned more at younger ages. In 1976 the best paid 10 per cent of professionals in management aged between 21 and 24 earned less than the median for the occupation as a whole: by 1990 they earned considerably more. The same was also true of professionals in science, and for managers. The erosion of the relationship between age and pay entails the erosion of status distinctions and the emergence of more youthful affluent sectors in the population (see also Egerton and Savage 2000).

The situation of manual and routine white-collar workers is very different. In 1975 earnings for these groups peaked when workers were in their thirties, so that by their forties they earned only slightly more than the occupational average. Those on labour contracts could expect to see their earnings peak in their early middle age, and then a slow process of decline: a very different situation than for professionals and managers. By the 1990s, however, manual workers in their forties earned a rather similar age premium to professionals and managers, while routine non-manual workers earned much more in their forties than their younger counterparts. Worker earnings peaked in their forties, rather than their thirties.[17]

There is little evidence here that 'prospective rewards' are now specifically linked to service class occupations. This marks the erosion of Goldthorpe's 'service relationship'. Managers and professionals can no longer expect rewards simply for 'service', while manual and routine white-collar workers in the right kinds of environment (which usually means working for a blue chip or public sector employer) may actually expect greater remuneration in middle age.[18] These figures offer modest support for the argument that organizational centrality, rather than occupation, is crucial for income prospects as a person's life progresses. Those who are organizationally central can expect improving pay, but those who are not, regardless of occupation, fare less well. This argument is strengthened by the findings, reported in columns five and nine of Tables 3.6a and 3.6b and columns four and seven of Tables 3.7a and 3.7b. This is the extent to which the income for the best paid 10 per cent in any occupation exceeds that of the occupational average. The tables indicate that, at least for men, this élite is pulling away from the average, and hence that there is growing income variation *within* occupational groups. Among men, in 1975 it tended to be élites working in literary, artistic and sporting occupations which earned much more than the median for the group as a whole. This is not surprising, since one would expect that the 'stars' would earn much more than their colleagues. Next were managerial groups, where élites also earned well above the median for their group. This may well reflect the fact that management is a heterogeneous and diverse group with senior managers of large companies classified in the same group as managers in small firms. In all manual groups, however, the élite of the top earning 10 per cent did not earn more than half as much again as the median for their occupational group.

By 1990, however, it is clear that the 'élite' within nearly every occupational group had pulled away from the median – in some respects by quite marked amounts. The only two exceptions are for professionals in education, health and welfare – who again stand out as being different from other occupations – and for workers in the security services. Both of these occupational groups are based nearly exclusively in the public sector, in which traditions of collective bargaining continue to operate, and this may have had the effect of reducing the ability of its leading members to demand higher than average pay increases. Among all types of manual workers it is clear that the élite groups were much more significantly better off than the average member of their group in 1990 than they were in 1975. The élite within every manual grouping earns more than the average professional employee. Although occupational differences in income are increasing, within any one occupation there is a growing diversity of income levels. The conclusion must be *that polarization is not simply an occupational process, but also one which operates within given occupations.* Tables 3.7a and 3.7b show that the same process operated in the 1990s, except among clerical workers.

The figures for women (Tables 3.6b and 3.7b) are somewhat different, in that in the white-collar occupations the relative pay of the élite actually tended to fall over the period between 1975 and 1990. This may reflect the 'pack' catching up with the leaders, given that this period saw a big increase in female pay in many of these occupations.

In general we can detect some difficulties with Goldthorpe's account of class positions which defines someone's class position in terms of their occupation and employment status (see Crompton 1998). One might expect that Goldthorpe's concern to theorize class in terms of employment relationships would lead him logically to focus not on occupations but on the organizational context in which people work (since there may be variability as to whether some occupations are organized through labour or service contracts according to the type of firm or enterprise in which the occupation is located). However, he in fact is wedded to occupations combined with employment status as the key measure of class position.

Yet, economists have shown that organizational factors are often critical: an electrician working for a large company may effectively be employed on a service contract whereas an electrician working for a small firm may not. To give a different example, Evans (1992a: 217) shows that 17 per cent of managers and professionals actually 'clock on' – which might be taken as evidence of working on a labour contract. By contrast, 21 per cent of skilled manual workers are employed on a salary, not a wage. Despite the fact that theoretically Goldthorpe recognizes the role of organizational factors, they do not register in his occupationally-based class schema. However, occupations are losing salience as markers of a person's economic position, especially the position of men. Organizational position, which can be related to one's occupation but which is subtly different, may be a more powerful way of basing class analysis. I return to this point later in the book in Chapter 6 where I explore the connections between class theory and organizational theory.

Class impacts on economic inequality not just cross-sectionally, as a kind of macro-structure which affects the income people can command, but also as something which individuals perform, by accumulating different potentials to unlock income sources which may operate later in their lives. Traditionally, the middle-class male career had allowed professionals and managers to expect higher incomes and greater security as they aged. This was one of the main contrasts with manual workers, where pay was greater in years of peak fitness and youth. By the 1990s such traditional expectations had declined. Instead, as we have seen earlier in this chapter, individuals have to accumulate income cumulatively both by developing the right skills and by working in the right kinds of organizational context to maximize the potential for skills to unlock rewards, both in terms of direct income from the labour market and in terms of the indirect rewards which might flow from this. Economic class inequality is, if anything, more marked than ever, but people need to put the resources of class to work: they do not convey rewards automatically.

Conclusions

It is undoubtedly true that economic inequality is both multifaceted (in that it has different causes), and graduated (since there are no absolute breaks in income or wealth levels). However, the power of class to shape economic inequality is clear. One way of illuminating this is to consider the respective roles of property, culture and organization in generating economic returns.

I have argued that property is increasingly important in allowing a small group of extremely wealthy households to have enjoyed boom times in the 1980s and 1990s. There is a small grouping – perhaps 1 per cent of the population at most – whose wealth rests upon revenues from accumulated property stocks of various sorts, and whose fortunes have soared in recent years. This group includes some members of a traditional establishment, but goes well beyond it. In many respects it is a rather heterogeneous grouping, and it seems unlikely that it functions as any kind of a social and cultural entity in the way that the traditional upper class, with its established social circles, did. It is also an invisible élite, because of the way that property itself has changed to fluid forms. I have argued that although other groups in the population draw to some extent on income from petty property interests, there is a clear dividing line between the small élite and other classes in society.

The cultural basis of income inequality can be thought of in numerous ways. If we define culture in Weberian terms as status, then its role is relatively unimportant. The 'traditional' upper class élite has been transformed into a 'super-wealth' group. Admittedly some of the old figures of the British establishment continue to be present among the new super-wealthy, though they by no means dominate this group. People do not generally accept the legitimacy of economic inequality. Economic inequalities, it would appear, are grounded in the naked workings of the capitalist labour market and its institutional supports. A second, more indirect way of thinking about the role of culture is through the role of skills in generating economic rewards. Human capital does have some impact on earnings, but only to a modest degree, and furthermore only in specific kinds of contexts. Perhaps a third way of thinking of the importance of culture is called for, which links it to organizational processes?

Organization is fundamental to understanding the generation of economic inequality. To a certain degree this idea is well captured by Goldthorpe's concept of a service class of professionals and managers. This group depends mostly on labour market earnings for its income, with money derived from property being of only subsidiary significance. This class, comprising perhaps a third of the population, has also done well: its incomes have increased both in absolute and relative terms (with some exceptions). There appears to be a clear economic division between this service class and the remaining two thirds of the population. Indeed, in economic terms it is rather difficult to detect an 'intermediate' class between the professionals and managers on the one hand, and the manual working class on the other. Income data shows that many routine white-collar occupations offer similar kinds of economic rewards to blue-collar occupations, and this suggests some kind of process of economic fusion between these two groups. Cowell *et al.* (1996: 68) have themselves commented on the extent to which income changes 'echo a phenomena that has generated considerable discussion in the United States, but which has not been given much attention in the United Kingdom, namely the "disappearing middle class"'. There appears to be a significant economic gap between professionals and managers and the 'rest'. In relative terms the position of manual and routine non-manual workers has been deteriorating steadily. Nor, at least in income terms, does it seem particularly helpful to distinguish a small 'underclass', substantially cut off from other members of the working class. To be sure, the bottom 10 per cent of the population have lost not just in relative but also in absolute terms, but there is considerable movement into and out of this bottom group.

I have also suggested, however, that the importance of organizational processes in generating economic inequality challenges Goldthorpe's approach to class. Taken seriously, it leads us to note that occupations cannot readily be seen as the building blocks of class. Individuals in situations of organizational centrality can accumulate advantages to themselves, so leading to processes of cumulative relative advantage and disadvantage that builds over time. Economic inequality therefore needs to be understood dynamically. Rather than economic polarization being about a cross-sectional rupture between winners and losers in the present, we should be aware of how these battles have implications not just for the present, but for the future. The ability of some groups to store their privileges, in the form of pension entitlements, accumulated share income, and through property ownership means that the full extent of class inequality can only be understood dynamically. Class is a longitudinal process rather than a cross-sectional one. Rather than people lining up on static class lines, with the results of their conflicts affecting the pattern of future social change, it can be suggested that people now have to achieve their class positions: their futures are linked to their own, as much as other people's, actions. Class becomes individualized.

Therefore, despite changing labour market and household dynamics, looking at inequality in household and life course perspective only amplifies and consolidates the kind of divisions I have examined above. Income inequalities among women are actually rather greater than they are among men, and because men and women tend to form relationships among their equals, so household relationships tend to multiply individual inequalities. Of course there are exceptions and complications, but the general picture holds. The same is also true for the life cycle. Old age, historically a period when most groups could expect to be in poverty, is now highly stratified, between those reliant on dwindling state pensions and those with access to occupational and private pension schemes.

I therefore conclude this chapter by adding a further twist to the impasse in class analysis. Evidence reviewed in Chapter 2 suggests that class is of limited cultural importance, and in Chapter 1 I showed that sociologists find it difficult to develop a satisfactory deductive concept of class. However, despite this, I have argued here that there is clear evidence of the hardening of class-related economic inequality. How is it that this divorce between these economic trends and popular recognition of class processes has occurred? How and why have sociologists, in general, found it less useful to use the concept of class at the very same time that economic polarization has reached unparalleled depths? These are puzzling questions which need to be resolved both theoretically – by reflecting on the nature of sociological theory – and substantively, by understanding better the nature of contemporary class processes. I make a start on these questions in the next chapter by visiting the heartland of British class analysis, the study of social mobility.

Notes

1 Readers seeking an example of this point might glance at Giddens (1990). This stricture does not apply, or at least not in any straightforward way, to some influential contemporary writers such as Beck (1992), Lash and Urry (1994) or Castells (1996, 1997, 1998). I consider these issues more fully in Chapter 5.

2 Though see the fascinating work of Cowell *et al.* which uses kernel density estimates to suggest that recent trends means that UK income 'does not have the standard textbook uni-modal shape. Rather, it has an intriguing bi-modal character' (Cowell *et al.* 1996: 65).

3 Though it can be argued that even in this period women's economic contribution to households was crucial. See Roberts (1984).

4 Between 1979–81 the proportion of the household income of cohabiting households earned by men was 73 per cent of the total: it was 61 per cent in 1989–91. In 10 the average share of household income earned by women was 15 per cent: in 1989–91 it was 21 per cent (Harkness *et al.* 1996, Table 7.2).

5 Though there are concerns regarding the reliability of data about the poorest groups in the population. Many of these appear to be self-employed and it is possible that there is systematic under-reporting of income.

6 This applies to the richest 200 people at these two dates, who may not be the same people.

7 See Scott (1997: 305): 'The predominant trend in the City, however, has been the thorough deregulation of its markets and their operations, leaving the core elements of the capitalist social class less cohesive and well-integrated than before'.

8 Adonis and Pollard (1997) have drawn attention to the development of what they call a 'superclass' of well paid, *salaried* employees, mostly professionals such as accountants, solicitors, local government officers, university professors, doctors etc. (see Adonis and Pollard 1997, Table 6). Although, as I discuss later in this chapter, most of these groups have indeed prospered in recent years, their salaries alone are nothing like enough to allow them membership of the wealth élite discussed here.

9 As long ago as 1980 Atkinson and Harrison (1980: 223–8) noted that the share price was a major factor in affecting the wealth levels of the top 1 per cent of wealth-holders.

10 Wealth from pensions is distributed somewhat more equally than is 'marketable' wealth, but is still distributed in favour of affluent earners. See Banks *et al.* (1996: 341ff.).

11 This is a different pattern from previous periods of house price inflation when all types of housing did rise in value, albeit at different rates.

12 1991 data from the British Household Panel Study (BHPS) indicates that managerial households have mean equity of £72,500 and partly skilled manual workers have equity of £42,400 (Hamnett and Seavers 1996, Table 14.8).

13 To give one example, much discussed at the time, when Reuters press agency was floated on the stock market in 1984, its three leading managers earned between £3 and £6 million for their shares. See Read (1998).

14 The best paid ethnic group in Britain, the Chinese, earned 79 per cent more than did the lowest paid ethnic group, the Bangladeshis, in the mid-1990s (Modood *et al.* 1997, Table 5.5). According to Table 3.3, the best paid occupational group, managers and administrators, earned 123 per cent more than the lowest paid occupational group.

15 For men the most important set of factors affecting their levels of pay is the type of occupation performed. This variable includes a measure of the number of hours worked, and therefore reflects in part the trite point that, all else being equal, people tend to earn more if they work more hours. Even allowing for this, there is also evidence that men in professional and managerial employment, by virtue of being in these jobs, have higher incomes than are due to them simply on the basis of their qualifications. The second most important factor affecting the variation in men's income is qualifications. Family background is the next most important set of factors, followed by ability (measured at age 11) and aspirations (measured at age 16), and the character of the respondent's work history.

16 Human capital theorists would recognize that human capital only leads to higher rewards where there is a market for the skill in question. However, there is a danger if the logic of this point is taken to its conclusion that human capital theory becomes tautologous. It simply amounts to saying that those earning the highest incomes do so because their skills are most in demand, without offering any explanation for this situation.

17 Arguably this is the reason why Gosling and Meghir (1994) find, at the aggregate level, a tendency for the wages of older workers to rise relative to those of younger workers. They do not however break down their analysis by occupation to establish this.

18 Having made this point, I should note that one possible explanation for the age premium for manual workers in the 1990s is that it reflects a cohort difference between manual workers recruited in the 1970s and those recruited in the 1990s. If this is true, young manual workers in the 1990s should not expect their earnings to rise in middle age to the level of those recruited in the 1970s. However, my general point concerning the growing complexity of the relationship between class, income and age still holds.

4 Social mobility *and the* 'Nuffield paradigm'

No other subject exemplifies the impasse of class analysis so well as the study of social mobility. Through the work of John Goldthorpe in particular, the class structural approach to the study of social mobility represents the finest intellectual achievement of the sociological class analysis tradition. However, the legacy bequeathed by this body of work is a problematic one. The exclusively quantitative and technical nature of these recent studies have reduced their appeal to non-specialists, while there has also been considerable confusion about the precise claims about class which Goldthorpe's work actually makes. Furthermore, there is an increasing disjuncture between the sophistication of the quantitative studies of social mobility on the one hand, and the much less mature analysis of the subjective experience of mobility and immobility on the other. We have here, in miniature, a tension that characterizes the field of class analysis in general: a lack of dialogue between research on the structural and cultural aspects of class.

This chapter is not so foolhardy as to claim to offer a comprehensive account of current issues in social mobility research.[1] My focus is restricted to considering the relationship between class analysis and social mobility. I argue that it is possible to build on the class structural perspective pioneered by Goldthorpe to develop a consistent account of social mobility and social class. However, it is necessary to critically rethink Goldthorpe's contribution to this subject. I take issue with some of Goldthorpe's critics, notably Saunders (1995) and Payne (1987a, 1987b, 1992), who claim that Goldthorpe overstresses the importance of class as a determinant of social mobility. I emphasize that Goldthorpe and his associates do not generally make strong *substantive* claims about the role of class. Rather, their contribution is best seen *methodologically*, in terms of their advocacy of a class structural approach to social mobility. In the second section of this chapter I argue that Goldthorpe's class structural approach has major virtues compared to the individualistic approach found in the American status attainment perspective. Several of Goldthorpe's critics misunderstand the central features of the class structural approach and thereby falsely charge Goldthorpe with exaggerating the importance of class. I go on to criticize Goldthorpe's claims about how the self-recruitment of their working class leads to their demographic 'maturity'. At the more methodological level I argue that Goldthorpe's conception of class formation rests upon a view of class formation as involving 'static' attachments to fixed class positions which makes it difficult to recognize that class formation is a dynamic process. I further argue that his advocacy of rational action theory leads to too rigid a distinction between the class structure and the rational individual which is ultimately unable to handle the cultural salience of class.

The final part of this chapter pulls together evidence from diverse recent studies of social mobility to develop an argument I left hanging in Chapter 3 – that class processes are best seen not as 'macro-social constraints', but as working biographically through the individual. I argue that this emphasis – which is consistent with elements of Goldthorpe's work as well as some of his putative critics such as Saunders – can recognize how class formation can take individualized forms. I flesh out what this rather nebulous hope might mean by examining how individual factors mediate the relationship between class position and social mobility.

Before starting my analysis I will begin – in the spirit of this book – by looking at what the lay population thinks about social mobility. For the study of mobility is as much about what people think about mobility as it is about objective mobility chances.

Popular understandings of social mobility in Britain

One of the enduring common-sense notions found in British society is the idea that hard work, effort, and talent are effective in leading to just rewards (see Harrop 1980). In 1949 David Glass' team found an almost universal endorsement of the meritocratic idea in their survey of attitudes to social mobility (Glass 1954).

Table 4.1 lists the kinds of factors which people from diverse social classes associated with (upward) social mobility in 1949. Meritocratic ideas claiming that hard work, good education, high ability and strong personality lead to upward social mobility drew support from members of all social classes, and from those with different class identifications. It is true that those manual workers who identified themselves as 'working class' were somewhat more likely to emphasize 'education' rather than 'hard work' or 'ability' as correlates of success. These working-class identifiers evidently embraced the meritocratic belief in the value of training and education more than did the middle classes who emphasized the role of motivation and working hard. Nevertheless both groups believed that individuals can 'help themselves' to get on by displaying the right attitude, work ethic, or by gaining educational qualifications.

Only a minority of working-class respondents referred to the role of 'contacts' (16 per cent) and 'money' (12 per cent) in affecting the prospects of upward mobility.[2] The overwhelming sense is that of a population which believed in the justice and legitimacy of the 'reward system' and the possibility of social climbing.

More recent evidence from 1987 British Social Attitude Surveys suggests

Table 4.1 Factors associated with social mobility, 1949

Factor	Background of respondent, by occupational group (and class identification)				
	Professional (%)	Salaried (middle) (%)	Salaried (working) (%)	Manual (middle) (%)	Manual (working) (%)
Hard Work	41	37	33	35	28
Training	22	32	33	33	43
Ability	27	22	15	12	17
Personality	20	18	19	14	10
Ambition	12	9	6	8	6
Contacts	8	12	4	5	16
Money	5	4	5	5	12
Good upbringing	5	3	4	5	3
N =	133	210	108	111	300

Source: adapted from Glass (1954, Table 20) (some unpopular responses excluded).

Table 4.2 Factors associated with getting ahead in life, 1987

Factor	Essential or very important (%)	Fairly important (%)	Not very or not important at all (%)
Hard work	84	14	2
Good education	72	24	4
Ambition	79	17	3
Natural ability	57	37	5
Knowing the right people	39	41	20
Having well-educated parents	28	45	27
Coming from a wealthy family	21	33	44
A person's race	16	31	45

Source: adapted from Brook (1992, Table P-5) (minority responses excluded). N = 1181

that not much has changed. Table 4.2 indicates the factors which respondents felt were 'important to get ahead in life'. Education and hard work figure as the most popular responses, exactly as they had done 40 years previously. Ambition is emphasized somewhat more in 1987, while ability ranks slightly less high.[3] There is some slight evidence pointing to a stronger emphasis on class-related and social processes in affecting one's chances of getting on. 'Knowing the right people' is ranked fifth in 1987, a similar ranking to that which working class identifiers had awarded it in 1949. In 1987 it was also felt generally important to have 'well-educated parents' and also 'to come from a wealthy family'. Neither of these responses were offered to respondents in 1949, but the nearest equivalent, 'good upbringing' ranked somewhat lower with only 4 per cent of the respondents selecting it.

Not too much should be made of these variations between 1949 and 1987, especially since the questions were asked differently and thereby elicited divergent kinds of response. The general finding is one of remarkable stability, even in a period of dramatic social change. The general 'common sense' revealed by Tables 4.1 and 4.2 is of a general belief in the virtues of there being a return for educational attainment, hard work and talent. People do not deny the value of social advantage (in 1987 only a minority of respondents thought it unhelpful to come from a wealthy or well-educated background) but nor do they stress it. The only significant division in the responses is between those emphasizing 'natural' or 'innate' factors as opposed to those emphasizing people's performance and motivation to work. The general endorsement is of the way in which individuals are able to make their futures.

We can, of course, question the sociological value of the kinds of answers represented in Tables 4.1 and 4.2. Evans (1997) disputes the idea that people endorse meritocratic views and claims that when people are asked to provide specific reasons why working- and middle-class people (rather than people in general) succeed, they show an awareness of class. Evans' analysis is problematic, however, since it frames mobility and success in class terms through its phrasing of questions. We certainly need to recognize that people's responses to these questions indicate a complex mix of wish fulfilment, scattered observation (both from personal knowledge and media representation), and defensiveness. And, even if we wish to claim that the endorsement of meritocratic perspectives is the product of 'false consciousness' related to the power of the dominant ideology (Abercrombie *et al.* 1980), it is still worth considering what aspects of the social world allow such meritocratic beliefs to have such currency. The remainder of this chapter takes up this question, by showing how class inequalities work through individualized processes.

Social mobility, individual mobility and class inequality

British research on social mobility continues to be indebted to the findings of the Nuffield mobility study. It is quite remarkable that 25 years after the fieldwork for this survey was carried out, and 20 years after the initial publication of its research findings, this study continues to dominate the British research agenda so completely. The situation in other countries, and especially the USA, is very different. In the USA the early hegemony of the 'status attainment' approach pioneered by Blau and Duncan (1967) lasted for only a decade or less, and subsequent research rapidly fragmented thereafter. In Britain, however, the influence of Goldthorpe's work has helped lead to a strong identification between class analysis and social mobility, and it is this relationship which needs careful unpicking.

Goldthorpe's work has generally been taken to be a strong argument for the importance of social class in influencing social mobility (see for instance

Payne 1990, 1992; Saunders 1995). However, there are two different kinds of claim about the relationship between class and social mobility. One *substantive* claim is that social class is a major influence on people's chances of social mobility: for instance, that those from working-class backgrounds are less likely to do well than those from the middle class. The other *methodological* claim is that social mobility is best conceptualized as mobility within a class structure. In this case the interest lies in understanding social mobility in terms of the flows of individuals between social classes. Either of these claims does not entail the other. Goldthorpe's major concern is methodological rather than substantive. He is not interested in explaining the correlates of individual mobility and weighing up the various determinants of the same.[4] Rather, his work can be seen, in deductive terms, as a consideration of how social mobility looks if examined from a class structural perspective.

A good example of a fundamentally different approach has recently been provided by Saunders (1997), which can therefore be considered here as a foil. Saunders assesses which factors correlate with an individual's upward social mobility. Although he does not acknowledge it (though see Bond and Saunders 1999), this leads him to tread in the footsteps originally laid by Blau and Duncan (1967) in their pathbreaking book, *The American Occupational Structure*. Here Blau and Duncan ranked Americans on a 17-point scale according to the standing of their occupation and considered what kinds of factors affected the level people attained on it. They found that there was a strong correlation of .405 between father's position and son's position. However, over half of this effect operated because the father's position influenced the kind of education that the son received which in turn influenced the son's job. Net of this educational effect, there was little direct relationship between father and son's position. They therefore claimed that the USA was organized more around the principles of achievement than ascription. Saunders claims that this same relationship also applies in the UK and that class processes are only of minor importance.

Empirically, Saunders' arguments are based on an analysis of the NCDS, which is a longitudinal survey which collects data on respondents (and, in the earlier sweeps, their parents) when they were 7, 11, 16, 23 and 33. Saunders distinguishes variables which differentiate *ability* (measured by respondent's performance on ability tests) from *motivation* (measured according to responses to attitude questions) and *structural factors* (for instance, whether the parental home was overcrowded, the attitudes of the respondents' parents, etc.), all measured when the children were living with their parents. Saunders then shows that the best predictor of upward mobility (measured by the type of job respondents were doing at age 33) is the 'ability' of the respondents, followed by their motivation and work attitudes (Saunders 1997: 271). Downward mobility is predicted most importantly by the lack of 'ability'. These results, interestingly, fully conform to the popular view of social mobility as discussed in the first section of this chapter.

There are however serious concerns about the way that Saunders conducts his investigation (see also Breen and Goldthorpe 1999). Leaving aside his problematic use of the registrar general's class schema, the most controversial issue is what 'ability' tests actually measure. Saunders claims that IQ tests are not a perfect measure of intelligence but 'are the best indicator we have of intelligence (certainly better than examination results), and the issue (addressed in psychology) of how far they measure innate against learned ability is largely irrelevant' (Saunders 1997: 277). In fact, the ability tests used in the NCDS are not IQ tests, but leaving this point aside, it is absolutely critical to know if these kinds of tests measure learned or innate ability. If they only measure learned ability, then it is not clear why their empirical significance can be seen as congruent with structurally based arguments which show that more advantaged households are best able to cultivate ability in their children.[5] It is certainly clear that – for whatever reason – middle class children appear from these tests to have more 'ability' than working class children (see Savage and Egerton 1998).[6] It is striking that Saunders' own analysis shows that measures of ability correlate less well with respondent's occupational outcomes when they are aged 33 than do measures of their educational attainment. A multiple regression model shows that the three variables which predict occupational outcomes most clearly are examination performance, qualifications and the social position of the first job (Saunders 1997: 275).

This is a particular example of a general problem. Saunders has the apparently enticing idea of separating out a host of different independent variables and seeing empirically which correlates best with a person's achieved social standing. However, such is the inter-correlation of these variables with each other that we can never be sure that they are in fact reliable measures acting independently of each other (exactly as I have noted in the case of 'ability'). This points to the problem of adopting an individualist paradigm, where structural processes are examined only in so far as they are measured individually (for instance, where overcrowding in the parents' home is taken as a measure of social disadvantage). Structural variables cannot be simply counterposed to individual ones and their relative importance empirically adjudicated. It is not surprising to report that 'able' young people from disadvantaged backgrounds will tend to do better then their less 'able' peers. However, in a society where there are growing numbers of middle-class jobs it is likely that working-class children will be drawn in to fill these new positions. It is quite plausible – indeed likely – that those who fill these jobs will be deemed to be 'brighter' than those who do not. However, in this case 'brightness' does not *cause* mobility, it is simply the filter that distinguishes those who are upwardly mobile from those who are not. The apparent correlation between an individual's ability and their upward mobility can be consistent with the power of social class.

It is in part because of major conceptual and methodological problems with 'individualistic' perspectives such as these that Goldthorpe chooses to organize his analysis from a class structural perspective. He makes it clear that his prime interest does not lie in examining how open British society is, but in the rather different question of examining how patterns of mobility affect processes of class formation.[7] This explains why Goldthorpe's unit of analysis becomes the aggregated social class grouping rather than the individual, with attention paid to the proportions of men[8] moving into and out of a given class (see Pawson 1993 for an overview, as well as Savage 1996b).

Table 4.3 Decomposition of total mobility rates (TMR) into total vertical (TV) and total non-vertical (TNV) mobility and of total vertical mobility into total upward (TU) and total downward (TD) mobility (%)

Nation	TMR	TV	TNV	TV/TNV	TU	TD	TU/TD
England and Wales	65	50	15	3.4	32	17	1.9
France	65	44	21	2.1	32	12	2.5
FRG	62	47	15	3.2	33	14	2.4
Hungary	76	45	32	1.4	35	9	3.8
Ireland	58	39	19	2.1	30	9	3.4
Northern Ireland	63	45	18	2.5	34	11	3.0
Poland	60	43	16	2.7	35	8	4.5
Scotland	64	51	13	3.9	33	18	1.8
Sweden	73	54	19	2.9	42	13	3.3

Source: Erikson and Goldthorpe (1992, Table 6.3).

Substantively, Goldthorpe's emphasis is on the high amount of mobility found in Britain and his account is therefore not at odds with that of Saunders. Table 4.3 provides cross-national evidence from one of the most comprehensive analyses of male social mobility, the CASMIN project (Erikson and Goldthorpe 1992). The table indicates that in England and Wales around two thirds of sons are in a different social class from their father. Some of these movements between social classes cannot be seen as moves 'up' or 'down' the class ladder, since they are moves between classes which convey similar economic rewards. Excluding these, 50 per cent of sons have moved up or down between social classes compared to their fathers, a proportion broadly in line with figures from other countries. The country with the highest vertical mobility, Sweden, saw 54 per cent of its sons in different classes from their fathers, while the country with the lowest vertical mobility, Ireland, had 39 per cent. (It is worthy of note that in some respects Goldthorpe detects much more social mobility than does the lay population. Recent survey research suggests only 10 per cent of the population think they have been socially mobile (Young 1992)).

England and Wales are characterized by a high degree of mobility. But aggregate figures of upward and downward mobility are perforce rather crude to indicate how much mobility there is between particular classes. Table 4.4, taken from Goldthorpe *et al.* (1987), and based on the Nuffield survey carried out in 1972, is an 'inflow table', which shows the proportions of fathers of respondents in given social classes who come from different social classes.

To recap well-known findings, Table 4.4 indicates dramatic social flux. Fathers *do not* tend to be from the same class as their sons. The highest proportions of fathers in the same class as their sons are for semi-skilled workers (where 42 per cent of fathers are in the same class), unskilled workers (37 per cent), the self-employed (27 per cent) and the 'upper service class' (25 per cent). The other middle-class groups have a considerable amount of mobility into their ranks. Only in the two manual classes do more than one third of respondents have fathers from the same class as themselves. There is

Table 4.4 Class composition by class of father[1] at respondent's age 14

Father's[1] class	Respondent's class (1972)							N	%
	I[2] Percentage by column	II	III	IV	V	VI	VII		
I	25.3 (24.2)	12.4 (12.0)	9.6 (9.1)	6.7 (6.0)	3.2 (3.0)	2.0 (1.9)	2.4 (2.0)	680 (688)	7.9 (7.3)
II	13.1 (12.5)	12.2 (11.8)	8.0 (7.6)	4.8 (4.4)	5.2 (4.9)	3.1 (3.0)	2.5 (2.2)	547 (554)	6.4 (5.9)
III	10.4 (10.0)	10.4 (10.0)	10.8 (10.2)	7.4 (6.1)	8.7 (8.2)	5.7 (5.4)	6.0 (5.3)	687 (694)	8.0 (7.3)
IV	10.1 (13.0)	12.2 (13.9)	9.8 (12.2)	27.2 (36.5)	8.6 (10.6)	7.1 (9.6)	7.7 (12.3)	886 (1,329)	10.3 (14.1)
V	12.5 (12.0)	14.0 (13.5)	13.2 (12.5)	12.1 (9.4)	16.6 (15.6)	12.2 (11.4)	9.6 (8.6)	1,072 (1,082)	12.5 (11.5)
VI	16.4 (15.7)	21.7 (21.0)	26.1 (24.8)	24.0 (19.2)	31.1 (29.2)	41.8 (39.4)	35.2 (30.3)	2,577 (2,594)	30.0 (27.5)
VII	12.1 (12.6)	17.1 (17.8)	22.6 (23.6)	17.8 (18.5)	26.7 (28.5)	28.0 (29.4)	36.6 (39.3)	2,126 (2,493)	24.8 (26.4)
N	1,230 (1,285)	1,050 (1,087)	827 (870)	687 (887)	1,026 (1,091)	1,883 (2,000)	1,872 (2,214)	8,575 (9,434)	
%	14.3 (13.6)	12.2 (11.5)	9.6 (9.2)	8.0 (9.4)	12.0 (11.6)	22.0 (21.2)	21.8 (23.5)		

Notes: 1 Or other 'head of household'. The two basic questions in the 1972 inquiry from which the data of the table derive were: 'What is your job now?' – following on from several questions on earlier occupations; and 'What was your father's (or other head of household's) job at that time (i.e. at respondent's age 14)?' – following on from several other questions about respondent's family circumstances at that age.
2 Classes are I: higher salariat; II: lower salariat; III: routine and non-manual; IV: *petite bourgeoisie* (including farmers and smallholders); V: lower-grade technicians and supervisors of manual workers; VI: skilled manual employees; VII: unskilled manual employees (including agricultural labourers and rank and file service workers).

Source: Goldthorpe et al. (1987, Table 2.1).

little inheritance of social positions in the way common in rural, agricultural societies.[9]

Goldthorpe's findings can be questioned for focusing on men, and they are also somewhat dated. Subsequent research suggests that if anything absolute mobility has increased over time. Heath (2000) finds that the proportion of upwardly mobile men has increased from 27 per cent for those born before 1900 to 42 per cent for those born after 1940, while downward mobility has fallen from around 20 per cent for men born before 1920 to around 13 per cent for those born between 1950 and 1959. Marshall *et al.* (1997) indicate that male mobility has increased in recent years. Their survey, carried out in 1990, indicates that 56 per cent of men had moved up or down the social class hierarchy compared to their fathers. Heath (2000) and Marshall *et al.* (1996) also demonstrate a high rate of female mobility, especially among younger women. 36 per cent of women born between 1950 and 1959 were upwardly mobile, and only 17 per cent stayed in the same class as their father. These high total mobility rates for women are not surprising given the nature of gender segregation in the labour market. Women tend to be employed in exclusively female forms of work (notably routine white-collar employment), and this entails daughters being more mobile than sons in relation to their fathers. Nonetheless it is still striking that daughters are marginally more likely to be in a higher social class compared with their fathers as they are to be in a lower social class. Class mobility is the norm, not the exception, for both men and women.

Substantively, Goldthorpe is not committed to the proposition that there is little mobility between social classes, and indeed he emphasizes the extent of mobility in England and Wales (see especially Goldthorpe *et al.* 1987, Ch. 2). Admittedly, there are times when Goldthorpe seems to emphasize the lack of mobility. He criticizes feminist writers who have argued for the need to classify the class positions of households, not just one of their members. He argues that a joint classification is 'bound to generate very high rates of class mobility' (Goldthorpe 1990: 409). Indeed, so high is the mobility to be found under this procedure, he claims, that it might 'call the whole project of class analysis into doubt' (1990: 409). This implies that class analysis depends on substantively demonstrating low rates of class mobility. However, this is an unusual aside. In general, Goldthorpe fully recognizes the extent of social mobility.

Controversy arises however when Goldthorpe takes the further step of distinguishing between relative and absolute rates of social mobility. Goldthorpe famously argues that while absolute rates show large amounts of mobility, relative rates (which compare the relative chances of members of one social class with those of another) indicate that sons of more privileged social classes have better chances compared to those of the working class. Furthermore, these advantages remain fairly constant over time. Goldthorpe's critics have argued that this focus on relative rates allows him to smuggle class back into his account. Payne (1992: 223–4) claims, in support of Saunders (1990a) that *'relative mobility constancy is less discomforting to a traditional "class" perspective than is the rise in absolute mobility rates'* (original emphasis). Having opened the door to recognizing the real extent of mobility, Goldthorpe slams it shut again to emphasize the persistence of class inequalities.

It is undoubtedly true that Goldthorpe's more recent work has shown him to be increasingly interested in relative rather than absolute rates of mobility. In *Social Mobility and the Class Structure in Modern Britain* (1980) he makes his prime interest in questions of class formation explicit, and five of the seven core chapters (2, 5, 6, 7 and 8) deal with absolute mobility rates and their ramifications. However, in his recent comparative work with Erikson (Erikson and Goldthorpe 1992), the focus does shift, with the three core chapters (3, 4, 5) examining relative mobility rates. Despite this, critics mistake his sociological interest in relative rates as a sign of his commitment to emphasizing the substantive power of class. In fact, so far as class formation is concerned, Goldthorpe is unequivocal on the need to focus on absolute rates (see generally, in Goldthorpe's defence, Westergaard 1990).

Admittedly Goldthorpe's shift is linked to his view that relatively little of sociological interest can be said about class formation. He came to doubt the existence of an association between the reality of social mobility and people's perceptions of mobility, notably when he found that the socially mobile were not much different from the immobile in terms of their attitudes and orientations (see also Marshall and Firth 1999). He became increasingly doubtful that any major claims could be made about the relationship between demographic class formation and cultural identity. However, it would be foolish to claim that this explains why he sets such store by relative mobility. The use of a measure of relative mobility is essential not 'to smuggle class back in', but to permit rigorous comparative analysis. Whether the comparison be temporal (i.e. comparing mobility over time) or spatial (comparing mobility between places, e.g. nations), methods of differentiating mobility due to structural factors (notably changes in the division of labour) and other factors (notably changes in social 'openness') need to be found. None of Goldthorpe's critics have found an alternative way of doing this to the use of relative mobility rates.[10]

It is undeniably true that Goldthorpe's use of odds ratios as the best measure of relative mobility can be challenged (see Payne 1992; Noble 1995; Saunders 1997; and see the reply by Breen and Goldthorpe 1999). Evidence does not always back up Goldthorpe's claim that there is no trend over time for such relative odds to change (Payne 1992; Miles 1999). But this is beside the main point. The analytical purpose of distinguishing between relative and absolute social mobility is to permit *comparative* research which allow researchers to abstract from peculiarities of specific kinds of employment structures. When Goldthorpe talks about the specific question of class formation in contemporary England and Wales (for instance in Goldthorpe *et al.* 1987, Conclusion) he focuses on absolute rates. It is only when he poses the comparative question of understanding persistence in relative rates over time that his focus changes, for quite understandable reasons.

There is a further issue here. Relative mobility rates report comparative differences between the chances of members of different social classes. They do not, in themselves, offer any kind of explanation of such differences, whether in terms of class or anything else. In this respect Payne's (1990: 301) assertion that 'Goldthorpe . . . treat[s] mobility as a product of class relations, to the virtual exclusion of other causal forces' is fundamentally misguided. It is in fact perfectly plausible in principle for the relative advantages of (for instance) service-class sons over working-class sons to be explained in terms of the superior 'merit' or 'ability' of service-class sons.[11] Goldthorpe *et al.* (1987, Ch. 4) and Erikson and Goldthorpe (1992, Ch. 4) construct a model to fit the patterns of relative mobility they uncover. Rather than assuming that class explains relative mobility rates, their model is multidimensional. Only one of the four processes it delineates, that linked to *inheritance*, can be seen as directly linked to class (see Savage 1994 for more detail). Erikson and Goldthorpe's (1992: 139) own gloss on their findings is that 'propensity for mobility within class structures, whether cross nationally common or variant, must, in our view, be treated as being more than one-dimensional'.

Goldthorpe's work does not offer particularly strong or emphatic claims about the *substantive* power of social classes to determine the mobility of individuals, and he cannot justly be accused of 'left wing bias' (Saunders 1995: 38). Read carefully, Goldthorpe's study of social mobility endorses the view that Britain is a highly mobile society in which there are few, if any, absolute barriers to class mobility.[12] This emphasis on the high degree of mobility should be at the heart of our understanding of class identities and class formation, as I now go on to examine.[13]

Class formation, rational action and the class structural paradigm

In my view, the important implications of Goldthorpe's work can only be discerned when his substantive claims about class and mobility are placed firmly in the context of his class structural methodology. I will press the implications of Goldthorpe's class structural perspective for understanding class formation in order to suggest that there are a series of problems in his formulations that need further consideration. I explore two issues in Goldthorpe's work with particular care. These are first, his approach to class formation, and second his advocacy of rational action theory.

Class formation

Goldthorpe's advocacy of a class structural approach to mobility has frequently been hailed as a major sociological triumph (e.g. Muller 1990; Pawson 1993). It directs attention to processes of 'class structuration' by examining the recursive relationship between the class structure, defined through the class schema, and the way that individual actions are both constrained by this class structure and also help to reproduce it (e.g. Pawson 1993). Goldthorpe's gloss on these intentions is best indicated by the following quotation:

> The achievement of a genuinely open society, would imply, it may be supposed, the decomposition or at all events the serious attenuation of classes in the sense of aggregates of individuals, or families, identifiable

in the extent to which they occupy similar locations in the social division of labour over time. However class relations are ones highly resistant to change: those groupings who enjoy positions of superior advantage and disadvantage cannot be expected to yield them up without a struggle, but will rather typically seek to exploit the resources they can command in order to preserve their superiority. Change is therefore only likely to be brought about through collective action on the part of those in inferior positions . . . The first consequence of the guiding interests that we have set out, so far as our treatment of social mobility in modern Britain is concerned, is then that this is carried out essentially in terms of mobility between classes . . .

(Goldthorpe et al. 1987: 28–9)

Demographic identity is crucial to class formation, which involves assessing the extent to which a class is self-recruiting:

To discuss the homogeneity and retentiveness of different classes is simply another way of treating their degree of 'demographic identity' . . . or, that is, the degree to which they have formed as collectivities of individuals and households through the continuity of their association with particular sets of class positions over time.

(Erikson and Goldthorpe 1992: 226)

One of the main conclusions that Goldthorpe and Marshall (1992: 387) draw in their manifesto for class analysis is that they have discovered common patterns of class formation. They note that 'across diverse national settings, classes have been shown to display rather distinctive "mobility characteristics"'. Professional and managerial classes come from heterogeneous social backgrounds but have good prospects for retaining their offspring in their own class. Members of the working class are more likely to come from working-class backgrounds, but their children are often upwardly mobile (see Table 4.3). Goldthorpe therefore points to the demographic 'maturity' of the working class (given its self-recruiting nature) and the lack of demographic unity of the service class (given the much more mixed social background of its members). This has clear affinities with his earlier arguments against the idea of the 'embourgoisement' of the working class (Goldthorpe and Lockwood 1968, 1969). There is continued potential for political solidarity among the working class. By contrast, the rapid expansion of service-class positions has meant that this class recruits widely, is composed of people from heterogeneous backgrounds, and therefore lacks a cohesive class identity. However, both these arguments are flawed.

Let me consider first the issue of middle-class formation. It is striking that Goldthorpe defines class formation in terms of stasis and continuity. The more the members of a class stay in its ranks (either between generations or over an individual's life), the more attached that people are to a class and the better formed is that class. What we have here is a definitional distinction in which class formation involves *static* attachment. However, by conceptualizing class formation in these terms, mobility and class formation are defined in terms of opposition. Rather than class formation being itself a dynamic process, involving a particular way of linking pasts, present and futures, it is posited as being based on a static attachment to fixed positions.[14] This view of mobility and class formation is more germane to understanding working-class formation rather than middle-class formation. Middle-class formation involves a dynamic relation to time, in which middle-class people expect prospective rewards, and in which work lives are embedded around ideas of individual progress and advancement in the longer term (often, as I discuss further in Chapter 6, around the narrative of 'career'). Therefore, occupational and class instability may actually be consistent with very marked patterns of class formation. Even though the members of a class may come from diverse backgrounds, they may nonetheless share a common belief and commitment to the 'career' in which their end point, rather than their starting point, helps define a class identity. Goldthorpe's notion of class formation rests upon a restricted understanding that is applicable to peasants and the working class.

The question of demographic working class formation poses different issues. Perhaps the major ambiguity in Goldthorpe's class structural approach concerns the definition of the *class structure*. Strictly speaking the idea of 'structure' refers to internally related positions in the division of labour, in which a given set of positions entails the existence of others, as, for instance, in the capital–labour relationship.[15] Goldthorpe clearly uses class structure in the stricter sense. He emphasizes that his own class schema is 'relational' with the result that the classes it delineates are defined with respect to other social classes, and he roots this class schema in the social division of labour.[16] However, Goldthorpe's analyses are not sampled from the entire workforce and are therefore not representative of the division of labour in its entirety. This is because the exclusion of women and dependants (or more latterly, whichever household members are in 'inferior' class positions) means that there are people who perform jobs in the division of labour, but who are not part of the class structure as Goldthorpe operationally defines it (see Crompton 1998). There is a systematic bias in Goldthorpe's work towards excluding some people involved in lowly positions in the division of labour.

This bears on Goldthorpe's substantive claims about the maturity of the working class. Goldthorpe is concerned that by including women carrying out intermittent or part-time work, spuriously high amounts of mobility are artefactually revealed. However, by not including them, he omits significant numbers of people carrying out various kinds of 'proletarian' work in the division of labour from his account of the demographic maturity of the working class. The sociological conclusions that he draws about working-class formation in general are likely to be skewed because they are only based on a sub-sample of those in working-class positions. We could choose to accept the logic of Goldthorpe's arguments and distinguish the 'core' manual working class (defined as the heads of their household) from those who are 'secondary earners' (other household members, mostly women). However, while this may allow Goldthorpe to rescue his claims about demographic unity among the 'core' working class as he defines it, this ignores potential tensions between 'core' and 'peripheral' working class. Goldthorpe has defined out of his analysis significant groups of 'workers' which most sociological theorists would wish to include as part of their speculations about working-class formation.[17] Since most of the sociological arguments about class formation – Marxist, Weberian and liberal – which Goldthorpe takes issue with take *the workforce within the division of labour as a whole* as their reference point, the sociological relevance of his arguments become problematic. The real problems in Goldthorpe's analysis lie not in his account of relative mobility rates, but in his conceptualization and operationalization of class formation. His work does not demonstrate either that the middle classes are not demographically formed as a class, or that the working class are.

The rational action approach

Goldthorpe's class structural programme is premised on making a sharp methodological distinction between the class structure on the one hand, and individuals moving (or remaining static) within it on the other. In making this distinction he draws on an honourable tradition in class analysis which distinguishes class 'positions' from the 'people' who may be contingently located in them (Carchedi 1977; Crompton and Gubbay 1977; Abercrombie and Urry 1983; Scott 1996). Whereas most of these writers endorse some form of structuralist analysis, in which causal emphasis is given to structural processes, Goldthorpe has been increasingly explicit in using the same distinction to argue for a form of methodological individualism which celebrates the capacity of individuals to engage in rational action within the costs and opportunities provided by the class structure.[18]

In his later work, Goldthorpe has become increasingly articulate in defending a 'rational action theory' (RAT) perspective on social mobility. I have elaborated the reasons for this intellectual move in Chapter 2, where I interpreted it as a defensive attempt to shore up a mode of class analysis whose inductive and cultural foundation had become unstable. RAT allows Goldthorpe to explain how individuals act in class ways even when they lack developed class awareness. He argues that rationally acting individuals from different classes will not engage in similar kinds of actions because the opportunities and constraints presented to them by virtue of their location in class positions vary. The same kind of attitude can thus lead to different outcomes. This formulation allows Goldthorpe to work with a mode of class analysis which makes little or no reference to claims about the salience of class cultures.

The most developed use of RAT so far is contained in Goldthorpe's (1996) account of how class differences in educational attainment are generated. He emphasizes that the greater propensity of middle-class children to out-perform working-class children is not due to the differing cultures of working-class and middle-class pupils (as for instance might be suggested by Bourdieu's emphasis on cultural capital or Bernstein's discussion of extended and restricted codes). Rather, the differing mix of constraints and opportunities facing middle- and working-class parents is decisive. As Goldthorpe puts it, 'persisting differentials are simply one expression of the way in which the unequal distributions of resources, opportunities and constraints that characterise a class society contribute to their own perpetuation through the quite rational adaptive strategies that they induce on the part of those who must act under their influence' (1996: 497).

Goldthorpe builds upon his class structural approach to develop a general picture of how class inequalities are reproduced through individual rational actions in ways which avoids references to class culture or structural determinism. As a piece of intellectual chutzpah this is a *tour de force*. However, careful reflection indicates a series of unanswered questions. First, Goldthorpe tends to waver between strong and weak versions of RAT. He avows a 'weak' version of RAT (see particularly Goldthorpe 1998) which champions it as an aid to deductive reasoning and involves no substantive claims that people do in fact act rationally. Indeed, he recognizes that many people are not, in fact, rational, but simply that different kinds of irrational action will balance each other out (Goldthorpe 1996: 485–6; though see Scott 1996 for some critical remarks). Rationality here operates as a kind of 'null hypothesis' – i.e. the most parsimonious assumption that needs to be disproved. Goldthorpe is prepared to recognize value-oriented rationality (rational action in pursuit of a norm) as compatible with a RAT explanatory framework. Despite the sophistication of these formulations, this amounts to an attempt to 'to have his cake and eat it' in an ultimately unconvincing fashion. Invoking instrumental rationality can provide explanatory accounts, but at the cost of reductionism. Casting the net wider to their include value rational action avoids reductionism but leads to description, since all RAT will do in this case is recast the actions consequent on any value in 'rational' terms.[19]

It is indeed striking that the substantive claims that Goldthorpe makes concerning the rational action basis of class differences in educational attainment take a narrower, instrumental form.[20] There are, however, problems with this. One concern, discussed within game theory, but not addressed by Goldthorpe, is the relationship between individual and collective rationality.[21] In Goldthorpe's case the issue concerns the relationship between the maximization of collective household good as opposed to the good of a specific individual (e.g. a child or parent) within it (e.g. Goldthorpe 1996: 495). But, what instrumental reasons might parents have for sacrificing their own well-being (in terms of childrearing work, financial support, etc.) to their children's disposal? Would parents in a rationally acting household choose to devote all resources towards one child's education, so minimizing the chances of other children in the household, or share the risk? It is not clear how the individual rationality of different household members could ever lead to the kind of collective household strategy which might actually result in the optimum chances for children, at least without placing the argument on a normative rather than an instrumental footing (e.g. without developing an argument along the lines that parents wish their children to have the best start in their lives because they 'love' them).

As numerous critics of RAT have insisted, and as Goldthorpe himself recognizes, decision making depends on specific kinds of cultural framework. Consider, for instance, Goldthorpe's argument that working-class parents do not tend to encourage their children into higher education since this would be risky if they fail to obtain a university place. Rather, 'less ambitious – and

less costly – educational options would be adequate to the goal of maintain-
ing class stability, while also providing quite good chances of some degree of
eventual upward mobility' (Goldthorpe 1996: 495). This rather peculiar formulation suggests that working-class parents prefer their children to remain
in the working class rather than move to a higher class. Interestingly, it
points to the class contextuality of strategies for class reproduction. The
'rationality' of service-class reproduction (where the instrumental service class
parent will wish to reproduce their own class position for their children) is
substantially different from the instrumentality of working-class reproduction (where the rational working-class parent may want to place their children in a different, higher, class).

But further, in order for either working-class parents or service-class
parents to pursue a rational strategy they have to have a sense as to which
class they are in. Goldthorpe's analysis proceeds as if the brute realities of the
class to which people have been objectively allocated are enough to elicit a
'rational' response. But in fact if working-class parents delude themselves
that they are part of the established middle class, then they will not, presumably, regard higher education as 'for' other social classes. And further, we
have already seen that significant numbers of middle-class people think they
are working class, but it is not clear that they adopt the 'working-class'
strategy which Goldthorpe delineates. The RAT argument depends not only
on the objective existence of a class-based cost and opportunity structure,
but also on an awareness of symbols and identifiers to allow people to devise
an 'appropriate' strategy. Yet, as we have seen, Goldthorpe's account is designed specifically to avoid appealing to such cultural terms of reference,
since he knows that people's class identities are actually rather weak. Without them, however, his explanatory framework falls apart.

This is a useful moment to take stock. Goldthorpe's critique of individualist perspectives on social mobility is powerful and effective. His emphasis on the value of examining mobility within the context of the class
structure remains a crucial step forward. However, Goldthorpe's subsequent
attempts to conceptualize mobility processes within a rational action perspective in which the class structure specifies the constraints and resources at
the disposal of individuals is too minimalist. It is simply not possible to
ignore the cultural frameworks which people use to make sense of their
social location and which will thus condition the kinds of rational responses
that they will make. It is preferable to operate with a closer understanding
of the relationship between the individual and the social context and to
examine the factors which intervene between the class structure and the
individual actor. This involves, among other things, examining the cultural
construction of differing kinds of rationality and recognizing the social
embeddedness of individuals. As part of this process we also need to work
with a more fluid conception of class formation which does not take the idea
of stasis – as in the 'traditional working-class' sense – as the litmus test of
class formation. Classes are formed through the actions of individuals, and it
is important to see not only whether individuals are mobile or not through
a fixed class structure, but also how class relations are themselves constituted
through different modes of temporal linkage. In order to carry this through

it is useful to turn our attention away from images of the 'working class', which still colour Goldthorpe's sophisticated attempts to examine mobility. In the last section of this chapter I try to illustrate what this might mean in more empirical terms.

Social class and middle-class reproduction in contemporary Britain

Three types of research provide valuable ideas on the kinds of mediating processes that intervene between the 'class structure' and the 'individual', and which thereby develop our understanding of contemporary class formation. First, following on from Goldthorpe's discussion of inequalities in educational attainment, I look at the intermediary role of educational qualifications on social mobility. Second, I return to consider some of the issues raised by Saunders (1997) by considering the role of individual 'ability' on social mobility prospects. Finally, I will examine how a focus on work life mobility might provide material of value. In all three cases I will emphasize that it is useful to look at these not as alternatives to looking at mobility from a class perspective, but rather from within a broad class structural approach.

Educational attainment and social mobility

There is no denying the central role of educational processes in stratification processes. However, rather than seeing this point as undermining the role of class, as Saunders (1997) suggests, it is more valuable to examine, from within a broad class structural perspective, how educational processes help class processes to operate. The most interesting starting point here is Bourdieu and Passeron's (1973) arguments concerning the role of cultural capital in middle-class reproduction. Bourdieu and Passeron argue that, as capitalism 'depersonalized' with the growth of large scale corporate ownership, it therefore became more difficult for middle-class families to pass on their advantages through direct inheritance of property. Other mechanisms have therefore developed which allow middle-class advantage to be reconstructed primarily through the education system. Even though middle-class parents may not be able to pass on their occupations to their children they can impart the right sorts of capacities to their children to enable them to do well in the educational system. The resulting credentials can then be translated into good jobs, entry to which is dependent on educational performance.

From this perspective, the reproduction of the modern class system depends on the existence of an educational system which allows middle-class children to do systematically better in the system than other children and subsequently gain advantages in moving into more privileged forms of employment. Evidence does indeed suggest that this process of middle-class reproduction is secure. Marshall *et al.* (1997) show that 89 per cent of service-class sons who attained degree level qualifications had succeeded in moving into the professional and managerial middle classes. However,

Table 4.5 Class distribution in Britain, by class of origin and educational attainment (percentage by row)

Class origins	Class destination						N
	I	*II*	*III*	*IV*	*V/VI*	*VII*	
Education level 1							
I, II	8	11	14	14	13	39	105
III	7	17	12	10	14	38	42
IV	7	6	8	28	15	36	177
V, VI	2	7	10	8	23	50	517
VII	2	8	9	8	16	57	507
Educational level 2							
I, II	12	19	27	10	11	19	315
III	15	14	29	16	10	17	93
IV	9	13	28	17	12	19	190
V, VI	6	13	25	9	25	21	564
VII	8	13	20	9	26	25	396
Educational level 3							
I, II	29	33	22	4	7	5	256
III	29	38	23	0	8	2	52
IV	28	32	11	15	8	7	117
V, VI	21	35	14	4	13	13	224
VII	18	29	21	3	14	16	117
Educational level 4							
I, II	48	41	5	4	2	0	227
III	52	40	10	0	0	0	42
IV	42	37	4	12	0	7	57
V, VI	38	43	12	3	0	5	112
VII	37	50	6	2	4	4	52

N = 4162.
Note: Classes are I: higher salariat; II: lower salariat; III: routine non-manual; IV: *petite bourgeoisie* (including farmers and smallholders); V: lower-grade technicians and supervisors of manual workers; VI: skilled manual employees; VII: unskilled manual employees (including agricultural labourers and rank and file service workers).
Source: Marshall *et al.* (1997, Table 5.1).

educational processes do not always work so smoothly to ensure middle class reproduction. Goldthorpe (1996), following Halsey *et al.* (1980), emphasizes that rather similar proportions of children from lower social classes with degrees also moved into the salariat. And since only 46 per cent of those with degree qualifications were from professional and managerial backgrounds it is clear that education does not simply reproduce social class privilege. It is possible for children from lower social classes to do well at school, obtain degrees and move into middle-class employment: it is a vehicle for social mobility.

Gordon Marshall and his colleagues (1997) have explored how educational attainment mediates the relationship between social class background and social class destination (see Table 4.5). They emphasize that even controlling for level of education, class differences are apparent: '[A]t each level of education, there is differentiation in the destination reached by individuals, according to the social backgrounds from which they originate. Persons having service class (or even routine non-manual) origins are more likely to arrive at relatively privileged positions within the class structure' (Marshall *et al.* 1997: 80). In fact Marshall *et al.* overplay their hand.[22] Class differences net of educational attainment are relatively modest. Thus 89 per cent of the highly educated children of the service class attain comparable positions themselves, compared to 87 per cent of the children of unskilled labouring fathers and 81 per cent of the children of skilled manual fathers.

Marshall *et al.* (1997) bolster their argument by using log linear models to consider whether the effect of a father's social class has any impact beyond its effect on children's education. Although they show that a better fit is obtained with a model which allows a father's class to affect the son's class independent of educational attainment (as in the 'merit–selection' model), the degree of improvement is modest.[23] Although it is clear that class does have an independent effect on children's social destination, only 8 per cent of cases are misclassified if no independent effect is assumed in the model. Furthermore, the merit–selection model in the British case is similar to that in many other countries: only in Bulgaria is the model significantly more effective.[24]

Marshall *et al.* (1997) go on to examine changes over time, comparing their survey (pooled with other surveys of the same period to increase sample size) with those carried out as part of the Nuffield mobility study. They show clearly that 'returns to graduation' continue to be very strong. The odds of graduates rather than non-graduates reaching the service class were in the order of 87:1 in 1972 and 82:1 in 1989. The returns to those with 'advanced' (A level and equivalent) education fall somewhat, a sign perhaps of the devaluation of such credentials in a period of higher education expansion. But the really striking findings concern the prospects of children from different class backgrounds. Whereas in 1972 the odds of the sons of higher service-class fathers moving into service-class employment compared to the sons of unskilled labourers (controlling for the effects of education) were 6:1, by 1989 they had more than halved to 2.2:1. As Marshall *et al.* (1997: 127) comment, 'while the direct effect of class origins on one's chance of obtaining salariat employment remains significant it has declined over the past twenty years or so'.

The implications of this striking finding are worth drawing out. Since we know that in the same period the association between father's and son's class stays roughly constant, class effects are increasingly being mediated through educational processes. The main way in which privileged households pass on their advantages to their children is by ensuring – through whatever means – that their children obtain better educational qualifications than their peers. To be sure, there are all sorts of other resources which the advantaged can bring to bear, but the most important would appear to be those which can be mobilized to improve the children's educational performance.

This finding may appear to indicate the declining salience of class, since the better performance of middle-class children in the educational system may reflect their superior innate capacities. Another argument may be that since educational attainment can to some extent be bought (through private schooling, private tuition etc.), or can be encouraged by appropriate cultural resources, this indicates that the power of social class operates through the educational process. Heath and Cheung's (1999) study of the effects of private schooling on educational attainment and social mobility shows that although private schooling continues to have a significant impact on the fates of children, its effects are now largely due to the ability of private schools to ensure their pupils perform well in educational tests. Whereas traditionally private schools had additional effects over and above this, pre-sumably through the mysterious workings of the 'old school tie', today these account for very little. Class effects are *increasingly* mediated through the educational attainment process.

'Ability' and social mobility

In the second section of this chapter I criticized Saunders' focus on indi-vidual mobility. However, I have also noted that Goldthorpe's class struc-tural approach is ultimately too minimalist to be persuasive, and there are therefore good grounds, as Goldthorpe himself now recognizes (and see Devine 1998a), to study the role of individual ability within a broad class structural perspective. Savage and Egerton (1998) carry out a relatively simple attempt along these lines and argue that it makes more sense not to examine the correlates of individual success or failure, but to see how the movement of respondents between social classes may vary according to their ability level. Ability is a mediating variable, rather than an independent one, as in Saunders' study.

This exercise reveals a number of points of interest, but here I focus on three. First, even controlling for the ability level of children, there are powerful class differences between the fates of high ability middle-class and working-class children. Only 7 per cent of the 'high ability' sons of large business owners and managers work in manual occupations when they are aged 33, compared to 38 per cent of the 'high ability' sons of unskilled manual workers. In contrast, over half of the 'low ability' sons of professional fathers join the middle class, compared to 10 per cent of the 'low ability' sons of unskilled manual workers. Class differences remain even for those of similar measured levels of ability. Middle-class children are better able to convert their high ability into middle-class jobs than are working-class children, and it seems highly likely that this is related to the superior re-sources at their disposal.

Second, there are marked differences in the proportion of children from different social classes who are judged to be of 'high' or 'low' ability. For the sons of professionals, the ratio with 'high' rather than 'low' ability is 87:13. For the sons of unskilled workers, the ratio is 32:68. For daughters the imbalance is even more marked. The ratio of 'high' to 'low' ability for the daughters of professionals is 94:6; for the daughters of unskilled manual workers it is 36:64. Class effects appear to be mediated through the 'ability' levels of individual children. The reasons for this are unclear. As mentioned earlier in this chapter, it may reflect the social bias of ability tests (the extent to which they tap learned rather than innate ability[25]), or possibly the different kinds of genetic endowments of middle-class and working-class children. The important point is to note that some of the processes behind class advantage and disadvantage work *through* the individual, rather than *on* them.

Finally, Savage and Egerton (1998) show that women's occupational destinations are considerably less affected than men's by the class of their fathers, once their ability levels are taken into account. The main exception is the daughters of professional fathers, whose chances of being located in professional and managerial employment are much better than those of (for instance) managers or small business proprietors. Women rely much more exclusively on having high ability and converting this into good educational qualifications, while the sons of service-class fathers have other resources at their disposal to allow them the chance of moving themselves into privileged classes.

Work life mobility and careers

I have argued that the effects of class work through the individual: both in terms of the performance of individuals (in educational processes) and in terms of individual 'abilities'. A further exemplification of this point concerns the role of individual work life mobility in generating class outcomes and affecting processes of class formation. The relationship between work life mobility and intergenerational mobility has been much discussed in recent literature (Sorensen 1986; Erikson and Goldthorpe 1992; Savage *et al.* 1992), and although I do not have the scope to enter fully into this debate here, it is useful to clarify some pertinent issues.

First, there is wide agreement that there is more diversity of work life mobility trajectories than might be assumed from the standard mobility tables which compare parent's class at one moment in time with offspring's class at another. The reason for this is not difficult to spot. Since intergenerational mobility is only based on a 'two point in time' comparison it is inherently less likely to register diversity than is the study of work life mobility observed on a 'many point in time' basis. It is possible to argue, therefore, that fluctuating mobility already revealed in 'standard mobility tables' would be considerably increased if work histories were focused on (Sorensen 1986), thus making claims about class stability even more difficult to establish. Goldthorpe's riposte to this point is that the diversity of work life mobility simply reflects different pathways to the same fixed position. However, if we take seriously the idea that class formation can involve regular and predictable trajectories we need not be wedded to the idea that high degrees of work life mobility need to be inimical to class formation.

Interest in work life mobility tends to have been confined to very specific topics. The most seriously researched area is the extent to which there is a division in the working class between an underclass and a broader working class (e.g. Marshall *et al.* 1997). Research indicates that in general there is considerable mobility between unemployment, casual employment and various kinds of proletarian jobs, and most sociologists doubt whether a distinctive underclass, separate from the working class, can be distinguished (Gallie 1988). An example comes from Gershuny's (1994) study of career histories of men and women aged between 40 and 60. He argues that there is a largely immobile working class, composed of various categories of manual workers. Although upward promotion is certainly possible from this group, nonetheless the overriding pattern is continued manual employment, punctuated possibly by periods of unemployment. Manual workers, both male and female, aged between 40 and 60 have spent on average over 90 per cent of their working lives in similar kinds of employment. Many of these individuals may move between different sorts of manual employment, and there is clear evidence of some movement between the ranks of skilled and unskilled manual work.[26] No distinct underclass, comprised of those only weakly attached to the labour market, was detected in Gershuny's analysis. Some sociologists disagree, and suggest that a small group of around 5 per cent of the population exhibit fundamentally different patterns of work life mobility from those in the working class (Buckingham 1999). However, Buckingham measures weak labour market attachment by the relatively generous criteria of having spent as little as 15 per cent of one's potential working life out of employment.

Gershuny's analysis supports the broad argument Goldthorpe develops about the demographic maturity of the working class. However, this aspect of his argument is problematic because it focuses on the earlier careers of those aged between 40 and 60. While it may be the case that most of those in this age group have indeed spent most of their earlier lives in manual employment, this has nothing to say about those workers in manual employment who leave such employment before the age of 40. Egerton and Savage (2000) show that since the 1970s manual employment has been increasingly defined as the activity of young men, many of whom subsequently move into other kinds of jobs (see also Chapter 6). Therefore it would be wrong to assume that most people at any one time in manual employment have necessarily had long periods of life in similar work. Many will be young people destined to work only for a relatively short time in manual work. Hence, there is no demographically coherent working class.

Gershuny also considers the structure of middle-class careers. He finds that there is a difference between those whose careers have mostly been in middle-class employment and those who move into middle-class employment after spending their younger years in manual or routine white-collar employment. The former tend to be professional workers, but also include technical workers and the 'semi-professions'. There are other members of the middle class, especially those in managerial jobs, who tend to be upwardly promoted after some years in the labour market. They occupy a 'liminal' class position between, and in uncertain relationship to, the other two 'core' classes which have much more regular patterns of job mobility or immobility.

The professional middle class appears to form the core of the middle class, in terms of the degree of its 'closure' from other social classes. Savage *et al.* (1992) argue that during the 1970s and 1980s there was a marked erosion of the 'organizational career'. Managers who had traditionally worked their way up the job ladder of a particular firm found themselves replaced by

managers recruited from outside, and as middle management itself was frequently undermined, so regularized promotion prospects deteriorated. Savage
et al. (1992) showed that growing numbers of managers had worked for more
than one firm. By contrast, however, they suggested that the professional
middle classes had been able to preserve their privileged position, much of it
based in the public sector. Economic trends were therefore working to accentuate the division between the core middle classes and the 'liminal' group.

Subsequent research suggests that there has been a significant increase
in mobility between professional and managerial ranks. Mills (1995) compared the 1949 Glass survey (Glass 1954) with the SCELI survey of 1986 (also
analysed by Gershuny). Mills found that in the earlier period well over half
of people moving into a professional job did so directly after leaving education. The majority of professionals were directly recruited into professional
careers, presumably after gaining the relevant qualifications. Managers, by
contrast, were much more likely to work their way up, being recruited after
having spent time in other jobs. Mills emphasizes that the situation had
changed considerably by the 1980s, and that only a few professionals were
now recruited directly from education. He also argues for growing convergence between professional and managerial work, with increasing numbers
of managers moving into professional employment and vice versa. Mills'
evidence is at odds with that of Gershuny because he suggests that the
boundaries between the core middle class and the 'liminal' middle classes are
becoming somewhat less distinct. The professionals now have more unpre-
dictable careers than previously, and there is considerable crossover into
management jobs.

This idea has been used by Goldthorpe (1982, 1995) to emphasize that
there is a more cohesive core 'service class' that is becoming increasingly closed
off from other social classes. However, questions can be raised about Mills'
and Goldthorpe's arguments. There continues to be a clear division between
those young people who move into professional and managerial jobs directly
after finishing their education, and those who work their way up the ladder.
This distinction can be less easily mapped onto the divide between professions and management than used to be the case, but this does not mean that
there are not two rather different kind of middle-class population. A distinction between core and liminal middle class is more accurate than that between professional and managerial, though there continues to be an overlap
between them, and it can be argued that the dominant cultural motif of the
core middle class continues to be defined in terms of professionalism.

In general there is considerable congruence with the evidence I reviewed in Chapter 3 on economic inequality. The one third of the population which I argued has become considerably more prosperous in the past
20 years tends to comprise the core professional middle class. On the other
hand, manual and routine white-collar workers, who have done less well in
economic terms, also have the poorest mobility prospects, at least in relative
terms. This having been said there is considerable movement, and a large
proportion of the population, designated here as the 'liminal middle class',
do experience upward social mobility, often by promotion into managerial,
lower professional, or technical employment.

Conclusions

In this chapter I have examined a further aspect of the impasse in class analysis: the gap between popular perceptions of mobility (which appear to endorse meritocratic values) and sociological analyses of the same (which appear to emphasize the role of class). I have suggested ways in which we can link these two more effectively, and in the process I have continued my arguments against the deductive approach to class analysis that I started in Chapter 1. It is in fact clear that there are many good reasons why people should think that the virtues of hard work, ambition and educational excellence should be so important in affecting their fates. It can safely be said that any individual endowed with any or all of these traits is likely to have better prospects than those who do not possess them. Thus, the lay perception of social mobility is largely correct, though the crucial rider should be added *that class is embedded in these virtues*. It is not that class is more important than individual abilities: it is rather that class processes work through the individual.

One way of registering the importance of class is to see the effect of class as everything else which is left over once the effect of education, age, ability etc. is taken into account. In this case, it has to be said, the effects of class on mobility are modest, as my discussion of Marshall *et al.* (1997) will have made clear. In fact, class does not stand like a puppet-master above the stage, pulling the strings of the dolls from on high: rather it works through the medium of individualized processes. I have shown that class affects both children's performance in ability tests, and their ability to secure high levels of educational attainment. There is no gainsaying the fact that one of the main factors affecting an individual's life chances is their level of educational attainment, not their social class. Indeed, it can be seen that the effect of educational attainment appears to be increasing somewhat. However, this point cannot just be taken at face value. Educational qualifications act as a kind of 'marker', a means of distinguishing, within any relevant sub-group of the population, who is to be successful and who unsuccessful. To be more specific, in a society where there is a demand for professional and managerial workers that cannot be supplied from the progeny of those already in such jobs, there is bound to be a need to recruit from below. In this recruitment process individual abilities, traits and capacities may be 'herding' devices which distinguish the sheep from the goats, the upwardly mobile from those confined to remain in their class of origin. But the use of individual traits does not operate in such a way as to challenge the balance of class privilege: rather, they strengthen it by providing superficial legitimacy for the system as a whole. A qualification does need to be added. There are downwardly mobile children from the middle class, with the implication that there are more upwardly mobile working-class children than are permitted simply due to expansion at the top of the occupational structure.

If we recognize the individualized role of class formation, and see class formation as related to the identification of trajectories rather than as an attachment to fixed positions, then a rather different perspective on class formation and social mobility is suggested than that which is evident in

Goldthorpe's work. Furthermore, if the influence of class works through grand social processes standing outside any one individual, then there is little that individuals can do to influence events, and no need to worry or reflect on its mechanisms. But it is precisely because class needs to be enacted through the actions of individual people that it is so important. Having now examined the impasse in class analysis I attempt, in Part 2, to take forward the points that I have developed in order to provide a more constructive account of the changing nature of class relations. I start, in Chapter 5, by reflecting further on the issue of individualization.

Notes

1 Useful surveys of British research include Pawson (1993) and Payne (1992). Savage (1996b) offers some general comments on the field of mobility studies, and Brieger (1990) offers a useful American overview of recent work. Heath (1981) is still the most useful introductory text, even though it is now somewhat dated.
2 Though it might be noted that the interview only asked respondents for largely individualized rather than structural factors.
3 It is difficult to compare directly since the questions were asked differently. In 1949 respondents were asked to list which factors were associated with social mobility, so encouraging them to pick only one or two, while in 1987 each factor was asked separately in turn, so encouraging respondents to pick as many as may be important.
4 '. . . we should also say that one matter which we do not pursue, or at least not in any direct way, is that of the explanation of mobility or of occupational attainment in terms of variation in individual attributes' (Goldthorpe *et al.* 1987: 30). Saunders' vituperative barb against Goldthorpe (and Marshall) that 'they *claim* to have demonstrated empirically that meritocratic principles cannot explain the distribution of individuals into classes, yet, like Glass, they never apparently considered it necessary to collect data on the differential "merits" . . . of the individuals they were researching' (Saunders 1995: 28, original emphasis) misses the target completely. Goldthorpe, at least in his reporting of the Nuffield mobility study, makes no claim to be testing meritocratic principles.
5 See Fischer *et al.* 1996 for an excellent critique of the use of IQ tests by Herrnstein and Murray (1993).
6 Saunders (1995) explains this in terms of the superior genetic make-up of middle-class households. However, this is not demonstrated empirically and could equally be explained in terms of socialization.
7 '. . . whereas our interest in mobility from the standpoint of openness will be repeatedly apparent in the course of the chapters that follow, *it is not in fact that which has been of greatest influence in determining the focus of our research.* Of prior importance has been an interest in mobility from the standpoint of its implications for class formation and class action' (Goldthorpe *et al.* 1987: 28, emphasis added).
8 I take up the question of gender later in this chapter.
9 This is not to say that it never occurs. Particularly in small, privately owned enterprises, it remains common for children to inherit their parents' business. In some economic sectors, notably farming, this tendency is especially marked as there also continues to be a strong ethos which emphasizes the need for a family farm to be kept in the family (see Massey and Catalano 1978). In modern Britain, however, only around 10 per cent of people work in their own businesses and are

thereby in a position to pass them on to their children. Furthermore, even among people in such situations only a minority of children do actually inherit a business from their parents. In England and Wales Erikson and Goldthorpe (1992: 219) show that only around 23 per cent of men from farming backgrounds are themselves farmers (and not all of these necessarily on their parents' farm) while around 21 per cent of sons from other small businesses are themselves small business owners. Even in the world of small business, therefore, direct inheritance is by no means the norm.

10 Saunders' work, based on the NCDS, only examines one cohort in one country and does not have to deal with this problem.

11 In this respect Saunders' (1997) arguments are not necessarily at odds with those of Goldthorpe. Using NCDS data, Saunders notes that 63 per cent of the children of professional and managerial parents were themselves in jobs of this kind when they were aged 33, compared to 28 per cent of the children of semi- and unskilled manual workers. Saunders (1995) contends that there are no necessary reasons to suppose that this difference alone testifies to the power of class. Rather, it may be that the children of the middle classes tend to be more able than those of the working class, with the result that sociobiological processes tend to lead to the reproduction of class differences.

12 The one main exception to this concerns mobility into the upper wealth élite, where there may be a considerable (though not absolute) degree of closure. This is not an issue which Goldthorpe examines since this class is not identified in his class schema.

13 In this respect my arguments differ fundamentally from those of Blackburn and Prandy (1997) who focus on the reproduction of inequality.

14 Linked to this criticism, it can also be noted that Goldthorpe's conceptualization of time, resting on a two-point comparison is rather limited. See Sorensen (1986), Savage *et al.* (1992), Abbott and Hrycak (1990), Stovel *et al.* (1996).

15 In a weaker sense the idea of class structure can be used as a kind of descriptive listing of different kinds of occupational class positions, as it appears to be within the registrar general's class schema, for instance.

16 For example, 'one could say that class analysis begins with a structure of positions, *associated with a specific historical form of the social division of labour'* (Goldthorpe 1983: 467, emphasis added). See also Goldthorpe *et al.* 1987: 61.

17 Goldthorpe's defence at this point might be that there may be gender (ethnic, etc.) divisions within the working class, but that these are gender and not class divisions. Even granting this point, it still seems that such divisions are likely to impact on the 'solidaristic' potential which Goldthorpe claims the demographically 'mature' working class possesses. Since Goldthorpe nowhere presents an analysis of the gender and ethnic divisions within the working class one can only assume that he does not feel that these considerations outweigh those of solidarism.

18 The development of Goldthorpe's thinking here can best be traced by considering his (1990) reflections on Johnson's (1990) discussion of his work. See especially Goldthorpe (1990: 419–20).

19 Goldthorpe is well aware of these issues (see especially 1998: 179).

20 And indeed Goldthorpe (1998: 179) notes, with respect to the problems of defining normatively-oriented rational action, that he chooses to 'hold on to the idea of rational action as being outcome oriented . . . in the sense that it derives from some kind of cost-benefit evaluation'.

21 The 'classic' rational choice problem is that of the prisoner's dilemma in which people seeking to maximize their individual chances thereby undermine their chances of maximizing their collective chances.

22 They are wrong to state that 'among individuals at the lowest level of educational attainment, those having service class origins are four times more likely to achieve service class employment than are their working class peers' (Marshall *et al.* 1997: 80). In fact they are only twice as likely to: Marshall *et al.* are referring to entry to the upper service class which is a minority destination for all the poorly educated, including the children of service-class fathers.

23 Contrary to normal reporting practice, Marshall *et al.* (1997) do not, in their Table 5.2, indicate the estimates for the main effects model and therefore do not allow the reader to evaluate the extent which the merit–selection model improves on it.

24 The G2 statistic is higher for the British case but this reflects the greater numbers of degrees of freedom in the British model compared to those of other countries. This makes the delta statistic a more useful measure for comparative analysis.

25 Fogelman (1983) show that class differences in the scores of children in ability tests increase between the ages of 7, 11 and 16, suggesting that these tests tap acquired ability.

26 More generally on the relatively weak division between the skilled and unskilled working class see also Evans and Mills (1998).

Part **II**

NEW DIRECTIONS *in* CLASS ANALYSIS

5 Individualization *and* cultural distinction
(*with Gaynor* Bagnall *and Brian* Longhurst)

In earlier chapters of this book I have argued that we should abandon an approach to class which roots it as a collective enterprise. In piecemeal fashion I have sketched out ways of thinking of class as an individualizing process, and in this chapter I develop this argument by considering the relationship between 'individualization' and class analysis. This issue is important because the leading exponents of individualization theory, Anthony Giddens and Ulrich Beck, have both situated their accounts as partial critiques of class analysis. In pointing to the way in which individuals reflexively construct their biographies and identities, they develop challenging arguments about the erosion of class identities in 'late modernity'. They see class not as a modern identity – as Marx and Weber did – but as a traditional, ascriptive one, which has no place in a dynamic, reflexive and globalized world.

Although, as my discussion in Chapter 2 will have made clear, I have considerable sympathies with their emphasis on the weakness of collective class awareness, I nonetheless argue in this chapter that Giddens and Beck radically misconceive the relationship between individual and class identities. While old models of collective class cultures are indeed dead and buried, we should not leap to the other extreme of positing thoroughly individualized beings who fly completely free of class identities. Analytical oppositions between traditional class cultures and new individualized ones, which themselves draw on many other well-rehearsed oppositions (between modernity and post-modernity, organized and disorganized capitalism, and so on) fail to capture the complex interweaving of class and individual identity.

The first section of this chapter examines the arguments of Beck and Giddens in order to show that the underpinnings for their ideas are in many ways deeply conventional and rather 'dated'. In the second section I turn, by way of contrast, to consider the contrary arguments of Pierre Bourdieu concerning the interrelation between individual identities and social class. I am in general sympathetic to Bourdieu's arguments. His emphasis on class as a 'relational' process, in which social groups differentiate themselves from others in various 'fields', allows us to recognize how class cultures can be usefully viewed as modes of differentiation, rather than as types of collectivity.

I am nonetheless critical of certain aspects of Bourdieu's analysis, especially his difficulties in theoretically registering the positive resources that attach to some aspects of working-class culture and the cultural power of populist motifs. At least in the British case, it is essential to recognize the positive cultural valuations that have historically been attached to certain aspects of working-class culture. These generate a certain cultural counterweight to the strategies of cultural exclusion that can be associated with claims to cultural capital, in all its diverse forms, and help to validate populist claims of 'ordinariness' as a central motif in cultural life. This leads me on, in the third section, to expand on and illustrate these theoretical arguments by drawing upon in-depth interview research examining popular narratives and rhetorics of class. I show how we can usefully see individualized identities as class identities. Although the way that explicit class identities map onto awareness of difference is in some respects arbitrary, it is still possible to show that individual identities and relational identities are more closely interrelated than theorists of individualization suppose. The final section of the chapter explores some of the broader issues concerning the changing nature of class identities and examines how we might think about the meshing of individualistic and class identities.

Class and individualization

No writer exemplifies the 'break' from class analysis in British sociology more than Anthony Giddens. His earlier work was preoccupied with social class. His theoretical reworking of Marx and Weber (Giddens 1971), his empirical interest in élites (Giddens and Stanworth 1974), and his synthetic ideas about the 'class structure of the advanced societies' (Giddens 1973), all testified to his concern with class analysis. It can be claimed, indeed, that Giddens' most influential idea – that of 'structuration' (developed most clearly in Giddens 1984) – was derived from his reflections on class analysis (Giddens 1973).[1] However, by the mid-1980s, Giddens' interest in class had waned. Although, as a card-carrying sociologist, Giddens continued to refer to the relevance of class,[2] it no longer played an important role in his thinking.

Indicative of this shift is Giddens' work is *The Consequences of Modernity* (1990). Here, Giddens sees a shift in the political agenda from one where 'emancipatory politics' held centre stage to one where 'life politics' jostles with it and possibly shifts it from its central position. For Giddens 'life politics' indicates a new role for the individual in politics: 'while emancipatory politics is a politics of life chances, life politics is a politics of lifestyle. Life politics . . . is a politics of self-actualisation in a reflexively ordered environment, where that reflexivity links self and body to systems of global scope' (Giddens 1991: 214). Class politics held sway when people mobilized to improve their life chances. In an era when the terrain of politics has become more reflexive, where politics is not oriented so much to the brute realities of the conditions of life, but reflects on the limits of old forms of political intervention, and devises new strategies, class has less purchase.

Admittedly, even in his recent work, Giddens continues to acknowledge the continuation of old-style 'emancipatory' concerns (e.g. Giddens 1994). It is clear from his brief statements that he has no ready theoretical handle on their relationship to life politics, and hence seems to see them simply as a 'throwback' to times past.[3]

Giddens is not alone in this intellectual drift. Ulrich Beck, perhaps the most prominent contemporary German sociologist, was more explicit than Giddens in settling his accounts with class as a means of articulating his distinct views about the nature of 'reflexive modernity'. Beck, like Giddens, insists that contemporary individualized cultures break from the ascribed culture of class. This is a major theme of Beck's book on *The Risk Society*: 'it is no longer social classes that take the place of status groups, or the family as a stable frame of reference that takes the place of social class commitments. *The individual himself or herself becomes the reproduction unit for the social in the lifeworld*' (Beck 1992: 130, emphasis added). And, '*class loses its sub-cultural basis and is no longer experienced*' (1992: 98).

Beck and Giddens are aware that their arguments pose difficulties in reflecting on theorizing 'individualization' in a sociologically convincing way. The 'individual' and 'society' is one of the classic, much discussed tensions in social theory and both Beck and Giddens are keen to search for a way to avoid positing a dualistic relationship between these two terms (for instance, by claiming that individual freedom entails breaking from social forces).[4] The way they do this is to argue that a culture of 'individualization' does not entail 'weakening' the power of social structural forces, but is premised on the way that large scale contemporary social change forces individuals to be reflexive.

In fact, this approach does not stop either of them from adopting, from time to time, conventional Enlightenment humanist ideas implying that individualization depends on 'freeing' people from social constraint.[5] Thus Beck happily makes reference to 'Enlightenment' notions of individualism whereby people free themselves from social ties, and at times sees late modernity as simply a democratization and extension of this long-term development (e.g. Beck and Beck-Gersheim 1996: 34, 38). Giddens also incautiously refers to lifestyle in terms of 'forms of self-actualisation and empowerment' (e.g. Giddens 1991: 6). However, in general both authors are clear in their intent to distance themselves from this 'humanistic' reading of individualization. 'Individualization' Beck argues, is a triple process involving 'disembedding, *removal* from historically prescribed social forms and commitments . . . the *loss of traditional security* with respect to practical knowledge, faith and guiding norms . . . and . . . re-embedding, a *new type of social commitment*' (Beck 1992: 128, emphasis added).

The first two points seem to draw on the classic sociological dualism in which individuals are freed from social constraints, and from social norms and values. However, Beck's final point insists that individuals are re-embedded, finally, back into society, albeit reflexively. Beck draws on Habermas and Luhmann to argue that individualization is not to be understood as a process which allows the 'free individual' to emerge, but rather, 'how one lives becomes the *biographical solution of systemic contradictions*' (Beck 1992: 137, emphasis added). What Beck appears to mean is that individuals are able to reflect on the implications of various structural processes that surround them, and can thereby choose how to act with respect of them. Individuals cannot escape structural forces in general, but they can decide which ones to act on, which to ignore, which to oppose and so on. Reflexive modernization does not create the 'free' individual. Rather, it creates individuals who live out, biographically, the complexity and diversity of the social relations which surround them.

Beck's arguments about individualization therefore attempt to avoid the excesses of methodological individualism and try to see the individual as embedded in social relations, albeit of a highly complex and global character. Here his arguments are linked to his claims about the 'universalization of risk'. In contemporary societies he claims that risks cannot be attributed or apportioned to specific social groups, but are universalized, so that anyone can, potentially, be affected by any risk. Since risks are not the attribute of social groups, so they cannot be shrugged off by individuals (in the way that individuals who thought that a danger was integrally related to membership of a specific social group could shrug off their own responsibility for dealing with that danger onto that group – even if he or she was a member of the group in danger). Thus Beck seeks to evade the classic sociological dualism: individualization depends on a particular configuration of social relations, not the collapse or erosion of society in general.

The idea of 'universalization of risk' is a controversial one. Beck himself is somewhat equivocal as to how this is played out with respect to class. At times, especially when talking about ecological risks, he appears to believe that risks have indeed become more shared between social classes – for instance, talking about the 'boomerang effect' whereby the risks bounce back and affect the privileged social groups who produce them (see Beck 1992: 37ff.). At other times, he seems to think that the reflexively educated middle classes, which have the intellectual skills to reflect on the problems around them, are actually more affected by risks.[6]

However, Beck's general line of argument, which surfaces especially when he talks about social and economic risks, is that individualization is compatible with continued inequality in life chances and therefore the risk society is both individualized *and* class divided. Beck does not demur that, for instance, middle-class professionals have fewer chances of losing their jobs than manual workers: the important point, for him, is that they nonetheless face that possibility, and therefore cannot rule out that possibility from their reflections. Indeed, by reflecting on these concerns and developing strategies to allay their fears, they may actually help to accentuate the kinds of inequalities I have explored above, so that individualization and social inequality can be mutually constitutive.[7] Despite its different theoretical lineage, this approach has rather similar substantive implications to that developed by Goldthorpe in his advocacy of RAT, which I discussed in Chapter 4, and it is open to the same objection. Individuals still need to situate themselves socially in order for them to assess what kind of 'risk category' they fall into. They cannot but involve themselves in a process of cultural differentiation that by necessity involves the making of social distinction. Individualization cannot but be a cultural process involving differentiation from others.

Giddens develops related, though subtly different, arguments. He links individualism to the growing problems in sustaining ontological security in a globalized world. Giddens is less cautious than Beck in avoiding teleological language to describe individualization and implies certain inherent self-developing processes to individuals which will be realized once the individual is freed from societal 'checks': the more tradition loses its hold . . . the more individuals are forced to negotiate lifestyle choices among a diversity of options' (Giddens 1991: 5). Nonetheless, Giddens is also keen to locate the contemporary 'dynamism of modernity' systemically, in terms of the separation of time and space and the disembedding of social life from face-to-face contact. He sees institutional reflexivity (and hence the decline of tradition) as fundamental to the development of a 'life politics' where we search to create a coherent biography in a fractured world. Once again we see the 'externalization' of the self from social relations so that the former can reflect, and plan its future actions, and then reinsert itself back into society.

The individuals of Beck and Giddens' social theories are lonely. They see the reflexive individual as the product of global and system-wide social conditions, rather than linked to more proximate social relations around the firm, family, neighbourhood, social network and social class. People's sense of individuality is constructed not with respect to other people or social groups, but as a reaction to the loss of security inherent in a de-traditionalized, globalized world system. To be sure, these people search out others, for instance as they seek the kinds of 'pure relationships' that Giddens (1991) emphasizes as a key feature of late modern identity, but such relationships remain contingent (see further Beck and Beck-Gersheim 1996). Giddens also suggests that people's need to strip away the kinds of social obligations and ties characteristic of traditional relationships means that pure relationships involve sharing[8] and hence equality between partners.

Giddens and Beck do not seek empirical support for their arguments. Indeed, it has been argued that their ideas are not of the type which seeks empirical adjudication (see Gregson 1991). Their arguments are, rather, designed to convince rhetorically, by setting themselves up as more plausible and 'commonsense' than other, discredited, accounts. These other accounts, I surmise, are not infrequently the kinds of 'collective class cultures' which I examined in Chapter 2. By setting up the idea of individualization against the 'Aunt Sally' of the traditional, collective class culture, some kind of plausibility for their own account can be mustered. Because we do not seem to live in a society with strong collective class solidarities, it may appear to follow that we are individualized. However, if we refuse the proffered starting point – i.e. the assumption that collective class cultures have ever been important – then individualization needs to be seen in a very different light (see Savage 2000). I will now spell out what an alternative approach might entail.

Individualization and social distinction

There are numerous sources for the idea that individualization involves making claims to social distinction through processes of defining oneself in relation to the other. Historically, the elaboration of ideas of individual freedom has involved invoking 'others' whose lack of individuality throws into contrast the meaning of individuality. Slaves, women, children, Jews (and other ethnic minority groups), those from the 'Orient' and so on have all served this purpose at various times, as have members of 'other' social classes (see e.g. Pateman 1988 for the case of the 'sexual contract'). Honneth (1994), for instance, traces one way of grounding this approach in his reworking of Hegel's idea of the master–slave dialectic (in which the slave comes to recognize himself by reference to his master). Here, I want to focus on the arguments of Pierre Bourdieu because of their centrality to recent debates about class and culture, and in order to show how Bourdieu offers a different vantage point for reflecting on similar issues to those raised by Beck and Giddens.

Bourdieu's best known claim is for the role of cultural capital as a different axis for class formation compared to economic capital (Bourdieu 1984). He recognizes the power of property as a central source of social inequality, but also emphasizes that culture is a separate axis on which class formation occurs. Cultural élites sustain their claims to distinction by either directly or indirectly denigrating other modes of cultural appreciation, thus committing practices of symbolic violence against them. Those with economic resources do not necessarily have access to cultural capital, and hence there are tensions between these two sources of social power. It is possible to convert one mode of capital into the other. Cultural capital can be converted into economic capital by socializing children into performing well in the educational system, thereby allowing them to acquire good qualifications and move into well-paid jobs. Those with economic capital can also attempt to acquire cultural capital, for instance by paying for the schooling of themselves or others. However, because the exercise of cultural capital is not simply a matter of intellectual taste but is inscribed in the way people act and deport themselves, it is not easy to move between the *habitus* which marks out a specific kind of capital.

Bourdieu has not infrequently been regarded as a cultural reductionist, since he sees cultural life as intrinsically related to processes of social conflict (Jenkins 1991; Alexander 1994; Chaney 1997). This charge is unfair. Indeed, Bourdieu's analysis of culture offers a way out of the impasse experienced in the British tradition that I discussed in Chapter 2. He neither sees culture as a set of widely accepted norms or values, in the manner of the structuralist functionalists, nor as arising out of social positions, in the way that Marxists conceived it in the base–superstructure relationship and Lockwood discussed as part of the S–C–A model. Culture is not a product of class relations but is itself a field in which class relations operate. Cultural battles are therefore recursively involved in class formation. This allows Bourdieu to operate with a considerably more fluid notion of culture than was present within the British tradition.

Bourdieu does not specifically address the question of individualization, but it is indirectly present in most of his work. Bourdieu's methodology emphasizes the need to examine the relationally defined character of processes in diverse social fields and he therefore sees claims to individuality as resting on social cultural and political struggles which permit some to claim the right to full individuality at the expense of others. In place of the humanist traces which remain in Beck and Giddens' work, Bourdieu insists on the thoroughly social character of individualization and the ways in which individuals are socially constructed by distinguishing themselves from the 'non-individual'. Much of Bourdieu's work, and especially his book *Distinction* (1984), examines the way in which intellectual middle-class culture is defined in relation to popular culture, and considers how it has articulated an aesthetic of distance and abstraction as a means of distinguishing itself from the sensuous, the immediate and the popular. Bourdieu discusses this with reference to the creation of 'high culture' and legitimate modes of art, and in particular their consecration within educational systems. Within this broad perspective, individuality – defined as self-control, autonomy and the ability to judge and hence be an agent – has emerged in association with the Kantian aesthetic (see generally Fowler 1996). The concern to distance oneself from the sensuous and everyday is a strategy which forms part of the move towards distinction, and as Bauman (1989, 1993), following Levinas, points out, this distancing is tied into a moral removal from the concerns of others. This suggests that the kinds of globalizing forces which Giddens see as a systemic, background feature of late modernity might be better seen as exemplifying the *habitus* of particular types of socially located individuals as they go about their daily projects. Rather than globalization being a 'brute fact' facing individuals, some culturally privileged individuals construct a globalized world to allow them to shrug off responsibility for their local, social activities (see further Bourdieu and Wacquant 1999).

Bourdieu's approach allows us to see class relationships as fundamental to claims to legitimacy and entitlement. However, his arguments lead not to an emphasis on class as heroic collective agency, but towards class as implicit, as encoded in people's sense of self-worth and in their attitudes to and awareness of others – in how they carry themselves as individuals. Social distinctions that Bourdieu sees as lying at the heart of class processes might not always be apparent to people themselves, since if the culturally advantaged recognized their taste explicitly as that of a privileged class, this would devalue it, by contaminating it with a pragmatic and instrumental meaning utterly at odds with its claims to be universal, which lie at the heart of the entire Kantian aesthetic. It is hence the very salience of class struggles over distinction which explains why it is so difficult for them to be explicitly named and identified by their protagonists, and to be tied down into a neat model specifying the relationship between social location and culture.

Recent research has illuminatingly used Bourdieu's arguments to consider features of contemporary class cultures. Skeggs' (1997) interviews with young women from working-class backgrounds in the North-West of England showed that they were generally unwilling to talk openly about class precisely because its scars and impact are so deep, and also so personal. Skeggs argued that it was the deep and pervasive effect of class which explained the very difficulty of naming it explicitly. This research has clear affinities with the American research reported some years ago by Sennett and Cobb (1971,

1993), in which the power of class was registered individually, in terms of the sense of failure it instilled in working-class people:

> This fear of being summoned before some hidden bar of judgement and being found inadequate infects the lives of people who are coping perfectly well from day to day: it is a matter of hidden weight, a hidden anxiety, in the *quality* of experience, a matter of feeling inadequately in control where an observer making calculations would conclude the workingman had adequate control.
>
> (Sennett and Cobb 1993: 33–4)

These studies suggest, in line with Bourdieu's thinking, that the absence of direct class awareness that I noted in Chapter 2 might actually demonstrate the hegemonic power of the dominant classes to stigmatize, and thereby undermine, working-class identities (Skeggs 1997; Reay 1998). Class cultures do not 'unite' people into a proud collectivity, but because of their power to mark individuals as lacking in appropriate tastes and demeanour, they raise fraught recognition of the extent to which promises of equality are not kept.

What Bourdieu's arguments point towards is the need to consider the nature of contemporary identities in ways which are not premised on simplistic contrasts between either class collectivism on the one hand, or individualized identities on the other, but which are attentive to their intermeshing. They expose Beck's and Giddens' arguments as a particular kind of intellectual manouvring, a kind of celebration of a cosmopolitan intellectual ethic that can only be realized by a small minority of people.

However, Bourdieu's arguments can be disputed in a number of ways (see also Longhurst and Savage 1996). First, Bourdieu's concept of cultural capital invokes the existence of a cultural hierarchy which clearly distinguishes 'high' culture from 'low' or 'popular' culture. Although Bourdieu is aware of the contested nature of this distinction, and has illuminatingly examined the emergence of new kinds of consumer cultures as linked to the aspirations of the upwardly mobile (see Featherstone 1988), it can still be suggested that his approach is reductive (see Lury 1995; Chaney 1997). To some extent, Bourdieu's work is marked by its formulation in a specifically French context. This may reflect French culture but has less application in other countries such as the USA (Lamont 1992; Halle 1993), or Britain (Savage *et al.* 1992). Lamont emphasizes that moral, cultural, and socioeconomic boundaries are defined in different ways, and cannot be conflated. It can further be argued that many people move between cultural practices with greater ease than Bourdieu's arguments about cultural capital imply. Petersen and Kern (1996) refer to the emergence of the cultural omnivore whose taste crosses cultural divides, so that some people may appreciate opera as well as country and western music, for instance (see also Bryson 1996; Erickson 1996).[9] Harking back to some of the themes raised by Beck and Giddens, it can be suggested that ideas of individuality can be more fluid and self-referential than is implied by seeing them simply as defined with respect to others. Bauman, for instance, draws attention to the fleeting nature of contemporary, contingent, identities and associates these with the emergence of consumer culture (Bauman 1988; 1998): 'The individual's drive to self assertion has been squeezed out from the area of material production. Instead a new wider than ever space has been opened for it at the new "pioneer frontier", the rapidly expanding, seemingly limitless world of consumption' (Bauman 1988: 57). Similar points about the fluid nature of consumer-oriented identities have been made by Munro (1996), though empirical research on consumer cultures does not support any strong claims about the potential of consumerism to sustain such new cultures (Warde 1994, 1997).

These points all direct us to be aware of the fluidity and complexity of processes defining cultural distinction. One important move to make here, in keeping with the arguments of this book, is to recognize the positive resources that inhere in working-class and popular cultures (see Jenkins 1991). While Bourdieu criticizes those struggles for distinction which lie at the heart of diverse modes of middle-class and élite culture, it can be argued that he nonetheless remains within their high cultural assumptions. His view of popular, working-class culture tends to be from within the Kantian aesthetic: he defines it as immediate and sensuous, rather than as sophisticated, moral, etc. Numerous critics have argued for the need to recognize a kind of popular cultural capital (e.g. Fiske 1987), or sub-cultural capital (Thornton 1995) which in a sense democratizes Bourdieu's notion and recognizes the extent to which popular culture contains cultural resources of its own. Bourdieu has in his more recent work shown a greater interest in examining popular culture (e.g. Bourdieu *et al.* 1999)[10], and he has a powerful defence of his general approach, which is that since the intellectual middle classes have always sought to define popular and working-class culture from outside, in the process helping define their own cultural identity, it is actually far more challenging to criticize middle-class culture from the inside.

One of the central arguments of this book, which will be further developed as this chapter progresses and in Chapter 6, concerns the central reference point of versions of 'working classness' in British culture, a feature associated further with modes of masculinity. It is striking that Skeggs (1997) and Reay (1998) who draw on Bourdieu's arguments concerning the stigmatization of working-class culture, examine the position of working-class women, who – as they fully recognize – are doubly disadvantaged by gender *and* class. The tricky theoretical issue is to find a way of recognizing both the stigmatization of working-class culture as well as its elevation to a significant place in British culture. One possible way of handling this tension is Fox's account of the internal dynamics of working-class culture in her (1994) account of the politics of twentieth-century British working-class novels. She argues that working-class writers have a 'double take' on dominant cultural forms. On the one hand they reject the assumptions of bourgeois culture, and provide some kind of political critique of class relations, sometimes using distinctive stylistic modes to make this point (for instance, the advocacy of 'realism'). On the other hand, however, they also distance themselves from working-class culture itself in order to provide a critique of it. Rhetorically, they need to point to the extent to which working-class culture is indeed degraded and impoverished, in order to explain why it needs to be changed. These writers therefore distance themselves *both* from the dominant culture *and* from their construction of working-class culture, and in the process they reinforce the dominant culture in stigmatizing working-class culture. What Fox points to is the tendency for dominated cultures to be fissured by the effects of the dominant culture, whereby efforts to culturally challenge those within the dominant culture constantly tend to divide the popular classes themselves. This has the paradoxical effect of undermining any latent class solidarity which might exist.

This line of argument provides a theoretical riposte to those (such as Halsey *et al.* 1980; Goldthorpe 1996) who claim that theories of cultural capital do not provide an explanation of why working-class groups value education. Within the parameters of Fox's argument this can readily be understood as testimony to the double-sided response of the disadvantaged classes themselves – to reject their own class cultures as well as those of the dominant classes.[11] Class identification is therefore complex and is not likely to lead to straightforward accounts in people's minds. Skeggs (1997) shows how one of the prime concerns of her sample of young working-class women was to establish their 'respectability', to distance themselves from those stigmatized by the dominant culture. She also points, therefore, to the importance of popular struggles which do not copy or imitate the middle class (possibly in bowdlerized form),[12] nor openly reject or flout it (as for instance discussed in Willis' 1975 account of young working-class boys' rejection of school culture). Rather, popular cultural struggles seek to situate individuals as both different from those stigmatized groups 'below' them, as well as those 'above' them.

These observations suggest that while Bourdieu's work gives us major insights into the kinds of processes which translate cultural hierarchies into social divisions, there are problems if his work is applied mechanically. Bourdieu's work cannot be taken as a warrant for saying that particular kinds of individuality, associated with specific kinds of class *habitus*, are the properties of specific occupational classes. Bourdieu underestimates the resources available to those from lower social classes in developing their claims to distinction. There is movement between cultural practices, with the result that social and cultural boundaries are porous. However, this does not detract from Bourdieu's main point concerning the power of social classification, as I now seek to show.

Individualization and class identities

In Chapter 2 I showed the fragility of class consciousness. I now want to turn to consider this issue again in a more positive light to reflect on how Bourdieu's general approach can help us identify certain repertoires of class talk. I draw on provisional findings from a research project I have been conducting with Brian Longhurst and Gaynor Bagnall.[13] This research project is primarily concerned with studying the social networks and leisure interests of different types of middle-class individual, and has carried out 200 in-depth, qualitative interviews with men and women living in or around the Manchester area to explore these themes.[14] Towards the end of the interviews respondents were asked first whether Britain was becoming a classless society, and second whether they saw themselves as members of a social class. A full analysis of class identities is provided elsewhere (Savage *et al.* forthcoming) and here I only illustrate how responses bear on the themes discussed in this chapter.

It is striking that, despite the relatively large sample size used in our research, as well as the fairly wide social range of people that we interviewed, there is remarkable consistency in people's articulation of class. Although there were important nuances which are reported where relevant below, a number of common features stand out. The first clear point is that most people are ambiguous about their class identity. Slightly under two thirds of our interviewees did not give an unequivocal response to the question asking them which class they belonged to. This ambiguity varies enormously. Minimally, it may involve a qualifying statement such as 'I'm middle class, I suppose'. It could also extend to a much greater degree of uncertainty.

D'you think of yourself as belonging to any particular class?

Well it's not the upper class, I'll tell you that. I, well I don't know whether you'd put us working class really or I should imagine, I don't think we're middle class but we, I don't know, I don't know where we come in that really.

No. D'you, would you think of yourself in those terms, you know, terms of class? You know, when you're describing yourself?

No I don't think I would really but, er, you know. No.

No. What ways would you describe yourself, you know, if you were thinking of . . .

I'd just say ordinary.

Yeah yeah yeah. There's no other, there's nothing you'd use to describe yourself?

No, not really.

This quote comes from a respondent who was much more hesitant than most, but it can also be taken as evidence of a second general point. Even though people tend to be ambiguous about which class they belong to, they have some knowledge of what the term 'class' means – of the idea that there is a working class, a middle class and an upper class. Very few respondents had no understanding of class terminology. In this respect the idea of class as a kind of set of benchmarks used to evaluate and 'place' people is well understood. People also tended to be well aware of the implicit politics of the kind of social evaluations which go alongside the class terminology. The responses of a 38-year-old male computer programmer indicate this point particularly clearly:

Do you think Britain's becoming a classless society?

That's a tough one. In many ways yes. In the sense that I think many of the old boundaries of class, the old distinctions and mechanisms that held the class system in place are being eroded by education, by change in the way we live, by other factors, but I think these things change very slowly. I think a lot of change might be superficial, and people might . . . my perception is that people who are middle class or above would seem to like to hold onto something . . . in conversation when you scratch beneath the surface sometimes you pick out people wanting to have this sense of 'Well, we've moved on', or 'We're not like that . . .', you know, and I like to pursue that often in conversation just to see what people mean.

How do they react when you pursue it?

Sometimes by . . . when they realize that you're on the hunt for something, by denial – 'Oh no, that's not what I meant' kind of thing and sometimes by being quite . . . by being defensive about it.

Do you think of yourself as belonging to any particular social class?

No. I was going to say . . . I didn't . . . I wouldn't put myself as . . . I'm working class . . . by background and upbringing and I'm still working so in that sense I'm working class. I find it a difficult area to make distinctions in. Again, it's a scale or criteria that I prefer not to use so I don't find it helpful or meaningful.

This man begins by providing an articulate account of issues around 'class-lessness' and of the nuances of class as a general cultural issue, along with the kinds of denials which are linked to claims about class. In his early statements he shows he has thought about class, indeed that he is interested in pursuing the issue in conversing with others. In the later parts of the extract, however, he exhibits the same defensiveness about class that he claims to find in others. He finds it easier to talk about class as a general social process than as an individually relevant one. However, this can be taken as evidence, in Bourdieu's terms, of the importance of class, rather than its reverse. Seeing class in general social terms, rather than as part of one's own identity, is less threatening. Here we see how a striking bifurcation between awareness of class as a social and political issue and class as relating to one's own individual identity might be explicable. What we see here is how individuals seek to evade placing themselves in terms of class, preferring to see it as a something outside them.

I've no experience of the class business, I couldn't comment on it.

Do you see yourself as belonging to any social class?

No, I'm fortunate, I'm not a man that worships money, I have enough money to keep myself comfortable but I don't wish for any more.

Fortunate indeed! And yet, in order to make sense of their own life stories, to ascertain which thresholds have been passed, the idea of class which at one level is denied, also needs to be invoked. This is the third point which I wish to emphasize. In around one third of interviews, respondents chose to talk about their class membership in terms of a life narrative. Here are two examples.

Which class do you belong to?

I knew this would come up. A jumped-up working class who has now entered the middle class. I hate to say it, I can't escape it, but I think we have become more middle class from humble origins. We're the working class that grew up with working-class parents keen on education who pushed us and we all went to grammar school and college and university and came out and suddenly found that we didn't belong where we came from.

So you wouldn't see yourself in any particular social class?

No, I'm a post-master's granddaughter, a railwayman's daughter. I've got no money.

But you wouldn't see yourself in any class?

My grandfather used to reckon he was middle class and my father was obviously working class.

I suppose I come from an upper middle-class family and in terms of the class I've probably slipped down. I always think it is quite funny with my family . . . I had access to people, landed gentry if you like, but I decided that I didn't feel comfortable with that and my parents would never have encouraged me further.

Here we see the individualization of class identity. The idea of class allows respondents to distance themselves from any strong claim to class membership. Instead, class operates as a benchmark by which people can measure their own life histories. We can also see how class is salient in terms of constructing an idea of difference, not in terms of defining a class which one belongs to. Very few people indicated that they had a sense of belonging to a class with a strong collective identity.[15] Those with ambiguous class identities defined their class in terms of who they were not. Even those respondents who had a strong sense of class identity defined their class membership in largely individualized terms, as a personal statement of who they were:

I'm working class. No airs and graces. If you're working class, you're working class.

Oh yeah, [I'm] working class. Yeah, yeah, I've got no pretensions to anything other.

Class identities invite people to situate themselves socially. This is a fraught process for many people who see it, rightly, as one which may undermine their claims to be seen as 'proper' people. As people make sense of their own lives they need benchmarks to do so, and class is a benchmark which people are usually aware of. But their use of these labels tends to be hesitant because taking the label too seriously would undermine their main aspiration to be an individual agent, not programmed to act in any particular way. Class is therefore both denied and invoked.

There is one important difference in the way people handle the idea of class. Some respondents felt confident in handling class labels and measuring themselves reflexively in terms of them, while others did not.

Which class would you say you belong to?

On the old ABC thing? I think I come from a C sort of working class, self-employed background, struggling to get the income and social life of a B, a profession, but if you look, like at the professions like teachers, when I was growing up, firemen and policemen and so on, they were all professionals.

This respondent is aware of market research class categories, and is confident enough to be able to reflect on how he might fit in in terms of them. Here is another example:

Middle class yuppie! Middle class, I suppose.

Do you think of yourself in these terms?

I like to think of myself as reasonably eclectic. I mean, I like pick and choose, you know.

Here the respondent playfully seizes on one of the most disreputable images of the 1980s before invoking a more ambiguous response and then emphasizing the diversity of his interests. Other respondents, however, were somewhat more hesitant in defining themselves in these terms.

If you had to describe yourself as belonging to any particular social class, what would you describe yourself as?

I wouldn't really . . . just for the reason again, with what I was saying . . . I generally know a lot of people from different walks of life and with different . . . I suppose some people would class some of these as very privileged and some less privileged. To me it doesn't really mean anything. I don't know where I would sit myself, probably working class.

But it's not a label you would pin on yourself?

Well, I don't put any label on myself really. I think labels are pinned on yourself by other people.

Whereas some people felt more confident at playing with class labels, trying them on and taking them off, this respondent betrays much more hesitancy. The class label is one which is pinned on and which is threatening, rather than an identity that can be used more positively. In general, those with a university education were more confident in reflecting on the use of class labels.[16] This is not to say that they were less ambiguous in placing themselves in terms of class. In general they tended to deny any clear class membership. Nonetheless, they were much more comfortable in reflecting on class than were those without cultural capital. Here is a 43-year-old cleaner:

There is some discussion going on about whether Britain is becoming a classless society, what do you think of that?

No.

And why do you think that?

I don't know really, I don't think it will ever be classless, I think there will always be filthy rich Conservatives.

And do you think of yourselves as belonging to any particular social class?

No, not really.

You don't think in those sort of terms? How would you describe yourself?

I would describe myself as a very normal lower middle-class person. [daughter interjects: 'I would say upper lower class, no working class, upper working class'].[17] I get on with most people – I have friends that I mean are very nice people but obviously have come from nice backgrounds, and I know people that are in the poverty trap, but I would not say that I treat them any differently.

Here the response to the question concerning class does not evoke an articulate response, but nonetheless does appear to tap felt beliefs about class inequality ('there will always be filthy rich Conservatives'). In her later responses to questions about self-identity it is clear that although she can give a class label to herself – in this case lower middle class – it is one which is relatively arbitrary and does not seem to be deeply felt. What was said with more feeling was the last sentence, where she says that she can 'get on with most people'. Here we see a concern not to use class as a basis for personal taste, with the subsequent concern to be 'outside class'. Class is something which this woman strives to leave behind. The final part of this quote indicates a determination to proclaim normality and to emphasize the arbitrariness of class to her own situation.

We can see a particular style of talking about class. The idea of class means something to people, even where the replies are hesitant. Crucially, rather than evoking a sense of *belonging* to a collective group, it invokes a sense of *differentiation* from others. In most cases it means they are not one of the privileged who have it easy, nor are they one of those at the bottom who are morally suspect. People's sense of self-identity is linked to a claim of 'ordinariness' or 'normality' which operates as a double reaction against both above and below. We see here the desire for claims to 'naturalism' which Strathern (1991) sees as lying at the heart of modern western identities (see also Anthias 1998). In some respects, this profoundly undermines the salience of class. However, in a complex double movement it also invokes class, since ordinariness only means something if contrasted with the non-ordinary – the snobs for instance.

This leads on to an important point about the lack of clear difference between middle-class and working-class self-identities. Of those who chose a class identity, around 60 per cent chose a middle-class self-definition and around 40 per cent a working-class self-definition.[18] However, it was clear in many cases that these two terms were not always seen as being in opposition. It is possible to use both terms as a means of trying to establish 'normality' between two extremes:

I suppose I'm middle, middle of the road really. I'm not a snob if that's what you mean.

> I don't give it a lot of thought really, but I suppose I am really just middle of the road.

'Middle class' here means you are average, normal, in the middle.[19] It means you are neither exclusive on the one hand, or part of the working class on the other. However, many of those invoking a working-class identity also claimed to be ordinary, which they did by claiming that the fact that they worked meant they were ordinary people, neither part of the work-shy at the bottom or the idle rich at the top:

> Well I vote labour so I must be working class. Like anybody who earns a hundred thousand or so, so long as they do a job they've got to be working class.

> I would say that I'm working class, I am working class, I sell my labour . . . it just happens that I get paid quite a nice salary, not as much as some but I am OK, and I don't worry about paying the bills, but I am working class.

> I'd say working class. What we've had, we've had to work for, everything. We've had to work and save up for it, we've had nothing given to us.

> *Do you think in these terms?*

> No, pretty average person, that does what everybody else does round here and copes.

People want to belong to a group of ordinary, average types, differentiated from a group above them and below them. The precise class label for this is relatively arbitrary. Some people see a working-class self-definition as compatible with this, since this is regarded as the least 'snobbish' case, but for others, middle-class self-definitions are preferred. Still others draw upon both resources at different points. This all suggests that Reay's (1998) and Skeggs' (1997) emphasis that 'working classness' is a stigmatized identity may overstate the case. Rather, these limited cases chime in rather better with Devine's (1992a, 1992b) study which shows that even among manual car workers the most common identity was that of the 'ordinary working people', which continues to offer some positive evaluations of working-class identification. Certainly in comparative perspective, it is the continued use of working-class identity as a means of announcing your independence that is striking.

In general there is little evidence that the respondents placed much store on defining themselves in strict class terms: what mattered to them was their emphasis on being 'ordinary'. In other ways, class continues to profoundly affect these self-identities, since people seem to see class as threatening to 'pollute' ordinariness. 'Ordinariness' is also seen as a relational construct in which people draw contrasts with others who place themselves above and below them. Class can be used in this context as a category that people use to differentiate themselves from others. While at one level individuals seek to 'escape' class in ways which have superficial resonance with the arguments of Giddens and Beck, it seems also to be the case that class reappears as a reference category which makes people aware of the possibilities of not being 'ordinary'.

Evidence from surveys and qualitative material is consistent (see Marshall 1988). People are ambivalent about class, but for consistent reasons. They wish to pursue 'ordinary' lives in which they are treated fairly and equally, as individuals on their own terms. The idea of class threatens this, and is therefore regarded with some suspicion as a term to use as a basis for explicit self-identity. However, since ideas of 'ordinariness' (or, less commonly, 'niceness', or 'respectability') can only be given substance by being contrasted with something else, discourses and idioms of class are smuggled back into people's thinking. It is, after all, members of 'other' classes who might *not* be ordinary.

Conclusion: individualization and class identity – critical issues

The evidence in the previous section suggests the need to modify Bourdieu's emphasis on the social legitimacy of cultural capital. A common theme in people's perspectives on class is their desire to be 'ordinary' and not to appear to be 'above' others. This marks something of a different angle from Bourdieu's emphasis on the struggles for cultural distinction, though it is not fundamentally at odds with his general approach. The focus on 'ordinariness' as a powerful cultural force allows us to redirect recent criticisms of Bourdieu's work that argue that established cultural hierarchies are being eroded in view of the rise of forms of cultural 'omnivorousness' (Petersen and Kern 1996). The assumption here is that traditional patterns of cultural distinction fragment as people sample different cultural styles with greater readiness. It can be argued that in so far as the evidence towards omnivorousness is convincing (see Warde *et al.* 1999) then it may reflect people's concern not to be labelled as being of any fixed social type. Because high culture can be characterized as uniform, fixed and predictable, omnivorous culture can be presented as a less hierarchical mode of acting. This is not to doubt that omnivorous culture can also allow new modes of cultural distinction (Bryson 1996), as people's skills which enable them to move between different cultural fields can themselves be a sign of expertise. However, what we see here is the ability to be both 'ordinary' and 'special' at the same time, an interesting indication of the changing intersection between class and culture.

It is important to take stock also of the lessons of individualization theory. They alert us to the way that people seem keen to invoke a distinction between their personal lives – in which class is rarely seen as a salient issue – and the world 'out there', the world of politics, the economy, the media, and so forth. Here class is often regarded as having a more important presence. Identities are relational constructs, in which individuals develop a sense of their own selves by comparing themselves with 'meaningful' others. There are some links between issues raised by Bourdieu and by the individualization theorists. Evidence indicates a strong populist critique of high culture which sees it as a violation of 'ordinariness', a mannered set of affectations which do not allow people to be themselves. In this respect it is possible to see how the need to 'perform' individual identity can be related to class-aware frameworks which celebrate the advantages of being free from power networks and hierarchical structures (see Savage 2000). Modes of individualization are therefore related to modes of class identity, and are not a departure from them. In the next chapter I seek to ground this populist, anti-élitist culture more fully in work and employment relations, in order to show how it has distinctive roots in class relationships.

Notes

1 The idea of structuration was used in Giddens (1973) to show, in Weberian fashion, how economic classes might become social classes in certain specific conditions.
2 See, notably, Giddens' textbook, *Sociology* (1997), which contains discussions of class and stratification.
3 See notably Giddens' uncertain statements about class and lifestyle in Giddens (1991: 5–6): 'One might imagine that "lifestyle" refers only to the pursuits of the more affluent groups and classes ... In some substantial part this is true ... yet it would be a major error to suppose that the phenomena analysed in this book are confined in their impact to those in more privileged material circumstances'.
4 See especially Beck and Beck-Gersheim's (1996) criticisms of the German writers Ostner and Roy and Mayer.
5 See for instance Lash's commentary on this work which refers to its 'core assumption' as the 'progressive freeing of agency from structure' (Lash 1994: 119). A not dissimilar refrain can be seen in Lash and Urry (1994).
6 'In the past, the affliction was dictated along with one's class fate ... Risk positions, by contrast, contain a quite different type of victimization. There is nothing taken for granted about them. They are somehow universal and unspecific. One hears of them or reads of them. The transmission through knowledge means that those groups that tend to be afflicted are *better educated* and *actively inform themselves*' (Beck 1992: 52–3 original emphasis).
7 This line of argument can also be traced through Castells' recent work (see 1996, 1997, 1998).
8 'Such processes help create "shared histories" of a kind potentially more tightly bound than those characteristic of individuals who share experiences by virtue of common social position' (Giddens 1991: 97).
9 In earlier work on British culture I classified this as post-modern culture, where people mixed and matched from different class *habitus* (Savage *et al.* 1992).
10 This brilliant book, which appeared after the manuscript for this volume was completed, raises important issues for considering how Bourdieu's ideas can be applied to popular culture. The book is largely composed of a series of long interview transcripts with people who have experienced suffering of various kinds. It is very different in tone from Bourdieu (1984), in which interview material is integrated more clearly into the analytical argument. This suggests that Bourdieu may sanction a more generous approach when looking at the dispossesed compared to those with large stocks of economic and cultural capital.
11 It also helps explain the tendency for mutualist self-organization and for demands for popular education which Johnson (1979) sees as a fluctuating though powerful demand within popular culture.

12 In the way suggested by those writers focusing on how upwardly mobile groups use new forms of consumer culture to enhance their social position. See Featherstone (1988).

13 This research has been funded by the Economic and Social Research Council, 'Lifestyles and Social Integration: a study of middle class culture in Manchester' project number R000236929.

14 The project does not attempt to interview a representative sample of the population, but instead has chosen four samples from areas picked for theoretical reasons to represent different types of middle-class lifestyle. These four areas are Wilmslow (taken to represent the high status, affluent suburban middle class), Cheadle (representative of the lower middle/upper working class living in semi-detached inner suburbs), Chorlton (typical of the young, gentrifying middle class living in inner Manchester) and Ramsbottom (taken as typical of mixed groups living in rural villages within commuting distances of Manchester). Here I say nothing about these local differences and concentrate only on the narratives of class used.

15 There were three examples of men who showed a strong sense of loyalty to the 'professional middle class', referring to their involvement in professional social networks, appropriate leisure pursuits, etc. There were others whose strong sense of middle-class belonging was predominantly negative in character. Here is the most striking example:

> *Do you think Britain is becoming a classless society?*
>
> No I don't.
>
> *Why?*
>
> Classless. Because I think there's a lot of people like me that enjoy a certain class. You'll always have the poor, you'll always have the lower working class, middle class and upper class; I think I'm . . . I like to think . . . I *never* class myself as working class. That's awful isn't it! But I have high values, I have high goals – I set my goals high. I don't want to be in this situation in another year's time – I want to be wealthy for many different reasons. Whether I will be, I don't know, but I always used to say . . . people used to say 'You set your sights too high Dave', and I'd say 'Yeah, but there's one little philosophy that I live by; if I set my sights very, very high and only reach half way and you only set your sights there and you only reach halfway, I'm an awful lot higher than you are'. So, you know, I'm always looking I suppose – I'm a dreamer. I'm definitely a dreamer.
>
> *Do you think of yourself as being . . . you mentioned you don't think of yourself as working class; would you think of yourself as middle class or . . .*
>
> I'd like to think of myself as middle class. I don't always think I have the money to be middle class; I certainly have the ideals and the dreams and I have a lot of class. I don't like common people, I don't like drunkenness, I don't like . . . I don't like a lot of things . . . oh, this is awful, it sounds terrible . . . that you see around you on a Saturday night when they're kicking people out of the pub; I can't stand bad language, can't stand women using bad language, can't stand swearing in the street, boozing – I just can't stand that kind of thing. Now whether that makes me middle . . . I like nice things, I like buying antiques, I like buying . . . I like a nice car, I like to eat well, I like nice things around me and my son says it's really strange when he goes into people's houses he says 'It's amazing what they don't have dad', I said 'Yeah, I know what you mean' and I can

only deduce . . . 'cos there are some of these guys are on decent money and that their life is spent, football, in the pub and that's where the money goes because they don't have things around them that would sort of denote that they enjoy the home, you know. My home is important.

16 Using other people's criteria I suppose I'm middle class because I've had a tertiary education.

> My background is, my father was a university lecturer and my mother was a teacher. We lived in a three bedroomed detached house with a garden . . . I like to think that I'm not marked by the way I speak, but again I probably am. If you were to pin me down I would say, pretend to be, lower middle class.

17 Although we attempted to conduct interviews with individuals alone, in some cases other household members were present and we made no attempt to exclude them.

18 This is what we would expect given that our sample is skewed somewhat towards middle and upper income groups. Indeed, as we argue elsewhere, what is striking is the extent to which working-class self-definition continues to be attractive.

19 Interestingly, those relatively few respondents who defined themselves as members of a middle class in a rather more élitist way often claimed that they were 'professional middle class'.

6 *The* organizational restructuring *of* class relations

In earlier chapters, especially Chapter 3, I alluded to the importance of 'organizational centrality' as a key force structuring social inequality. It is a central contention of this book that if we are to understand the interrelationships between economic inequality, social mobility and the cultures of individualization, work and career, it is essential to recognize the active role of organization. However, although the importance of organization has lurked behind much class theory since Weber's pioneering writings on bureaucracy, it has rarely been given satisfactory treatment as a central plank of class analysis. As Esping-Andersen (1994) quips, 'orthodox class theory is nested in an institutionally naked world' (quoted in Witz 1995: 56). In the first section of this chapter I therefore consider how organizational analysis can theoretically be brought into dialogue with class analysis. I refer to the uneven deployment of organizational theory within class analysis, which I attribute to the persistence of neo-Weberian organizational sociology within class theory, while pointing out that the sociology of organization has now moved onto different, richer, terrain. I briefly outline new issues within organizational theory which offer the potential to cross-fertilize elements within class analysis, focusing particularly on feminist arguments about the gendering of bureaucracy and the application of Foucault's arguments about capillary power.

The argument in the second section of the chapter is that the creation of class thresholds, especially the 'collar divide' between manual and non-manual labour, anchored organizational authority in work cultures which had historically been characterized by traditions of male manual worker autonomy and control. As the organizational 'career' developed during the twentieth century, career progress was defined as movement between classes. Socially visible biographical referents were thereby organizationally sanctioned through grading schemes and internal labour markets. In this way, the organizational construction of class was closely related to ascriptive and life course identifiers of gender, age, social background and race.

In the third, fourth and fifth sections I focus on the significance of the contemporary restructuring of organizations. Historically, skilled manual labour was identified with masculine independence, so that attaining manhood status was linked to taking up a recognizable, manual, working-class identity. Such was the strength of this cultural association that the middle class career emerged historically in reaction to it as organizations sought to wrest authority from skilled, autonomous, male manual workers. Career movement into the non-manual world of the 'middle class' took men out of the cultural orbit of manual work and also emphasized that white-collar workers had to exhibit modes of 'responsibility' which differed from working-class 'independence'. Career mobility into middle-class occupations was thereby defined in terms of a movement across a well-recognized and symbolically charged class threshold that also embodied different modes of individuality.

Over the past two decades, the restructuring of organizations has reduced the salience of manual work as the key cultural reference category. Manual work has not been eradicated, but its cultural significance has been redefined as an increasingly 'dependent' state. In the space for reconstructing the association between work and forms of individualism that this opens up, new career technologies have radically reworked traditional class boundaries and have created new ideas about the relationship between the individual, hierarchy and organization. New kinds of class distinction are embodied in these processes, while at the same time organizational hierarchy itself becomes less publicly visible.

Organization theory and class analysis

In modern capitalist society, dominated by large corporate, state and hybrid organizations, the study of class patently requires a theory of organization. However, despite frequent points of contact over the years, there is relatively little intellectual exchange between researchers within the fields of organizational studies and social stratification. While organization has been a largely unacknowledged foundation for much recent class analysis, there have been remarkably few attempts by writers within this tradition to reflect critically on organizations; nor is there sustained interest in recent intellectual developments in the study of organization. This has limited the capacity of those studying social class to recognize the way that organizations are both a cause and an outcome of class relations, and to see how organizations encode and embody cultures of class.

This is a sweeping statement that demands instant clarification. A few have little analytical place whatsoever for the role of organization. These would include those Marxists who reduce organizational forms to the capitalist social relations in which they are embedded.[1] These are, however, rather few in number today. Most Marxists, as I discussed in Chapter 1, are more open to reflecting on the significance of organization, as attested by recent currents of regulationist work that emphasize the role of institutional frameworks in regulating and organizing relations of capital, as well as by Wright's (1985) discussion of organizational assets. Pierre Bourdieu offers a more striking, and perhaps surprising, instance of the neglect of organization. While his work firmly establishes the theoretical salience of economic and cultural capital, he does not consider the role of organizational position

in structuring class other than that which operates through the role of economic and cultural capital (see Savage *et al.* 1992, Ch. 6).[2]

In general, however, the dominant tradition of class analysis has long
recognized the significance of bureaucratic structures. This is particularly
true within Weberian scholarship, since Weber's emphasis on bureaucracy
as a defining feature of modernity led logically to a consideration of the
relationship between classes and bureaucracies (Scott 1996). However, this
Weberian argument has left a problematic legacy for thinking about class. By
defining bureaucracy instrumentally, as the most 'technically efficient means'
of achieving any given set of ends, Weber took bureaucracy as a 'given',
rather than as a mutable, complex, social construction which enacted different kinds of relations of domination and power.[3] This instrumental perspective is linked to Weber's well-known 'ideal type' of the modern organization
which offered little historical specificity to bureaucracies themselves (see
Clegg 1989). The danger (once this approach was loosened from Weber's
ideal type methodology) was that this model of organization might become
reified and lead to an overly simplistic account of how class depended on an
organizational base.

The idea that bureaucracy is a foundation for class became a hallmark
of class theory from the middle years of the twentieth century. Dahrendorf
(1959) claimed that 'imperatively coordinated organizations' were an essential bedrock of social class, and similar arguments were used in theories of
the 'service class' from the time of Renner (1978). Goldthorpe's (1980, 1982)
arguments are the most sophisticated and best known, since his claims about
the distinctiveness of the 'service relationship' depend on the distinctive
bureaucratic basis of professionals and managers. There are parallels here
with the arguments of Erik Wright (1985, 1996) who also sees organization
as a distinctive axis of stratification. By virtue of their position, managers are
able to accrue surplus product to themselves, at the expense of other organizational members. Wright's arguments have considerable affinities with
managerialist claims that in large corporations managers may pursue their
own interests rather than those of the owners, and that there is a demarcation between property and managerial power.

The key issue here is whether there is a 'zero sum' power relationship
between the owners of organizations and their managers. Both Marxists and
Weberians have pointed to the continued power of shareholder interests in
the running of corporations and the extent to which managerial decisions
are still organized around the making of profit (e.g. Scott 1997). Interestingly, Goldthorpe fuses together capitalist and bureaucratic processes: the
service class is a bureaucratic class but also one which has to serve its (frequently capitalist) employers. Wright, by contrast, distinguishes the two
(though his arguments about organizational assets are primarily designed to
explain the role of state or public sector bodies, rather than private sector,
capitalist, organizations). Wright (1996) shows that organizational position
affects (albeit modestly) outcomes (such as social mobility chances, or friendship patterns) holding constant the forces of property ownership and skill.
Similarly, Savage *et al.* (1992) showed that in the British case there was
evidence that managers of organizations had some distinctive properties

compared to university educated professionals (for instance in their leisure patterns, social mobility prospects, etc.) (and see the debate in Butler and Savage 1995). This does not, however, entail seeing managerial and capitalist interests as necessarily zero sum. Shareholders may benefit from the actions of a managerialist élite that are able also to secure additional rewards for themselves.

Class analysts looked to organization to provide a 'base' for class, and tended not to stress the diversity or complexity of organizational forms. Rather, the Weberian account of bureaucracy, or a variant of it, was used as a hook on which to hang an account of class. This is problematic because organizational theory has itself experienced a profound rethinking of many of its assumptions in recent years. The challenge is partly theoretical – a repudiation of the instrumentalist perspective of Weberian accounts of bureaucracy – and partly empirical, linked to arguments about the declining relevance of fixed bureaucratic forms in an unstable, post-Fordist social order (e.g. Ray and Reed 1993). Given this challenge, to seek to anchor class analysis in an outdated account of organization is, to say the least, unfortunate (see further Savage *et al.* 1992; Halford and Savage 1995b).

Because class theorists looked to organization to provide an account of the 'base' for class processes, there has been little interest in how organization could also be seen as the outcome, the product, of class relations. However, in the past 20 years organization theory has developed a remarkable range of intellectual perspectives, many of which offer considerable potential for thinking about the social construction of class. There is an interesting comparison to be made here with gender and feminist studies. Traditionally, feminists were even less interested in theorizing organization than were writers on class (see Witz and Savage 1992). However, in recent years there has been a remarkable convergence of interest in the study of gender and organization (see Hearn and Parkin 1987; Savage and Witz 1992; Halford *et al.* 1997; Wajcman 1998). Much of this recent work emphasizes the interaction between gender and organizations, and the ways that organizations 'embody' gender relations. Despite the appeal of this body of work, this kind of analysis has not been used to any great extent in considering social class (though see the remarks of McDowell 1997 for the case of the upper-class male culture of the financial institutions in the City of London).

These feminist developments have valuable lessons for class analysis. Organizations are not just a base for class, but also the outcome of class relations. They are ways of sedimenting and storing social advantages in the form of established processes, routines, procedures and technologies. They provide ways of linking activities in diverse kinds of networks and are devices for bringing together and keeping apart. Recognizing the fluidity and contingency of organization thereby allow a more subtle rendering of the ways that classes are themselves organized and made culturally salient. Recognizing this point means breaking from the Weberian ideal type, and focusing on the extent to which organizational forms and cultures are subject to contestation and change (see Clegg 1989).

I do not have the space here to provide a developed account of how the relationship between organization and class can be theoretically elaborated. I only seek to elaborate points that will be sufficient (I hope) to allow me to trace the empirical connections between class and organization in the British case.

One important source is Foucault's (1977) analysis of modern capillary power and its association with bureaucratic modes of surveillance (see in general terms MacKinlay and Starkey 1998). It is striking that most attempts to see organization as a 'base' for class distinguish a group of beneficiaries (senior managers, for instance) from a group of disadvantaged organizational members (manual or routine white-collar workers, for instance). This is certainly true of Wright's arguments about organization assets, and there are traces of it in Goldthorpe's conception of the service class. Foucault's well-known claim that we should displace power from a visible point of origin at the top of an organization tree, and see how capillary power relations run through organizations is, by contrast, a useful reminder of the fluidity of organization.[4] Ideas of capillary power direct our attention to the kinds of discursive, institutional and technical ties that secure organization, and which work *through* organizational agents, rather than just *between* them. There are, of course, dangers here. One much discussed problem concerns the way that Foucault allows the concept of power to become so diffused that it becomes synonymous with social relationships of any kind. A way of manageably restricting the definition of power is to note that although organizational power can be fluid, it can be stabilized and fixed around key nodal points or thresholds. These thereby allow specific people (devices, rules etc.) to have decisive powers of agency, albeit in ways that are contingent and contested, and subject to reformulation. Class might, in specific situations, be an important 'stabilizing' device in particular organizational forms (see more generally Clegg 1989).

A second useful aspect of Foucault's work is his emphasis on the relationship between power, surveillance and the construction of subjectivity. Foucault (1977) argues that the human subject is a specific historical creation, associated with the modern era. This modern self should not be unambiguously celebrated as the freeing of the human spirit, but should rather be understood as the product of particular discursive and institutional forms which have ushered it into being.

Many of the details of Foucault's arguments about the panopticon, surveillance, and the human subject can be questioned (e.g. MacKinlay and Starkey 1998). Here I just want to note that the extent to which organizations are prime vehicles for the construction of the subjectivity of their members can be exaggerated. There is a certain 'stickiness' in the way that organizational members are affected by organizational restructuring. This is due in part to the fact that organizational members embody older ways of belonging to an organization even though the organization may itself change, and in part to the fact that their lives usually extend beyond the confines of any particular organization (see Halford *et al.* 1997). Du Gay (1996) has usefully drawn on the work of de Certau to emphasize the ability of organizational members to contest organizational authority through their deployment of diverse 'tactics'. I will now show how these insights can be used in the British case.

Masculinity, independence, and manual labour

In the 1960s Huw Beynon interviewed assembly-line workers at Ford's
Halewood plant in Liverpool. He noticed that although working conditions
were grim, most workers had no interest in escaping the line through promotion to more senior supervisory jobs. The shop stewards he talked to were
especially insistent on this point: 'The [shop] stewards weren't interested in
promotion, in becoming "dedicated Ford men". For them to take the white
coat at Halewood would be to join the other side. "I couldn't do that. Leave
the lads? Not in this firm anyway. They're a crowd of gangsters here"'
(Beynon 1975: 123–4).

Such attitudes were not restricted to men, though they clearly embodied forms of masculinity. At an even earlier period (the 1950s), the industrial
anthropologist Tom Lupton found a similar set of attitudes among a rather
different group of workers, in this case semi-skilled women garment makers:

> The distinction between 'them' and 'us' . . . was marked in the work-
> shop. The managers were called the 'higher ups'. The place where the
> 'higher ups' worked when they were not in the workroom was covered
> by one term 'the office'. To make the distinction between 'them' and
> 'us' was not to express resentment against managers as a class, nor
> envy. The workers I knew never wanted to become one of 'them'.
>
> (Lupton 1963: 36–7)

The women in this case were less militant than the car workers studied by
Beynon (or at least, so Lutpon's study implies). Nonetheless, the same basic
point concerning the lack of contact between the worlds of manual labour
and that of the 'higher ups' is apparent. What is striking is that these workers
attached the values of individuality and autonomy to manual, rather than
white-collar, jobs. Leaping across time to the early 1990s, I came across similar attitudes espoused by an elderly male bank clerk (see more generally
Halford and Savage 1995b, 1997; Halford *et al.* 1997). Despite the fact that
he was a white-collar worker rather than a manual worker, he also endorsed
a strongly-held view about the importance of the divide between staff and
managers:

> Q: Do you identify more with the staff of the branch or with the
>   managers?
> A: I would personally identify with the staff, I mean I have never
>   wanted to go beyond where I am now.
> Q: Why is that?
> A: It has never appealed to me, because of the way I look at work it is
>   only a means to an end to me. It has always seemed, for many
>   years, it has always seemed to me that if you aspire to the manage-
>   ment side of it you have to devote more of your own time and
>   personality to the bank, which I am not prepared to do.

John's views are in part 'instrumental', in the sense which Goldthorpe and
Lockwood (1968a, 1968b, 1969) depict in the new affluent workers of the
assembly-line industries. But this instrumentalism embodies both complex

strains of individualism and class awareness. The individuality of the ordinary staff member was compared with the servile status of managers (see my
elaboration of this argument in Savage 2000). John thought that becoming a
manager involved losing part of himself, a core sense of his own individuality and autonomy, becoming, in some sense, a 'company man'. Individuality, by contrast, involved being an 'ordinary' worker. This sentiment is
interesting in view of the abundance of evidence which shows how many
British workers show little interest in 'advancement' and prefer to be manual
workers. Glass' (1954: 69) study of social mobility showed that more
manual workers wished their sons to be manual workers than to move into
the professions. Runciman's (1966) study of *Relative Deprivation and Social
Justice* noted that British manual workers tended not to see management as a
salient social category – as a group which had any major relevance to their
lives. Beynon and Blackburn (1972: 89) found that the vast majority of
manual workers they interviewed in one factory had not applied for promotion to a supervisory position. Workers pointed out that they would lose
friends and have to take on more responsibility, an idea that they disliked.
Gallie's (1983) study of class radicalism also emphasized how the British
working class appeared more satisfied with its general position. In the-mid
1970s only 21 per cent of British workers (compared to 62 per cent of French
and Italians) thought that the reduction of inequality was 'very important'
(Gallie 1983: 86).

The link between manual work and cultures of independence, the cultural distance between labour and management, the association between
notions of labour and independence and masculinity helps explain how
manual labour was invested with distinctive moral values in twentieth-
century Britain. The roots of this distinctive culture are very deep. Biernacki
(1995), indicates that they can be traced to conceptions of labour and work
going back to industrialization. His comparative analysis of the meaning of
labour in nineteenth-century British and German textile industries demonstrates that in Britain employers and workers defined work not in terms of
the 'service' of workers to their employing organization, but in terms of the
actual output of work:

> Despite compelling similarities in the settings in which matching Ger-
> man and British textile mills developed, economic agents in the two
> countries applied different concepts of labour as a commodity to carry
> out the process of production. German employers and workers indeed
> acted as if the employment relation comprised the purchase of labour
> effort and of disposition over worker's activity . . . Through quotidian
> practice British employers and workers defined the factory employ-
> ment relation as the appropriation of workers labour concretised in
> products.
>
> (Biernacki 1995: 43)

In Germany, work was seen as the embodied activities of workers at the
workplace. In Britain, work was seen as materialized in the finished product.
Employers were not properly expected to lay claim to any particular forms of
worker deportment during working time itself. Biernacki's contrast can be

challenged (largely because its focus on the textile trades ignores the complexity of payment systems and industrial relations in other sectors). It is nonetheless an arresting argument, which fits well with those analyses of British industrial development that emphasize its labour-intensive character and the extent to which handicraft skills and worker autonomy persisted well into the twentieth century (see Savage and Miles 1994). It helps to explain why British workers have been unusually persistent in resisting control and authority in the workplace, and why they have frequently opposed management intervention. Manly independence and autonomy thus became central features of manual working-class culture. Here is Beynon (1975: 70) again on the shop stewards who came to the fore on Merseyside in the 1960s:

> The stewards were young men. They wore sharp clothes; suits with box jackets. They thought of themselves as smart, modern men and this they were. They walked with a slight swagger, entirely alert and to the point of things. They walked, talked and looked as they were. They knew what their bit of the world was about and they were prepared to take on anybody who challenged it.

The notion of the 'traditional working class', which I discussed in Chapter 2, is related to this emphasis on independence and autonomy. These images focus predominantly on male industries whose masculinity and heroism depended on presenting their workers as autonomous, free and not constrained by direct supervision. Coal miners, above all, came to be seen – however wrongly – as 'archetypal' proletarians (e.g. Harrison 1978). In a somewhat less exalted but still privileged position stood dock workers, shipbuilders, printers and railway workers. In all these cases workers were overwhelmingly male, worked in individual environments with no supervision (in the case of footplate workers or signalmen), or in gangs of closely bonded men where little *de facto* control was exercised over them (in the case of coal miners), and were strongly unionized. In some of these cases (for instance, among coal miners, dock workers and shipbuilders) the workers were also deemed to live in occupational communities, in tightly-knit neighbourhoods. The textile trades, however, which employed a predominantly female workforce were not given the same cultural weight, nor were the metal-bashing trades of the Midlands, organized in small workshops. Most glaringly of all, domestic servants – the largest occupation in Britain in 1931 – were never regarded as part of the heartland of the working classes, since their characteristics violated the symbolic ideas attaching to working-class independence (see Glucksmann 1990).

Bureaucratic expansion in Britain took place in an economy that was already well organized (informally) by manual workers, and this had major historical repercussions for the way that large organizations developed. As large organizations developed in the UK during the twentieth century they formed a historical compromise with the informal world of manual worker autonomy. Large firms could leave training to the workers themselves (see More 1980). Apprenticeship was the key institutional process by which boys became both men and skilled workers and thereby members of the working class. As late as the early 1970s there were more than twice as many apprentices as university students (or students in any form of higher education). Apprenticeship offered a training whereby young men rubbed shoulders with older, skilled men, and thereby learned the skills of the trade alongside the cultural mores of the trade itself. Thus Thomas Lupton (1963: 2) reflected autobiographically that: 'In the 1930s during my apprenticeship as a marine engineer, I spent some years in an engineering workshop. This experience brought home clearly to me the influence of customary workshop standards of conduct upon individual behaviour and the subtlety of sanctions employed to enforce conformity'.

Apprenticeship offered distinctive 'rites of passage' which melded occupational socialization and the acquisition of full manhood so that the two became intertwined. It offered to young men a recognition of the perils of the labour market. During the years between 1918 and 1939 apprenticeship became less regulated by customary practice and became a device whereby employers could employ cheap labour, which they might then dispense with on completion of their terms. Men were therefore forced to learn early in their lives that they had to stand up for themselves – both in relation to older male workers and to their employers. Apprenticeships were not the first rung on an internal labour market ladder on which young men could expect to be looked after by their employers. Rather, they forced young men to recognize that they might have to fight for their own future once they had completed their term, and hence helped generate a culture which associated the acquisition of manual skills with the display of masculinity (Willis 1975). From the employer's point of view the attraction of apprenticeship lay in its cheapness and adaptability. Without having to provide formalized provision of training, they could nonetheless be assured of the production of skilled workers (Littler 1982).

The position of women in this male working-class culture was highly problematic. To some extent women could take over the idea of autonomy and independence and apply it to a different realm – the home and family life. However, such was the degree of practical subordination of domestic life to male demands, this proved difficult to live with without recognizing the idea of female independence in the household as a sham (see Dennis *et al.* 1956). In some labour markets (for instance, some of the textile areas) it was possible for more egalitarian forms of gender relations to take root (Glucksmann 1999) and a rather different kind of class identity developed as a result. In general, however, male working-class culture proved resistant to women's politics (Savage 1987). This cultural legacy explains the difficulties that women had in identifying with the positive aspects of working-class identities (Skeggs 1997).

The development of the middle-class 'career'

Middle-class notions of the 'career' were generated against the backdrop of the cultural dominance of skilled male labour. The modern idea of the 'career', as a set of occupational transitions through job ladders, is a recent one, the meaning of which can only be traced from the 1850s or so (Williams 1975). Job mobility was historically common in most forms of capitalist employment, when workers moved between employers, or into and out of self-employment. The idea of the career, by contrast, invoked a notion of individual development linked to structured mobility through a hierarchical sequence of jobs (both inside organizations, and between them), and has become a crucial way of linking notions of individual development with organizational processes (see more generally Savage 1998). In place of the autonomy of the skilled manual trades, which measured itself in terms of its refusal to become incorporated into an organizational hierarchy, the idea of the career involved a mode of individuality which defined self-development through taking on the responsibility of hierarchy.

The emergence of career systems was in fact hesitant and uncertain in Britain. It was only when patterns of job mobility took on clear class, gender and age connotations in the early twentieth century that they became fixed in terms of their social meanings and in terms of the kinds of prospective rewards which became attached to them. Early models of the career were indebted to the military model which distinguished between the plebeian ranks and gentlemanly officers, and which etched this distinction into virtually every aspect of military life, including uniform, modes of conduct, payment, dress, housing and training. The military model was drawn upon in many developing bureaucratic sectors in the nineteenth century, notably the railways, which created its own distinction between officers and 'the ranks' (Savage 1998; and more generally Dandeker 1988). However, we should not overemphasize the relevance of the military model. This model was premised on the need to exercise punitive control over employees through direct visual surveillance. On the railways, this punitive system was challenged from the 1870s by the emergence of a managerial emphasis that workers should be encouraged to become responsible by being offered the prospect of 'career' progress, so obviating the need for direct visual control. Newer modes of career offered the potential of structured mobility into positions of responsibility, so defining the career in terms of its removal from the orbit of manual labour.

As these new forms of career developed, they crystallized new kinds of class distinction. The pivotal civil service reforms of the 1860s marked one highly influential alternative to patronage-based 'gentlemanly' careers. They linked civil service careers directly to educational attainment, and institutionalized the distinction between 'mechanical' and 'intellectual' labour, which was to be used to define the grading system and which was to earn widespread admiration and emulation elsewhere (Zimmeck 1988).

The crucial historical period for the crystallization of this intersection between 'careers' and 'class' was between 1880 and 1914. In those industrial sectors in which internal labour markets for manual workers had been introduced, manual job ladders were increasingly demarcated from white-collar positions, and promotion prospects for manual workers deteriorated (Miles *et al.* 1995; Savage 1998). On the railways, footplate workers and signalmen, who had traditionally enjoyed considerable scope for promotion and incremental earnings, saw their prospects worsen as railway expansion halted, with the result that there were fewer vacancies in more senior positions to fill. A similar process took place in the post office, and the prospects for postmen fell away steadily.

By contrast, in white-collar sectors, 'middle-class' career prospects were enhanced by the introduction of female workers whose routine labour allowed men to be 'freed' for rapid promotion, so allowing middle-class, white-collar men to expect high promotion prospects (Crompton 1986; Savage *et al.* 1992). This was particularly clear in banking where a dip in male promotion rates in the inter-war period led to the deliberate introduction of female clerks (Savage 1993; Stovel *et al.* 1996). Data from the Glass mobility survey (Mills and Savage 1998) indicates that whereas a clear majority of managers in the 1920s had worked previously in manual jobs, from the 1930s the majority had begun work in non-manual environments.[5]

Of course, as I discussed in part in Chapter 4, there was considerable work life mobility across the collar divide. However, it is likely that such movement only helped to reinforce the symbolic charge of the general class divide. Within this symbolically charged class cultural framework the key threshold was that between the 'ranks' and management. Moving into management was a key marker of career 'success', with success being defined in terms of removing someone from the world of manual labour. The centrality of this threshold was emphasized by the extent to which the nature of organizational belonging was fundamentally changed on either side of the line. Movement into managerial employment usually meant moving from a wage to a salary system, brought the privileges of staff status (such as better holidays, sick pay and fringe benefits), the use of exclusive facilities (dining rooms, toilets, etc.), and changed the cultural remit of the job.

A number of important implications follow. First, movements between salient career categories were linked to various ascribed characteristics, and to movements through the life course. I have already pointed out the importance of gender in this context. From the late nineteenth century to the 1960s, British employers tended to employ women on 'women only' career lines with little, if any, prospects of promotion, and limited incremental salaries (Crompton 1986; Savage 1993). Equally, there was a significant association between men's life course and their career progress. In some areas, promotion into management was seen as related to the acquisition of family responsibilities, and the leaving behind of 'laddish' attitudes. In banking there was surveillance over whether clerks could marry, and bank managers, alongside other 'respectable' middle-class professionals (such as the clergy and doctors) could live in employer-provided housing oriented towards families.

British employers also were unusual in developing incremental salary systems, which automatically related annual increases in income to the age of workers concerned. In this way career progress could be related to life course development. As male middle-class workers aged, so they could come to expect more security, responsibility and status, almost as of right. Career structures became intertwined with progress through the life course, so that middle-class men could identify their own lives partly in terms of their own career development.

During the classical period of the industrial revolution British enterprises tended to be small. During the twentieth century the large, multi-unit
enterprise developed, so that by the 1960s the amount of industrial concentration was equivalent to that found in the USA or Germany. The crucial
feature of the late emergence of these managerial hierarchies in Britain was
that in order to differentiate managers from the autonomous world of manual
work, employers sought to culturally differentiate themselves from labour.
While, as I have discussed, frequently allowing manual workers significant
degrees of *de facto* control, they were forced to reassert symbolically their
right to manage, and needed to culturally differentiate managers from workers.
One of the striking developments during the twentieth century was the way
in which class relations were embedded within organizational forms and
boundaries. Although workers were given considerable amounts of autonomy to organize their work (for instance, to directly recruit their families
and friends through extended internal labour markets), emergent management structures extracted their own quid pro quo (Littler 1982). This took
the form of a set of management structures distant from the world of manual
employment, which defined themselves as resting 'above' the dirty world of
manual work. Managerial hierarchies attempted to reassert symbolically the
control which was contested on the shop floor.

This imperative led to a peculiarly English determination to symbolically mark off manual from non-manual work and to emphasize the distance
between the two forms of employment (see also Massey 1994). At the core of
this system of symbolic differentiation lay the difference between the wage
and the salary. I have already suggested that the culture of manual work
emphasized that work was about the production of output, not about loyalty
to the firm, or working with a particular attitude. Work was output, not
'service'.[6] The piece rate was the archetypal indicator of this relationship, but
even where manual workers were employed on an hourly or weekly rate the
basic assumption was the same – that payment was in exchange for *things
produced*. Central to the ethos of management, by contrast, as Goldthorpe
recognizes, was the idea that employees had to be made dependent on the
firm, in order to ensure that they realized where their loyalties lay. The
precise way in which these distinctions were constructed varied. But this
general point allows us to understand how the division between workers and
staff became so powerfully engrained in organizational cultures and how
organizations strove to use this distinction to their advantage.

Manual cultures in contemporary Britain

I have argued that the idioms of male manual working-class culture have
been pivotal in defining class relations in twentieth-century Britain. Many of
these features persist today: indeed given the scope and scale of economic
and social change their resilience is remarkable. But, while elements of these
manual work cultures survive, their defining role in shaping social identity
has collapsed, and they play a far less important role in structuring organizational culture. This constitutes a profound social change whose full impact is

Table 6.1 Great Britain: percentage distribution of employment by occupation, 1961–90 (%)

Occupational category	1961	1971	1981	1990
Managerial	2.7	3.7	5.3	11.0
Professional	8.7	8.6	11.8	21.8
Technicians	^	2.4	2.0	^
Sales	9.7	8.9	8.8	6.6
Clerical	13.3	14.1	14.8	17.3
Crafts and operators	43.1	34.2	27.9	22.4
Semi-skilled service workers	11.9	12.7	14.0	12.8
Semi-skilled transport workers	6.5	10.0	9.1	5.6
Farm workers and managers	4.0	2.9	2.4	1.6
Not classifiable		2.6	3.8	1.0
Total	100	100	100	100

Note: ^ signifies that figure is included in the category immediately above.
Source: Census (1961, 1971, 1981, 1990, Spring); *Labour Force Survey (1991).*

still unravelling. The obvious starting point for this argument is simply the brute fact of the numerical decline of manual labour, however measured. Even those who emphasize the maturity and persistence of the working class do not dispute this basic fact. The decline affects manual labour in general and 'traditional' manual jobs in particular, as Table 6.1 indicates.

By the 1980s manual workers were a clear minority of the British labour force, with the result that the kind of populist claims to ordinariness and typicality which I explored in Chapter 5 clustered less obviously around manual work. Manual work was an increasingly exceptional and unusual activity. More than this, the traditional industries which had nourished 'heroic' images of manual labour were the ones which declined most dramatically. Table 6.1 shows that the traditional industrial sectors, such as mining, shipbuilding, railways, and iron and steel ('crafts and operators'), which had all helped generate ideas about the power of manual labour, experienced particularly steep losses. These sectors had mostly been declining since the 1950s, and their eclipse represented the end of a distinctive Labourite political project. This project had been based around masculine work identities in heavy industry, trade unionism and strong Labour loyalty. Although the Thatcherite period saw the final curtain falling on this project, there had been a longer term process of decline on which Thatcherism built. The state-owned industries of the post-war period had rationalized ruthlessly and in the process helped to undercut a vision of publicly owned enterprise, sapping manual worker energies from within. Indeed, Beynon (1991) has shown that rates of employment decline were higher in the nationalized industries than in other parts of the manufacturing sector, and he sees the erosion of manual working-class Labour loyalties as related to the developments of this period.

However, the decline of manual labour is a more complex process than the foregoing paragraph, with echoes of the crude idea of the 'Forward

March of Labour Halted?' (Hobsbawm 1980), might suggest. Manual labour continues to be a significant source of employment, with around 30 per cent of those active in the labour market being manual workers, a number roughly equivalent to those in the much-vaunted managerial and professional ranks. It is not only the stark decline of manual employment that is significant, but also its re-articulation into different kinds of work cultures. The cultural value of 'manly independence' traditionally associated with manual labour has been redefined. Manual labour has become increasingly identified as a form of subordinate and dependent labour. This has allowed white-collar and middle-class work to become more hegemonic in claiming to be the repository for individualistic values. A number of points can be made to develop this argument.

First, the route into manual work had traditionally been based around a direct transition from schooling to a manual environment with the subsequent socialization into male occupational cultures, either through apprenticeship or some other form of training through peer groups. As I showed above, this culture of training was of fundamental importance for sustaining notions of worker independence and autonomy, and can be traced back to pre-industrial, handicraft traditions.[7] This culture was sustained beyond the period of the Second World War and indeed experienced something of an expansion in the 1950s as it lost its association with the exploitation of youth labour and became linked to day release schemes and accreditation through the City and Guilds. However, it began to decline in the late 1960s and then cracked, with remarkable speed, in the late 1970s and 1980s. Gospel (1998) estimates that the proportion of manufacturing workers who were apprentices fell from 2.5 per cent in 1970 to just over 1 per cent in 1990. Various bureaucratized forms of training, notably the Youth Training Scheme, replaced the largely autonomous transmission of skills through male occupational cultures (e.g. Ashton 1990). When 'modern apprenticeships' were re-introduced in the 1990s, they were conceived in a radically different way, as a bureaucratically organized form of training with little role for independent manual worker input (see Gospel 1998).

There is more to this matter than apprenticeship alone. During the 1980s young men became increasingly concentrated in manual work (Egerton and Savage 2000). Despite the apparent aggregate decline of manual employment, large numbers of young men (45 per cent in 1981 and 37 per cent in 1991) were still employed in this form of work, albeit often only temporarily. This had the inevitable consequence of defining manual work increasingly as 'starter jobs' for young men, something to be left behind if possible, rather than as a proud badge of adult male independence. Rather than acting as a marker of achieving independence, manual employment became a mark of continued dependence. Indeed, the concentration of young men in manual work took place at the very same period that the economic position of young men in the labour market generally declined. Men aged between 21 and 24 earned 83 per cent of the average male wage in 1980, but that had fallen to 71 per cent by 1990 (Irwin 1995: 113).

The pay of young women converged with that of young men (Irwin 1995: 110), and by 1991 their share of professional and managerial employment was nearly on a par with that of young men. Of women aged between 23 and 27, 23 per cent were in the service class in 1991, compared to 25 per cent of young men (Egerton and Savage 2000, Table 1).

Whereas young women in their twenties tended to be in better paid jobs than older women in their thirties and forties, for men the reverse was true. Young men were becoming 'proletarianized' while young women were becoming 'embourgoisified'. Irwin (1995) also shows that young men took considerably longer to leave their parental home and set up independent living arrangements, so they tended to be doing manual work while still 'at home'. The result of all these trends is to help define manual work as the kind of work which dependent young men do, so undermining its association with images of independence.

Second, the increased immigration of ethnic minorities into Britain from the 1950s has helped to 'racialize' manual work, to the extent that in some industries and regions a close association between 'blackness' and manual labour has developed. This development is important in changing one of the key cultural signifiers from that of the collar divide to that of the racial divide (Modood *et al.* 1997). The Policy Studies Institute 1994 survey shows that Caribbean, Pakistani and Bangladeshi men were considerably over-represented in manual employment, with around two thirds of their number being manual workers.[8] This might be seen as the 'racialization of status'. Rather than white, non-manual, middle-class groups identifying against white manual workers, they are more likely to use race as a cultural signifier. This allows the potential for repositioning among white people, in which white workers – both manual and non-manual – can find some common cause with each other by defining themselves against ethnic minorities. The position of white manual workers becomes somewhat more detached from traditional class-based associations. This point is considerably complicated by the very different occupational profiles of various ethnic minorities, as well as by recent evidence pointing to the successes of young people from some ethnic minorities in obtaining good educational credentials and moving into middle-class professional employment (Modood *et al.* 1997; Iganski and Payne 1999). Nonetheless, the way that race now acts as a key cultural divide changes the symbolic importance of traditional class divisions.

Third, manual cultures of independence rested traditionally on the notion that workers could sell their skills elsewhere and that they were hence not beholden to any particular employer. This affected trade union policy, for instance through support for apprenticeship controls, migration schemes, etc. (see Penn 1981). During the twentieth century, manual workers became more reliant for job security on one firm. By the mid-twentieth century Vincent (1993) has shown that up to half of manual workers worked all their lives (or nearly all their lives) for one firm. Yet even where it was difficult for workers to move to different jobs, psychological independence remained important, as for instance in the well-known tendency of car workers to refuse to buy their own products (Beynon 1975: 109ff.).

During the 1970s and especially the 1980s the dependence of manual workers on their firms was however underscored by a number of developments. The rise of unemployment made it more difficult for workers to find alternative employers, and made them more reluctant to challenge their firm's autonomy. The chances of unemployment fell relatively heavily on manual workers – both skilled and unskilled (Gallie *et al.* 1994; Gallie *et al.* 1998, Ch. 5) – and so eroded the potential of manual work to be identified with independence.

The evidence I reviewed in Chapter 3 suggests that there is increasing variety in income levels attaching to particular occupations, implying a growing division between 'insiders' and 'outsiders' in internal labour markets. By the early 1990s almost as many manual workers expected 'internal progression' within their company as did professional and managerial workers.[9] This process is also related to the development of human resource management, the construction of core and peripheral labour markets, and various management initiatives which attempted to incorporate workers more fully into their firm's culture. Although it is doubtful that these schemes are entirely effective (see Gallie *et al.* 1994) their tenor is still significant. Gallie *et al.* (1998: 58) show that 'social skills' were the single most quoted attribute by a sample of managers for getting work done.

Fourth, as Cockburn and Ormrod (1993) have demonstrated, male work cultures traditionally depended on a particular relationship with technology, whereby manual workers could 'master' and 'control' the work process. Admittedly, this notion was very fluid, stretching from the physical hard labour associated with dock work or coalmining, to the detailed technical knowledge of engine drivers or skilled toolsetters. In some cases, male craft workers were actually able to 'masculinize' a set of work tasks that elsewhere might be seen as potentially feminine – notably in the typing work carried out by compositors (Cockburn 1983). These associations of the mastering of technology were steadily 'stretched' from their original base in the handicraft trades, and in the new assembly-line factories it is possible to detect the arrival of a very different notion in which mastery could be asserted with respect to technology. Here, 'surviving the line', and finding strategies to cope with the routines of mass production and new technological demands, became a covert sign of reasserting skill and mastery (see Burawoy 1985 for an American example of the way that 'making out' becomes a way of coping with deskilled engineering workplaces).

Willis (1975) has famously explored how notions of masculine 'hardness' could be imported into school contexts, a particularly important development as the school leaving age was raised. In some industries technology could be used to reconstruct modes of independence, notably in the railways, where McKenna (1980) shows how the idea of the 'bailiwick', the area which workers had effective autonomy within, was coded into the meaning of signal boxes and railway engines. Nonetheless, the development of computerized production (for instance using computer aided design and manufacture techniques) has stretched this idiom still further, in large part because computer technology lends itself to communicative and networking metaphors rather than 'mastery' ones. Of course, even here, it is striking how the language of labour has been inflected by male manual cultures, as in the designation of 'software engineers', 'hardware' etc.

However, one of the striking features of computing and information technology (IT) related work is the speed with which it is updated, meaning that ideas of mastery, with the assumption that skills learned through apprenticeship or youth training are thereby 'established' and embodied in the independent adult male who needs no further training, are inappropriate in ever-changing technical and occupational environments.

Fifth, the changing gender division of labour affects class cultures. The trends here are complex and by no means uni-directional. Women have always worked in the labour market, not only in traditional 'female' jobs such as domestic service and catering, but also in various forms of manufacturing. The gender division of labour has therefore never been one that was unchallenged, but was always contested and flexible. Nonetheless, it is clear that for much of the twentieth century a distinctive gender 'contract' prevailed, characterized by marked sex segregation in the labour market between men and women. In those sectors of manufacturing where women were employed, they were either employed in 'women-only' operating units (sometimes supervised by other women), or in family settings (as in textiles, see Glucksmann 1999). The extent to which women in these environments could partake in their own version of the male culture of independence varied. In some workplaces 'girls' managed to carve out forms of independence which had parallels to those found in the male trades. However, it was more usual for female shop floor culture was overridden by male forms of dominance and control, as for instance in the use of familial controls which in some sectors, notably textiles, might be direct forms of family labour, while in others might draw upon paternalist cultures (e.g. Bradley 1989).

Since 1945 there have been marked changes in the gender division of labour, though there is also considerable debate as to the extent and significance of such changes (see Hakim 1995; Ginn *et al.* 1996). Egerton and Savage (2000) show that one of the striking differences between the occupational profile of men and women is the fact that young women tend to be in higher status jobs than do older women. This is partly due to the well-established tendency for women to be downwardly mobile after they return to work from childbearing (Dex 1987), but it also reflects the extent to which young women have moved into professional and managerial jobs in remarkable numbers over the past two decades (see Crompton and Sanderson 1990; Crompton 1998). Here again we see a redefinition in the meaning of proletarian employment on the one hand, and professional and managerial employment on the other. The values of youth and independence become associated with the latter, while the former is associated with having familial responsibilities and dependence of various kinds.

Sixth, there are conflicting views concerning the changing role of trade unionism. Trade unionism came to play a particularly important part in helping to reconstruct notions of worker autonomy in mechanized work environments in which workplace independence was far removed from its handicraft origins. Loyalty to trade unionism in these sectors could be a way of symbolically reasserting some kind of 'rights' in the production process. Industries that used assembly-line methods, employed largely non-craft workers, and had strict supervision at the point of production, frequently witnessed considerable union growth in the years after 1945 (often following a difficult period between the two world wars when such sectors proved difficult to unionize). In the years after 1940, forms of work control were introduced in most assembly plants, mainly through the emergence of a powerful shop stewards movement which reasserted the right of workers to organize the pace of the line (Beynon 1975; Tolliday and Zeitlin 1987). Indeed, this process of informal modes of work control through workplace collective bargaining was seen as typical of the British system of industrial relations as late as the late 1960s, in the influential Donovan Report. Even in settings where high degrees of mechanization and automation seemed to indicate that traditional notions of craft independence should have little remit, in fact modes of informal control survived.

Since the late 1970s industrial relations have been transformed, and in particular the number of trade union members has been in steady decline as the Conservative government's offensive against trade unions attempted to reduce their powers in the collective bargaining process. Most commentators suggest that the real pace of change has been rather slow, and evidence from the mid- and late 1980s suggests that shop steward organization and informal union politics continued to be resilient in many workplaces (Batstone 1984; Darlington 1994; Gallie *et al.* 1996).

Gallie *et al.* (1996) have argued that the decline in union membership in the 1980s was largely to be explained by structural factors such as the loss of manufacturing and manual jobs rather than by a decline in employee commitment, while Rose (1996) shows that even in new modern enterprises, employers have made little attempt to erode union influence. However, it seems that these authors may have overstated their case. The decline of militancy after the early 1980s made it less pressing for employers to undermine union controls, and Rose shows that most union membership is explained in highly instrumental terms with little general commitment to unionization in general. More recent research suggests that the economic recession of the early 1990s did considerable damage to unionization (Geroski *et al.* 1995). It is a striking fact that by 1994 only 23 per cent of workers in the private sector were unionized (Morris 1996). Certainly, by the 1990s, the heartlands of trade unionism had changed from the male manual working class to the public sector white-collar workforce. By 1992 professionals were the most densely unionized occupational group, and trade unionism could no longer be readily identified as a core part of manual work cultures.[10]

Lastly, one of the major challenges to traditional cultures of manual labour comes from the rise of 'servicing' employment, where individuals deal with the public in face-to-face situations, as well as more recently by remote means, notably through call centres. In 1992 the main type of work of 32 per cent of men and 57 per cent of women was concerned with dealing with other people (Gallie *et al.* 1998: 52). By contrast, only 27 per cent of men and 8 per cent of women were directly involved in technically-oriented work activities.[11] The increasing importance of these social skills problematizes the relevance of older models of manual workers' autonomy, even though old handicraft idioms of worker autonomy did migrate from craft sectors to mass production. Despite the poor working conditions of many employees in the service sector, it seems most unlikely that there can be any direct transference of older work cultures because of the very different nature of the 'product' and of the working relationship.

I have emphasized that traditional manual cultures rested upon distinguishing work output from conduct ('dressage') during work time. Because labour was defined in terms of output it was culturally acceptable to 'lark around' at work. This distinction depended on the workplace being a private world away from the public gaze. As numerous sociologists have pointed out (Hochschild 1985; Lash and Urry 1994), in servicing environments it is much more difficult to distinguish work output from comportment while carrying out the work, since the meaning and definition of effective work is more directly 'embodied' in the conduct of workers. The whole culture of 'facework' is one on which older manual codes have little purchase. Rather, it is the kinds of social skills associated with etiquette, femininity and even cultural capital that have greater significance.

Taken individually, each of these points suggests specific changes have occurred in the organization of labour. Taken together, it seems clear that the cultural association between independence, masculinity and manual labour, and the subsequent cultural salience of the collar divide, has been fundamentally sundered. There are still manual workers, unions and forms of handicraft skill, but they do not mesh together in a structured way that allows them to serve as a cultural marker of major social significance. We should not underestimate the historical importance of this fact, since these developments constitute a break not just with industrial working patterns but with those stretching back even further in historical time before the nineteenth century. And, in the cultural vacuum that this sundering has allowed, I now want to argue that the cultural salience of the 'career' takes on new and unprecedented meanings.

The 'individualizing' of the middle-class 'career'

The declining salience of manual labour removes one of the defining anchors of career mobility and allows a new idea and model of the career to open up, one which is less organized around transitions across class-based thresholds. This new model of career can be seen as breaking from older established class cultures at the same time that it re-encodes class in new, though implicit rather than explicit, ways. While the traditional career linked occupational movements to class thresholds and to life course shifts, so anchoring careers in biographies, contemporary restructuring has disembedded the career from the life course and removed the salience of manual labour as the fundamental point of reference. In this final section I briefly explore this reconstruction of career and examine the main ways in which it challenges established work cultures.

There continues to be a perception that the career is a 'middle-class' phenomenon. Goldthorpe, for instance, claims that 'it is indeed the distinction between jobs and careers that is in some ways involved in many of the more striking class differences in mobility chances and experience that we have shown up' (Goldthorpe *et al.* 1987). Yet, while the association between the 'middle class' and the 'career' remains, this relationship has become more complex in recent years.

Two developments are particularly worthy of comment. First, increasing numbers of 'middle-class' people do not pursue 'conventional', bureaucratic careers but instead opt for a variety of entrepreneurial strategies, pursuing self-employment, consultancy etc. (see Savage *et al.* 1992; Fielding 1995; Savage and Butler 1995). Trends in the 1980s and 1990s have been striking in this respect. Between 1981 and 1991 all occupational groups saw increasing rates of mobility into self-employment compared to the period between 1971 and 1981. No less than 11 per cent of managers in 1981 were in self-employment in 1991, a rate higher than for any other occupation. The kinds of entrepreneurial strategies involved in this shift to self-employment may still be imbued with career motives (people seeking to 'get on'), but they nonetheless de-couple the career from bureaucratic hierarchies, and help define career advancement as being about 'proving yourself'.

Second, organizational restructuring allows a bifurcation within the manual workforce between those core employees of large firms who are employed on some kind of internal labour market, and those who are peripherally employed. Evans' (1992b) study indicates that significant proportions of manual workers felt that they were on 'career ladders', so tending to undermine the association between manual employment and jobs.

The de-coupling of the career from its anchorage in bureaucratic hierarchy tends to reduce the salience of crossing class thresholds. Within organizations there are also a series of organizational innovations that have offered a new way of viewing the career. Rather than the career being a means by which white-collar workers could distance themselves from the 'dirty' world of manual work, it has been redefined as a 'project of the self', allowing individuals to pursue their own 'life projects' in an environment offering them the resources and scope for self-development (see Grey 1994). Fundamental to this redefinition of the career is the development of organizational technologies that disembed individuals from their organization sufficiently to allow them to see organizations 'tactically', as vehicles which allow them to contingently 'develop themselves'. This implies the erosion of the kinds of organizational loyalty and commitment which Goldthorpe sees as a defining feature of the 'service class'.

This argument draws considerably on the work of Grey (1994), du Gay (1996), and Casey (1995) who have all emphasized how organizational processes allow the creation of new modes of discursive construction of subjectivity. Du Gay, for instance, argues that organizations use the discourse of 'enterprise' to encourage their employees to be proactive: 'Within retailing organizations, store managers and shopfloor employees are increasingly represented as enterprising subjects: that is, as individuals who calculate about themselves and work upon themselves in order to better themselves; in other words as people who live their lives as "an enterprise of the self"' (du Gay 1996: 145).

Gallie *et al.* (1998: 254) have indicated that the greatest loyalty to organizations exists where employees feel that their personal development can best be enhanced. Performance-related pay means that the rewards of a job are at least partly detached from seniority and status, so encouraging all staff to be proactive in meeting their targets. There has been a move away from incremental salary systems, which automatically linked career progress both to changes in the life course and to a clearly recognized yearly temporal parameter, and a rise in individualized payment and reward systems. In much of the private sector, salaries are negotiated privately and it is possible for considerable discrepancies between managers of similar age to open up. In the public sector the basic structure of the incremental salary has largely been left in place but has been overlain with various forms of merit pay (see Marsden and Richardson 1994) and performance-related pay which allow some individuals to accelerate their income more rapidly than others. According to Fernie and Metcalf (1995), 31 per cent of firms now operate merit pay schemes, where the rewards are tailored to the performance of individual employees.

Another important shift here is the declining role of symbolically sanctioned status divisions between various organizational members. Although the pace of change is uneven, many organizations have reduced or eliminated the salience of 'staff status' for managerial and professional employees. In practice this means that canteens and toilets are provided for all members of staff, not separately for manual and white-collar workers. Pay and benefit packages may be spread through the workforce as a whole (for instance, the basic principles of occupational pension schemes and sick pay schemes may be provided to *all* members of the organization, even though different levels of pay may affect take-up and the kinds of rewards offered). The removal of such demarcatory devices between different kinds of employees means that one cannot measure career progress in terms of moving between organizationally sanctioned, visible markers. Career 'progress' becomes internalized and lacks the same degree of visible public anchorage.

This goes alongside the weakening of the anchorage of careers in ascriptive markers, especially with respect to the role of social background, age and gender. Rather than career prospects being open to those who have met certain ascriptive criteria, they are geared to those who show that they have the potential to 'rise to the challenge' and to show the kind of 'enterprise' that career advancement demands. As Halford and Savage (1995b) indicate, this redefinition involves defining promotion as moving from a 'secure' environment to a 'risky' one, in which career advancement is defined as a Faustian gamble. In banking for instance, earning promotion from clerical to managerial grades leads to only a slight increase in basic salary, but brings with it the expectation that managers work overtime unpaid, that their pay increases are linked to performance, and that their job security is lowered. The most striking recent change consistent with this argument is the growing number of women in professional and managerial jobs (Crompton 1998). Halford *et al.* (1997) show how women are not *formally* barred from career progress within organizational cultures, though in practice they may be less likely to choose the Faustian gamble involved in taking on professional and managerial work because of other domestic commitments.[12]

The reworking of the relationship between individuality and the career can be attested to in a number of striking ways. First, one of the traditional ways in which the dependence of traditional middle-class professionals and managers on their employers was marked out was through the provision of housing, so demarcating the dependence of even senior employees on their company. Consider the example of clergy-tied housing, and houses provided for stationmasters, bank managers, industrial managers, and even the lodgings of Oxford and Cambridge dons. Today, such forms of subsidized tied housing for the middle classes have been largely eradicated, and in so far as companies support the housing of their senior staff it is through subsidizing their owner-occupied housing which becomes an additional financial perk rather than a mark of dependence.[13]

Consider also the use of uniform. There has been a striking recent expansion in the 'uniformed working class', especially for routine white-collar workers in areas such as retail and banking, and this can be seen as a mark of the servility of such staff. Professionals and managers, however, rarely wear corporate uniform, and in recent years there has been a reduction in the extent to which any are expected to wear uniforms.[14] Rather, they wear the kinds of business suits that mark them out as members of a professional and managerial class, which are transferable between employers, and in which employees are expected to demonstrate their own ability to self-monitor their own dress to be appropriate to their job, rather than just rely on the uniform handed out by their organization.

There are therefore some far-reaching implications in the changing culture of the career. The 'new' careers disembed individuals from social markers. They are careers with no absolute top or bottom. Individuals are encouraged to define their own salient thresholds and targets. In some respects this may reinforce class differences, as more ambitious employees from middle-class backgrounds may set themselves higher targets than do those from the working class, but by individualizing the career in this way class itself becomes invisible. The power of class *habitus* becomes more powerful in that it is the implicit assumptions held by individuals from different backgrounds about what constitutes a 'good' career which play a key role in leading individuals onto different kinds of career pathways.

Let me illustrate this point by comparing two different ways of talking about careers. These examples are taken from my study of banking and indicate rather crisply how different cultural perceptions can be attached to job movements. Here is Steven, who reports how the idea of career as progress through a hierarchy was conveyed to him in the early 1980s as he sought his first promotion to the managerial ranks: 'It was explained to me that you can't go from being one of the lads, and I was definitely one of the lads in those days, to being a manager in the same branch, it was felt it was a hurdle to get over in terms of being one of the boys to being accountable, making decisions, giving instructions and so forth'. Note the references to hurdles, to the independence of the 'lads', and to the idea that career progress involves the acquisition of responsibility. Moving up the ladder means shedding autonomy.

Compare now David, and the way he talks of his own career:

My personal philosophy is I have not been one of those who have sat down and said, right, that's where I want to be in ten years' time, so to that extent one could say that I am not career oriented...So one could say that my first aspiration once I had sort of developed through a clerical grade was to get my first management appointment, an accountancy appointment; having got there my next aspiration was I reckon I could do a managerial job and having got there it developed. If you want my aspiration is based on age, so I targeted myself at age 40 to be a G5 position, and I was on course to do that until the bank changed the goal posts, right, as it happens I have now achieved a G7 which is a senior management position.

(Halford *et al.* 1997: 164)

I am not interested here in comparing the typicality of David's response with that of Steven, but simply in the different narratives of career. For David there is no one key transition point: having reached management he sets himself further targets. These grades and targets are detached from notions of responsibility or hierarchy. They are abstract targets – 'goalposts' – for an individual to aim at. The organization appears as a setting in which David can pursue a game-playing project without limits and is talked about in terms that detach the career from its social context. Steven by contrast talks about a key transition – into management – which is also related to changing his relationships with other people, and making a transition from 'laddish' status.

New career cultures encourage an instrumentalist attitude towards employing organizations. Organizations are valued in so far as they provide the right opportunities for their staff to pursue 'careers of the self', but do not necessarily command broader allegiance. This development is interesting in view of evidence suggesting that levels of job satisfaction and organizational loyalty tend to decline at more senior levels of organizations. It is apposite to point out that the new culture of the career is possibly not one which organizations themselves endeavour to spread among their staff but is more an unintended consequence of these new developments. Nonetheless, the effects are profound. The new culture of the career is related to the declining propensity of professional and managerial employees to work for one company 'for life' (Savage *et al.* 1992; Mills 1995).

The new culture of the career depends on the defeat of older models of individuality. Only by shattering the older association between manual work, independence and individuality does the idea of the 'career' take on its full meaning as a 'project of the self'. The new model of individuality does not encourage employees to look at those above or below them as their reference categories. Rather, it encourages them to look sideways, at those they see as their competitive rivals. Rivalry in organizational contexts is of course nothing new, but in traditional organizational settings had been held in check by the ascriptive nature of the career. An emphasis on seniority as a marker for promotion, and the high probability in some sectors, such as among bank clerks, that nearly all long-serving men would win promotion to a managerial post (see Stovel *et al.* 1996), or alternatively that almost no one would, tended to take the heat out of the career. The new model of individuality is important in indicating something of a break from that emphasized by

Bourdieu in which the prime focus is vertical. It suggests that those close to you are also those you are most in competition with, and in some respects are those with respect to which you define yourself.

Since individuals no longer see a relationship between ageing and income, and therefore no longer anchor the career in the progress of linear time, they instead see rewards as linked to performance and thereby construe the career in terms of 'game playing'. Individualized forms of payment are not necessarily either economically effective, nor are they generally desired by workers (see Marsden and Richardson 1994), but it is the way they change the meaning of career which matters. Grey (1994) has written about the way that the career is increasingly being defined as a 'project of the self' – a project which individuals should pursue and which they internalize, through developing various kinds of career strategies and tactics (see further Halford *et al.* 1997). I am sceptical about the extent to which people internalize career values. Indeed, people's identities come largely from reacting against the idea of the orthodox career, but this does not change the fact that they perceive the career in 'game-like' terms – regardless of whether they approve or disapprove of the game.

This also helps to explain the reconfiguration of hierarchy around cultures of teamwork and accessibility. This involves changes in style, and also the deployment of some procedures such as briefing groups, workforce meetings and problem solving groups. A recent survey found that around half of private sector workplaces had schemes of this sort in operation by the early 1990s (Fernie and Metcalf 1995), and research by Gallie *et al.* (1998: 96) indicates that around half of the workforce was in 'quality circles' in the early 1990s. Culturally, this shift may involve the use of first names, or working from the same office. One engineer, who had recently been recruited to a modern factory in Swindon after a long time in an old railway workshop was clearly amazed by the cultural shifts involved:

> In BREL [British Rail Engineering Ltd] it was totally different. There was, like, pictures of Isambard Kingdom Brunel everywhere . . . though that did teach you a bit of respect for your superiors at work, that was the theory. Here I even call my own boss 'Robert', his first name. At BREL you would never dream of calling even a foreman anything but 'Mister' something. In a manner of speaking, they all but wore bowler hats still.
>
> (Rose 1996: 90)

What this shift represents is a new way of linking individuals and hierarchies. As individuals pursue their project of the self they are able to draw upon those around them, including those 'above' and 'below' them, as resources to help them pursue their tactical moves. This leads to the 'informalization' of hierarchy, in which hierarchy depends less on visible markers and much more on the implicit cultures of the organization.

It is important to recognize what this trend says about the definition of management in relation to its workforce. It goes hand in hand with a greater specification of management activities and responsibilities, which therefore means that management is defined less in terms of its generic supervisory role. A good example of this shift is in banking. Traditionally, managers of bank branches had a considerable degree of autonomy over all activities within the branch and the manager was therefore a general source of authority within that unit. Today the specification of managerial jobs is more exact (e.g. responsible for lending, or for operations), and line management structures have been made more transparent with the result that diffuse figures of authority have less role.

Conclusions

The most important point that I wish to stress in conclusion is the scale of the cultural remaking of the meanings of work, employment and the career over the past two decades. My emphasis has not been on the structural reworking of employment, a topic much discussed in various theories of post-industrialism (Kumar 1995), post-Fordism (Amin 1994), etc. Although there are some specific areas where the employment relationship has been changed in important ways, my main emphasis, consistent with my account of economic inequality in Chapter 2, and social mobility in Chapter 4, has been on the deepening of inequalities in established employment divisions (see also Gallie *et al.* 1998).

It is in the cultural reworking of organizations, and in particular the different ways in which people are attached to organizational positions that I think the most profound change has occurred. Although broad class inequalities between professional and managerial work on the one hand, and manual and routine non-manual work on the other hand have not changed fundamentally in conveying unequal life chances, the cultural meaning of these forms of work has. Whereas manual work used to convey notions of male independence while salaried work was consistent with organizational dependence, there has been a profound reworking of these cultural terms so it now appears that various forms of professional and managerial work allow people to pursue individualistic projects, while manual and routine non-manual work is defined as 'dependent labour'.

There is, then, considerable value in the arguments of writers such as du Gay (1996) and Casey (1995) concerning the remaking of work cultures. However, it is important not to overemphasize the power of organizations to 'make up people' (Hacking 1983), but to recognize the powers of 'embodied' individuals in organizations to resist and influence change (see Halford and Savage 1997; Halford *et al.* 1997). It is important to recognize the persistence of older, embodied work cultures and the limits of new forms of organizational discourse to fully inculcate their members with the appropriate forms of organizational commitment. Newer forms of organizational culture are not simply concerned to exhort their members to work harder, to develop the appropriate enterprising activities, etc. Rather, the prospect of enterprise is held out to those who wish to partake of it, so placing the emphasis on individuals to choose to opt in, or opt out, of the game-playing culture. Rather than the broad class division within employment being culturally marked by its association with ascriptive identifiers of age, gender, ethnicity, social and educational background, etc., it is marked by the type of attitude that individuals adopt to their work.

In this type of organizational culture there is a rather different articulation between class and occupational position. The kinds of cultural confidences, which encourage some people to seek to 'play the game', to take on a greater role allow the purchase of cultural capital to be enhanced within organizational hierarchies (see also Brown and Scase 1994). Rather than class being visibly marked out in organizational hierarchies, it is the embodied dispositions of class – confidence, personal authority and skill – that come to be held to be the prerogative of those destined to rise up the organizational ladder. In this respect class becomes individualized and loses its direct presence in organizational hierarchy.

Notes

1 The most vociferous work of this kind is that which developed as a critique of managerialist arguments which claimed that there was a separation of ownership from control within capitalist organizations – see Zeitlin (1974) for one influential statement.
2 Though in his more recent work, he does consider the role of the state with more emphasis than in his older work – see Bourdieu (1994).
3 Weber's interest, in his ideal type of bureaucracy, was to emphasize the distinctively modern feature of bureaucracy compared to organizations that preceded it. He would not aver from the need to rethink his ideal type to consider differing organizational forms within the long duration of modern capitalist society.
4 Though there are no doubt other ways of arriving at the same point, for instance Deleuze and Guttari's (1982) distinction elaboration of the rhizome in contrast to hierarchical thinking.
5 Of the birth cohort born in the 1880s, 92 per cent of those who were managers (at age 40) had begun work in manual employment (though numbers for this cohort are small). For the 1890s cohort this figure dropped to 48 per cent and 47 per cent for the 1900s birth cohort. A less marked trend is apparent for entry into supervisory work. See Mills and Savage (1998).
6 This cultural idiom continues to have significant sway even today, and often in work environments very different from those of handicraft production. Consider the way that the Higher Education Funding Council (HEFC) judges the research carried out in British universities through a research assessment exercise in which the research 'output' of members of staff is given major significance.
7 The most ambitious claims are made here by E.P. Thompson (1995), who sees apprenticeship as fundamental to plebian culture in eighteenth-century Britain and roots early trade union development around these concerns.
8 Though the PSI survey includes foremen among manual labour, and also seems to somewhat overrepresent manual labourers among white men.
9 In 1992 44 per cent of skilled manual and 34 per cent of semi- and unskilled manual workers expected internal progression compared to 44 per cent of professional and managerial workers (Gallie *et al.* 1998: 68).
10 In 1992 47 per cent of professionals were unionized compared to 43 per cent of technical and supervisory workers, 42 per cent of skilled manual workers and 37 per cent of semi- and unskilled workers (Gallie *et al.* 1998: 103).

11 These figures probably underestimate the extent of socially-oriented work since 21 per cent of men and women are listed as having an 'other' or 'no' main activity.

12 In an interesting paper, Adkins (1999) points to the continuation, indeed development, of practices whereby women are incorporated as wives into organizational hierarchies – for instance, where families are hired in toursim to run particular units. If this example is generalizable then it would suggest a serious qualification to the argument developed here, but my view is that trends are working towards the individualized employment of professionals and managers.

13 It would be interesting to consider the symbolism of those tied housing schemes which remain, for instance among university vice-chancellors. It is likely that this represents a further demarcation of élite groups from 'rank and file' academics.

14 Consider the declining use of hoods and gowns by university academics, the way that senior railway staff do not wear uniform, and even the informalization of dress among the clergy.

Conclusion: class formation *and* social change

The aim of this book has been to investigate whether the idea of class continues to have a useful role in showing the interconnectedness of various social processes in contemporary capitalism. Each chapter has considered a specific aspect of class analysis, Part 1 by discussing research in established areas of class analysis, and Part 2 in a more speculative mode. Each chapter has tried to be informative and even-handed in indicating where the idea of class may have a role, as well as where it may not. The aim of this concluding chapter is to link together the various arguments into a coherent statement about class formation in contemporary capitalism.

I begin with some general comments about the kind of class analysis that I have tried to recover in this book. The second and third sections consider the working class and middle class respectively, but in a way which sees them relationally. In the second section I examine the dissolution of the working class as a salient cultural identifier and argue that this has far-reaching implications for the dynamics of class relations more generally. In the third section I examine debates about middle-class formation, taking up themes I have myself considered in earlier work (Savage *et al.* 1992; Butler and Savage 1995). Here I seek to show how the dissolution of the working class has left the way open for new kinds of individualized, fragmented, middle-class cultures to gain greater presence.

What kind of class analysis?

At the start of this book I noted that class analysis has become defined as an increasingly technical and arcane specialism within sociology that finds it more difficult to engage with the broader issues of the 'sociological imagination'. I will therefore have achieved one major objective if I have convinced readers that it is still possible to discuss a multitude of empirical questions, theoretical perspectives and pressing social and political issues in the name of class. I have sought to recover a mode of class analysis that is not concerned to legislate in the name of class, by defining a particular true way of doing class analysis, but which defines it as an intellectual space which allows synthesis and dialogue between otherwise disparate research traditions.

My book exemplifies this approach in practice. I have attempted to link together diverse themes that are rarely interrelated in contemporary sociology – social mobility, economic inequality, class cultures, work relations, and so on – not around an overarching meta-narrative (whether this be globalization, post-Fordism, post-modernism, disorganized capitalism or whatever), but around more mediated, complex, local and ambivalent social processes. Seeing these as linked by class does not involve 'reducing' these disparate processes to a crude class base – for as I have endeavoured to argue, there clearly are no class actors in contemporary capitalism – but allows us to tease out contingent interconnections and threads running between different topics.

I wish to emphasize three general points about class analysis threaded through this book. The first is class analysis as a mode of *cultural* analysis. The traditional strengths of class analysis, I argued in Chapter 2, lay precisely in interest in the cultural meaning of class. In recent years, however, the apparent weakness of class consciousness, together with formidable theoretical problems in specifying an adequate theory of class and identity have eclipsed this current of thought. Some proponents of class analysis have tried to regroup by placing class analysis on a different footing, relying on a deductive brand of RAT that attempts to bracket-out questions of culture. I have argued that despite the attractions of this approach it is ultimately deficient. It leads to intellectual closure which draws up more narrowly defined research questions and internalized debates that do not interest those outside the (ever dwindling) research tradition of class analysis. Furthermore, it is unconvincing. It is simply not possible to bracket-out issues of culture from class analysis. Even RAT needs to operate with some notion of the cultural frames used by people as they make their rational decisions. My suggestion is that we can actually take the evident fragility of class awareness and identity, which I discussed in Chapters 2 and 5, as a starting point for contemporary inquiry. The ambivalence of class awareness is not an embarrassing fact that should discomfit proponents of class analysis but can be treated as an issue that points the way to telling issues of contemporary importance concerning individualized cultures, reflexivity, and the culture of ambivalence. Bourdieu's class theory allows us the best way of developing an appropriate starting point for this venture.

My second major claim is that we need to eradicate a mode of class analysis which takes the working class as the *archetypal* class. Due to the legacy of Marx, class analysis has emerged, as David Lockwood (1995) has noted, as part of the 'problematic of the proletariat'. Even though class analysis broadened its remit, much unconscious intellectual baggage has been weighed down with the image of manual labour and its liberatory potential as the palimpsest of class. This is particularly true with respect to the idea that class cultures are inherently collective. To concede this idea is to give the game away. If they are seen in this way, any indication of individualism, of whatever type, can be taken as evidence of the decline of class. The work of Giddens and Beck, despite its apparent novelty, is simply an intellectual unravelling of a long-standing intellectual assumption that has existed for 30 years or more. I have argued that we should see class cultures as contingently embodying forms of individualized identities which operate relationally. Thereupon we can find a way of reclaiming, albeit cautiously, the contemporary relevance of class analysis.

One of the central endeavours of this book has been to sketch out, albeit highly speculatively, what an individuated mode of class analysis might look like. When I discussed economic inequality in Chapter 3 and social mobility in Chapter 4 I emphasized how class 'rewards', in terms of claims to superior income, or advantaged positions in the division of labour, should not simply be seen as due to the working of an overarching class structure, or the rational workings of markets, but should be seen as the accomplishment of individuals, drawing on diverse resources. Subsequent advantages and disadvantages that accrue are cumulative over a person's life. Class structures are instantiated in people's lives. This argument is compatible with that of Giddens (1984), Goldthorpe and Marshall (1992), Bauman (1988) and Bourdieu (1984) and offers a more promising way of situating class analysis within contemporary theoretical debates than sterile attempts to map out class structures.

My concern about taking the working class as the archetype for class analysis goes beyond this issue of collective class cultures. I have pointed out in various parts of the book that contemporary class analysis, for all its sophistication, frequently still takes the idea of working-class formation as its bedrock. Thus Goldthorpe's argument that class formation is organized around the static attachment of people to class positions (Chapter 4) is premised on the traditional organization of working-class cultures of manual labour, rather than on more dynamic modes of middle-class formation. The very concept of occupation as the unit of class analysis, enshrined in different ways by Goldthorpe and Wright, depends on the idea that class formation is organized around occupations rather than around structured trajectories through occupational positions – as in the idea of the middle-class 'career'.

This leads on to my third general point concerning the importance of time and space in class analysis. I should start by noting that I am in a broad measure of agreement with many sociologists who emphasize the scope and scale of contemporary social change. Most chapters of this book have endeavoured to indicate that fundamental social changes are taking place. Chapter 6, in particular, offers an account of the changing nature of employment that suggests that there has been a major redefinition of the culture of work. One of the adjustments I have endeavoured to make to class analysis in many of the preceding chapters has been to strip away its residual tendency to cast its formulation of class in static and fixed terms, both in terms of time (where persistence of class is emphasized) and space (where class is defined in fixed spatial terms, with reference to national boundaries).[1] I am bothered by attempts, such as those of Goldthorpe and Marshall (1992) to defend claims of the value of class analysis in terms of arguments about the persistence of class. This is not because I disagree that there have been important continuities, but because if class is cast in these terms we are ultimately writing its obituary, since in this case the value of the concept depends on denying social change. The challenge for class analysis must be to allow a way of examining change as well as persistence, and this means providing a more fluid approach to the subject.

A class-focused account of social change has major advantages over the kinds of 'epochal', or apocalyptic, veiws of change that currently abound in the sociological literature. There are now any number of competing theories of change, all of which offer versions of a 'before' and 'after' narrative (though in some of these accounts the 'after' is left hanging as an account of the 'not-before'). This brand of sociological analysis has many dangers. It can conflate cyclical with epochal trends.[2] It involves imposing narrative closure onto a more complex social field. Most current accounts ground their arguments in macro-structural developments, such as globalization (Giddens 1991), new modes of capital accumulation (Harvey 1989), new types of technology, seen as an exogenous to social relations (Castells 1996, 1997), and so on. Of course, each of these perspectives can, and has been, contested (see for instance Hirst and Thompson 1997 for the case of globalization). Their main problem is that they locate the springs of change away from the proximate worlds of everyday life and over-stress the systemic logic of social change (see Latour 1994). A reformulated class analysis, I argue, offers a means of understanding social change in a more mediated fashion, as a particular articulation of local and global, individual and social dynamics, as a phenomenon that is attuned to continuity and change and recognizes our complicity in the social world we inhabit.

Central to this book is the idea that understanding social change lies in the restructuring of social class relations, rather than in the grand narratives of 'globalization', 'individualization' and so forth. These latter ideas should be seen for what they are, which is projects for intellectual grandizement. Bauman's (1988: 25) reflections on the politics of intellectuals are highly pertinent here:

> People who theorize models of society are intellectuals – on the whole distinguished members, yet members nontheless, of the knowledge class ... as intellectuals, they are engaged in a specific kind of productive practice which constitutes the mode of existence, a position in relation to the rest of society, and understanding of their own role, and a set of ambitions ... entirely of their own. It is these practices, perspectives and ambitions which are processed and theorized into model images of society.

Bauman has illuminatingly observed that the declining relevance of intellectuals for capitalist reproduction (which he relates to the rise of consumerism) frees them from their legislative role. It permits them to stand back from the need to directly account for their own writings to non-academics. One of the consequences of this, it might be said, is a temptation to write accounts of social change that locate the sources of change as beyond anyone's direct purview or control, so assuaging any remaining moral conscience of academics. This problem can only be redressed by recognizing people's situatedness in a world that is changing around them.

This approach to class analysis may well sound relatively innocuous. In fact, it is no easy matter to provide an account of social change that avoids the 'grand narrative' approach. Indeed, although Bauman is well aware of the problems of intellectual aggrandizement he himself falls prey to the temptation to provide overly simplistic historical sketches in his account of the decline of the work ethic and the rise of consumerism as one of the dominant motifs of contemporary social and cultural change (e.g. Bauman 1982, 1998; see the critical discussion in Warde 1994). Let me end this book by spelling out more specifically how a more modest account of social and cultural change might be constructed.

The dissolution of the working class

My central argument is that much contemporary social and cultural change can be seen as the fallout from the eradication of the defining role of the working class in British culture. This argument will be disputed and I want to clarify it immediately by distancing myself from three claims that might be viewed as integral to an argument such as this.

First, I am not claiming that working-class occupations have disappeared or that people do not occupy proletarian social relationships. There is no gainsaying the decline of manual employment in the UK, but there is good evidence that much routine service work exhibits all the qualities of 'proletarian' employment (see Esping-Andersen 1994 who refers to the 'new service proletariat'). Significant numbers of people continue to carry out recognizably 'working-class' jobs.

Second, I am not arguing that the working class has become middle class, as in old arguments much discussed in the 1960s about 'embourgoisement'. The dissolution of the working class simply refers to a process of working-class decomposition, and makes no reference to them becoming middle class. As I suggest in the next section, the middle class continues to be defined in exclusive ways and there is little evidence that it has become significantly democratized.

Third, I distance myself from claims about the fading of the golden, collective, working-class 'community'. My argument in no way depends on making realist claims about the development and sociological centrality of a 'traditional working class'. It is well established that the twentieth-century working class was fractured by gender, ethnicity, region, industry and occupation. My point is different. The idea of the working class served as a moral identifier for much of the twentieth century, and thereby helped consolidate a particular notion of the working class which had sustained importance in British society.

My argument is that the link between dominant notions of individuality and citizenship, which in Britain were closely associated with the working class, has in recent years been sundered, with profound social and cultural implications. As I argued in Chapter 6, notions of individuality, autonomy and mastery were tied in the British case to the image of the adult male worker who had learned a trade, and thereby was beholden to no one. In many respects I draw here on a very old argument. This is the claim I traced in part in Chapter 1 that the working class has historically played a key role in defining the nature of citizenship in Britain. Its most important forebear is of course Edward Thompson (1963) who has pointed to the umbilical link between the formation of the working class and the development of modern citizenship, and we might add by way of extension, modern views of individual identity itself.

More recently, historiography has indicated how this process has impacted on middle class formation. Wahrman (1994) (following, in some ways, the arguments of Briggs 1960) points out that in Britain middle-class identities emerged after those of the working class and therefore developed in reaction to them. He points out further that discursive strategies to stablize middle-class identities fluctuated in the early nineteenth century, but that the crucial moment for fixing the idea of the middle class was around the time of the 1832 Reform Act. Wahrman argues that the 'middle class' became espoused as a new interest group which needed political representation. By this means, it was possible to extend the franchise without using a democratic rationale to do so. The middle class were essentially consolidated into a status based, territorial and exclusive culture. Thus, as Thompson argues, it was the working class who were left, almost by default, as the bearers of modern democratic politics, not just through their role in political movements, but through their role in defining cultures of independence and respectability. This idiom had many overtones: it drew on ideas of the 'Freeborn Englishman', and articulated notions of masculine independence. Some historians (Joyce 1990) have seen it as a populist rather than a class based culture, but what is striking is the way that this culture was embedded in work cultures of autonomy, craft and skill. Notions of independence were related to ideas of male mastery of a trade.

It is the collapse of this association between dignity, individuality and the working class that is fundamental to understanding contemporary social and cultural change. The corrosion of these cultural associations has a number of facets, discussed in various parts of this book, and especially in Chapter 6. To summarize, working-class work has been constructed as 'servile' work, which no longer bestows mastery or autonomy on its incumbent. Manual labour is increasingly carried out by young men (Egerton and Savage 2000) rather than by adult men, with the result that it loses its connotations as the bearer of independent adult male status. There is also evidence that the traditional association between reaching adult status and full wage-earning capacity has faded: manual workers now take a longer time to reach their maximum earning capacity.

Consequently I dispute Goldthorpe's arguments concerning the demographic maturity of the working class. Goldthorpe's claim is premised on observations about intergenerational mobility, which show that most manual men are the sons of manual fathers, and hence can be expected to share common cultural traits. However, this possibility is confounded by other processes. First, the extent of work life mobility means that significant numbers of manual workers move away from manual employment. Second, Goldthorpe does not adequately address issues of gender and ethnicity, and their potential role in fragmenting the working class. As I showed in Chapter 4, Goldthorpe's sampling strategy permits him to concentrate on heads of household, with the result that those doing shadow proletarian jobs – young workers, women who work part-time and so forth – are simply not considered. Furthermore, if the focus is broadened to include new kinds of proletarian service employment, then the picture changes. Many workers in these areas are transitory and have no fixed working-class situation. Many are female, and furthermore, the meaning of such work, which lies in dealing with and 'serving' clients, undermines the potential for proletarian work to carry the connotations of independence. Lastly, the deployment of ethnic minorities in proletarian employment means that there may be very different cultures of manual employment, confined to specific ethnic minorities rather than any binding together of different groups within the working class.

I have emphasized the importance of seeing working-class culture as historically powerful because of its articulation with individualistic motifs. It would be wrong, of course, to assume that this was inherently anti-collective: I am not trying to turn ideas of working-class collectivism on their head so much as to look at them from a different vantage point. The collectivism of the working class, which was in certain times and places considerable, depended on the recognition of the dignity and autonomy of individuals (though largely male individuals). This can be powerfully witnessed in the various self-help and mutual aid organizations characteristic of the working class (see Savage 1987), and can also be seen in trade union cultures, whose organization depended not on submerging individual identities into collective ones, but on interweaving individual identities into collective organization through rituals and processes that recognized the role of the individual within the collectivity. It follows that an important feature of contemporary change is the way that trade unions, the principal post-war embodiment of claims to worker autonomy and self-respect, have been largely eliminated from many areas of manufacturing and service employment. Trade unions have increasingly become the vehicles of professional, public sector workers, and embody the values of public service rather than manual worker autonomy. The role of the Labour movement has thereby changed. So, while class alignments in voting patterns do continue, though in an attenuated form (see the discussion in Evans 1999b), the working class has largely exited from the field of organized politics, which has become a field for the middle classes.

It is important to say a few words about divisions among the working class. The working class has always been divided, but traditionally along the axis of individuality. The distinction between rough and respectable (Klein 1965) differentiated those who could look after themselves, and who were self-reliant and autonomous, from those who, for one reason or another, could not. The recent debate about the existence of an underclass covers very similar terrain, and is not of fundamental importance to my argument, for even if the argument for an underclass is true, it is not clear that this is a new departure in British society. What is new, however, is the division between those manual workers whose conditions of employment are increasingly approximating those of the service class, and those whose conditions of employment are not. Although Evans and Mills (1998) demonstrate that it is considerably more likely that professionals and managers are employed on internal labour markets, a significant minority of manual workers also share this position, and hence have no necessary reason to perpetuate the manual culture of retaining independence from their employing organization. I noted in Chapter 3 how there is growing variation among manual occupations in pay levels, and signs that the age–wage curve is increasing. This is an indication of a fracturing of the association between independence and manual employment.

However, I have also argued, in Chapters 2 and 5, that if the working class has lost it central role in defining 'individuality', it retains a ghostly presence at the heart of British culture. Many people still claim working-class self-identification and the values of ordinariness and unpretentiousness continue to dominate, albeit without a firm anchoring in employment relations. While many people are attracted to 'working-class' self-identities, these are largely memories of old class identities, expressed in narrative form. The attraction lies not in the idea of working class-ness itself, but more in the anti-élitist and populist connotations that the term has historically possessed. It is still attractive for people to claim working-class roots, while nostalgic images of working class-ness continue to be important refrains in staking out 'ordinariness' (Beynon 1999). What this points to is a cultural frame floating free from its traditional historical anchor.

Middle-class formation in contemporary Britain

Debates about middle-class formation have in recent years centred around claims concerning the possible existence of a 'service class' (Goldthorpe 1982; Abercrombie and Urry 1983), or, by contrast, the idea that the middle classes are fractured along various axes, which in earlier work I have characterized (adapting Wright 1985) as assets of property, organization and cultural capital. The stakes between these different ways of conceiving middle-class formation only become clear when the middle classes are relationally defined with respect to the working class. Only when this is fully appreciated can we gain a framework for the analysis of contempoary middle-class formation.

The middle class historically emerged in Britain as a servile class. This concept is well captured by Goldthorpe's idea of the service class, in which professionals and managers are ultimately dependent on, and morally committed to, their employer. The culture of the middle class therefore involved the removal of men (and women) from the arena of autonomy and individuality characteristic of manual work. It entailed defining them as dependents of their employer. The particular contract at the heart of British middle-class formation, as Goldthorpe rightly recognizes, was the promise of secure employment and incremental rewards, so that individuals could accept that their interests would be protected by their employer, not by their own actions, as was the case for the working class. Servility involved removing the middle classes ritually from the world of independent manual labour and symbolic reinforcement of their dependent position within organizational hierarchies, as I discussed in Chapter 6.

I depart from Goldthorpe's analysis of the service class when more contemporary issues are considered, however. This is because the 'service relationship' has been fundamentally recast and the association between class and individuality has been transformed. I have argued that the meaning of 'career' and 'work' has been radically changed so that while historically manual workers had the autonomy to pursue their tasks and managers and professionals were servile dependants on their organization, the restructuring of employment has turned these definitions around. The activities of managers and professionals are defined in terms of their ability to be entrepreneurial, while manual work is an increasingly dependent status. Today, individuality is a property of the professional and managerial middle classes, while working-class independence is but a memory, albeit still a powerful and nostalgic one.

Of course, as Beck and Giddens remind us, new modes of individualization differ profoundly from older versions. In place of the ascriptive, gendered and aged notions of the autonomous and dignified individual who set limits to what he or she could do, new modes of individualization focus on the self-developmental and transformative capacities of the self. As I argued in Chapter 6 this culture is invested with a Faustian sense of risk-taking and the assertion of individuality through game playing. Whereas traditional modes of individuality involved defending the self from outside influence, new versions involve striving for more – a quest for self-fulfilment that can never be finally achieved.[3]

To adapt, perhaps clumsily, Berlin's (1969) distinction between positive and negative conceptions of freedom, working-class ideas adopted negative versions, and middle-class ideas adopted positive versions. We can here see why this new kind of individuality, rooted in new modes of work organization, tends to efface class while at the same time it reproduces modes of class inequality. Whereas traditional modes of individuality depended on defining clear class boundaries (as well as those of gender, ethnicty, status, etc.) and policed clear thresholds, newer modes of individuality do not refer to fixed thresholds since the individual pursues a project of the self in each new situation so that old games recede once they have been played.

These arrangements are amenable to capital accumulation as the competitive actions of these workers help to reproduce, more intensely, social inequality as firms restructure in capital-intensive ways. There has, then, in Britain been a profound remaking of the relationship between class and claims to individuality. Class is effaced in new modes of individualization, by the very people – mainly in professional and managerial ocupations – whose actions help reproduce class inequality more intensely. But class cannot be completely effaced. Class creeps back, surreptitiously, into various cultural forms, though often in oblique ways. Let me unpack the reasons for this by considering how this remaking of the middle classes is related to the structuring processes of property, organization and culture (Savage *et al.* 1992).

We should not think that clear and distinctive fractions of the middle class can be delineated, each drawing on a different kind of 'asset'. Here I would distance myself from my earlier formulations where I implied that particular occupational groups within the middle classes drew on particular ones of these three assets, a formulation which I think is wrong.[4] As Bourdieu has emphasized, it is the historical mutability and interconnectedness of these axes, and the conversion strategies adopted to change one kind of asset into another, which is key. I will briefly discuss each of the three assets.

The central role of property in contemporary class formation is discussed in Chapter 3. In a period of major capitalist expansion and transformation, property has proved an exceptionally important vehicle for the accumulation of economic rewards, through its *rentier* modes. Drawing on the arguments of Chapter 3 it is possible to distinguish three groups of people who rely on property. First, there is a very small group, the 'very wealthy', perhaps 1 per cent of the population, who can exclusively rely on property assets for their income. Second, there is a group of around half the population who derive very little from property in any form. Third, there is a middle class, who rely predominantly on income from employment, but who also gain significant additional income from property, in the form of housing equity and investments. The important point is that for this group the ability to gain additional income from property depends on their employment relations, and in this respect property assets are only a significant axis of class formation for the very wealthy. Property assets remain the main dividing line between the wealthy and the rest. However, because of their relative invisibility, this does not necessarily turn into a clear class division between upper class and the middle and working class.

It follows that the roles of organization and culture remain crucial for contemporary middle-class formation. The question of cultural capital is a complex one, and Bourdieu's analysis cannot be straightforwardly imposed in the British context. One of the themes of this book has been the enduring vitality of populist, working-class motifs in British culture, with their enduring criticisms of cultural élitism. This general point is useful in considering the fortunes of the professional middle classes which in earlier work I saw as the leading repository of cultural distinction, the occupational group best able to translate its cultural distinction into privileged occupational position. There is recent evidence that professional hegemony has been challenged in various ways, though the association between educational achievement and class privilege remains strong. Professional identities are interesting in that they are the most salient of any contemporary class-like identifier. People voluntarily identify as being 'professionals', or espouse the idea that people should act 'professionally'.[5]

Traditionally, claims to professionalism draw on arguments about social exclusivity (see, for the case of the USA, Brint 1993, and more generally Savage *et al.* 1992). The contemporary appeal of professional identification undoubtedly continues to draw indirectly on this idea, but more importantly it appears to register an individual's claim to be able to act responsibly. This is associated with Bauman's recognition of the unbounded milieux of the contemporary individidual. In an uncertain world, reference to professionalism provides some kind of an anchor. It is a claim that – whatever the temptations of a particular work, or even social, setting might be – a person has the embodied traits to act responsibly and within recognized limits. This is a model of professionalism less directly concerned with distinguishing itself from those below it, and more concerned with dealing responsibly with those alongside it. Professionalism, I suggest, has taken over from manual labour the dominant motif of contemporary individuality, allowing individuals to claim distinction (through being well rewarded for the delivery of professional services) while also being 'ordinary' (in that the skills of the professional rely less on social background and more on work competences). The continued centrality of professionalism in class formation depends less on its claims to uphold cultural and social hierarchy, and more on its ability to powerfully appeal to how the individual in contemporary capitalism should 'be'. We should not, however, mistake the economic and social privelege that continues to be associated with professionalism. Professionalism is but one example of the emergence of cultural repertoires that use populist refrains to enhance their cultural privelege.

Let me now turn to consider the importance of organization. Much recent research demonstrates the weak position of those who rely exclusively on their standing in organizational hierarchies for their superior life chances. Corporate restructuring has entailed the stripping out of career managers and 'organization' men, and a growing reliance on outside appointments and consultants. However, while organizational hierarchy conveys fewer rewards in itself, organizational centrality remains fundamental for class formation. I have deployed the idea of organizational centrality (in preference to the rather formalist idea of the organizational asset) to note how those culturally central to organizations are best able to take advantages of restructuring. Halford *et al.* (1997) show how it is those who are able to position themselves at the centres of organizational cultures who often benefit from rapid promotion as organizations restructure. Organizational centrality is key to being able to reap additional rewards of property. Securing organizational centrality depends less on ascribed characteristics either of people (e.g. having a certain gender) or organizational position, and depends more on the ability of individuals to show they have the right 'approach'. These points illustrate the profound ambivalences in contemporary middle-class formation. In some respects it appears that anyone can become part of the middle class given the right 'perspective' or 'outlook', yet the distribution of the relevant traits is in fact highly unequal, and thereby social inequality is reproduced. Once again direct reference to class is effaced at the same time that class inequalities are more powerfully reproduced.

A good example of the implications of this new form of middle-class formation is posed by considering the role of gender and ethnicity. Whereas traditionally both organization and cultural axes distinguished directly on these lines, with women being formally barred from gaining access to educational qualifications and positions within managerial hierarchies, this is no longer the case. However, women and members of many ethnic minorities continue to be under-represented in advantaged positions. As Halford *et al.* (1997) argue this is because the individualized traits desired in managerial positions continued to be premised on the cultures and lifestyles of white men. Thus those women and members of ethnic minorities who do take up the challenge of participating in professional and managerial hierarchies differentiate themselves from most of their peers and so flout their claims to 'ordinariness', which I have shown have powerful cultural appeal. Thus it is quite possible that inequalities are reproduced by organizational processes that appear to be formally open to all.

New modes of class formation therefore efface direct reference to class while they simultaneously reproduce class inequality – indeed, in more naked and marked forms. The fading of hierarchy, both at the bottom (in terms of the dissolution of the working class) and at the top (through the invisibility of property assets) places greater emphasis on a culture of 'looking sideways'. Rather than there being clear hierarchical class thresholds, the focus switches to the different ways in which middle class individuals act. Rather than seeing middle-class division as tied either to structural divisions within the middle class (for instance between professionals and managers), or as the product of individual differences of temperament, taste, etc., we can see it more as different motifs expressing different kinds of middle-class lifestyle.

In Chapter 4 I referred to the distinction between the core and liminal middle class, and this distinction usefully establishes the tension at the heart of middle-class culture. The contemporary middle class sees itself as an 'open' class. But if it is entirely open, then how do people know they have succeeded? How can you 'flip' between being ordinary and distinctive at the same time? We can see middle-class differentiation as a cultural oscillation within the lives of middle-class individuals, rather than an oscillation between firm distinctive middle-class blocs defined in terms of occupational groups (though in some circumstances such differences may be identified). Contemporary modes of class awareness do not draw contrasts hierarchically, between those above and below, but they draw the gaze sideways, between yourself and others in similar situations. They draw attention to the need to develop a lifestyle that is both able to be exclusive and yet is ordinary, simultaneously. The impossibility of achieving such a closure helps explain the dynamism of contemporary cultural forms.

In conclusion, it seems apposite to reaffirm the ambivalence of social class. In one important sense we have reached the end of a long era in which working-class culture served to anchor social identity. Now, the very nature of class analysis needs to be rethought. One of the causes of this restructuring is the fact that the processes producing class inequality can actually now continue in a more naked way than before. While people were routinely aware of class cultures they had more scope to act on and change them: the history of socialist and Labour politics is about the partial success in modifying capitalism in a more egalitarian direction. However, the remaking of the culture of individualization transforms the cultural landscape. It allows the creation of a society that routinely reproduces social inequality at the same time as deflecting the attention of its key agents sideways rather than upwards and downwards, so making the issue of social inequality largely 'invisible' and somehow 'uninteresting'. If there is still a role for class analysis it is to continue to emphasize the brute realities of social inequality and the extent to which these are constantly effaced by a middle class, individualized culture that fails to register the social implications of its routine actions.

Notes

1 Substantively I have said relatively little about space in this book. An early chapter which applied the arguments of this book to the remaking of urban space has had to be sacrificed to keep the book within its word limit. I will return to the issue of space in future publications.

2 Consider for instance the way that some of Lash and Urry's (1987) prognostications about the character of disorganized capitalism now look rather dated as the balance of power has shifted decisively to large corporate interests.

3 We can still learn from Weber's (1948) influential account of the inability of modern individuals to be happy in 'Science as a Vocation'. Bauman's recent work covers similar territory (Bauman 1998).

4 To be precise, theoretically, I made it clear that assets did not map neatly onto occupational groupings, but in several chapters an equation between professionals, relying on cultural assets, and managers relying on organizational assets, was made (Savage *et al.* 1992). As I explained, given British historical development, it was contingently the case that these occupations did tend to draw on these distinct assets, but I would now emphasize further that these distinctions are unusual.

5 One of the most interesting facets of this is the way that significant numbers of those (and especially women) who advertise in 'lonely hearts' sections of newspapers and magazines describe themselves as 'professionals'. On 29 January 1999 16 (out of 71) women advertising in *The Guardian* stated that they were either professional, or seeking a professional male. Thirteen others gave an occupational identifier, all of which were professional or semi-professional. Eleven men (out of 78) mentioned they were professional. It is striking that only one person volunteered a manual occupation. It is equally striking that although there are almost as many managers as professionals in the labour market, virtually no one seems to think of describing themselves to a potential mate in these terms.

Bibliography

Abbott, A. and Hrycak, A. (1990) 'Measuring resemblances in sequence data', *American Journal of Sociology*, 96, 144–85.

Abercrombie, N. and Urry, J. (1983) *Capital, Labour and the Middle Classes*. London: Allen & Unwin.

Abercrombie, N. and Warde, A. (1994) *Contemporary British Society*. Cambridge: Polity.

Abercrombie, N., Hill, S. and Turner, B. (eds) (1980) *The Dominant Ideology Thesis*. London: Allen & Unwin.

Abrams, M. and Rose, R. (1960) *Must Labour Lose?* Harmondsworth: Penguin.

Adkins, L. (1999) 'Community and economy: a retraditionalisation of gender?', *Theory, Culture and Society*, 16(1), 119–38.

Adonis, A. and Pollard, S. (1997) *A Class Act: The Myth of Britain's Classless Society*. London: Penguin.

Aglietta, M. (1987) *A Theory of Capitalist Regulation: The US Experience*. London: Verso.

Alexander, J. (1994) *Contemporary Social Theory*. London: Verso.

Amin, A. (1994) *Post-Fordism: A Reader*. Oxford: Blackwell.

Anderson, P. (1976) *Considerations on Western Marxism*. London: New Left Books.

Anderson, P. (1980) *Arguments Within English Marxism*. London: Verso.

Anthias, F. (1998) 'Rethinking social divisions: some notes towards a theoretical framework', *Sociological Review*, 46(3), 505–35.

Arrighi, A. (1994) *The Long Twentieth Century*. London: Verso.

Ashton, D. (1990) *Restructuring the Labour Market: The Implications for Youth*. Basingstoke: Macmillan.

Atkinson, A.B. (ed.) (1980) *Wealth, Income and Inequality*. Oxford: Clarendon.

Atkinson, A.B. and Harrison, A.J. (1980) 'Trends in the distribution of wealth in Britain', in A.B. Atkinson (ed.) *Wealth, Income and Inequality*. Oxford: Clarendon.

Atkinson, A.B., Gordon, J. and Harrison, A.J. (1989) 'Trends in the share of top wealth holders in Britain, 1923–81', *Oxford Bulletin of Economics and Statistics*, 51, 315–31.

Bales, K. (1994) 'Charles Booth's survey of *Life and Labour of the People of London*', in M. Bulmer, K. Bales and K.K. Sklar (eds) *The Social Survey in Historical Perspective, 1880–1940*. Cambridge: Cambridge University Press.

Banks, J., Dilnot, A. and Low, H. (1996) 'Patterns of financial wealth-holding in the United Kingdom', in J. Hills (ed.) *New Inequalities: The Changing Distribution of Income and Wealth in the United Kingdom*. Cambridge: Cambridge University Press.

Baran, P. and Sweezy, P. (1966) *Monopoly Capital: An Essay in the American Economic and Social Order*. New York: Monthly Review.

Barrett, M. (1980) *Women's Oppression Today*. London: Verso.

Batstone, E. (1984) *Working Order: Workplace Industrial Relations Over Two Decades*. Oxford: Blackwell.

Bauman, Z. (1982) *Memories of Class: The Pre-history and After-life of Class*. London: Routledge.

Bauman, Z. (1988) *Legislators and Interpreters*. Cambridge: Polity.

Bauman, Z. (1989) *Modernity and the Holocaust*. Cambridge: Polity.

Bauman, Z. (1991) *The Ambivalences of Modernity*. Cambridge: Polity.

Bauman, Z. (1993) *Post-modern Ethics*. Cambridge: Polity.

Bauman, Z. (1998) *Work, Consumerism and the New Poor*. Buckingham: Open University Press.

Beck, U. (1992) *The Risk Society*. London: Sage.

Beck, U. and Beck-Gersheim, E. (1996) 'Individualization and "precarious freedoms": perspectives and controversies in a subject oriented sociology', in P. Heelas, S. Lash and P. Morris (eds) *Detraditionalisation*. Oxford: Blackwell.

Beck, U., Giddens, A. and Lash, S. (1994) *Reflexive Modernisation: Politics, Tradition and Aesthetics in the Modern Social Order*. Cambridge: Polity.

Belchem, J. and Kirk, N. (eds) (1997a) *Languages of Labour*. Aldershot: Ashgate.

Belchem, J. and Kirk, N. (1997b) 'Introduction', in J. Belchem and N. Kirk (eds) (1997a) *Languages of Labour*. Aldershot: Ashgate.

Bell, D. (1973) *The Coming of Post-industrial Society: A Venture in Social Forecasting*. London: Heinemann.

Benjamin, W. (1973) *A Lyric Poet in the Era of High Capitalism*. London: Verso.

Berle, A. and Means, G. (1968) *The modern corporation and private property*. New York: Harcourt, Brace, Janovich.

Berlin, I. (1969) *Four Essays on Liberty*. Oxford: Oxford University Press.

Beynon, H. (1975) *Working for Ford*. Harmondsworth: Penguin.

Beynon, H. (1991) *A Tale of Two Industries: The Contraction of Coal and Steel in the North East*. Buckingham: Open University Press.

Beynon, H. (1999) 'A classless society?', in H. Beynon and P. Glavanis (eds) *Patterns of Social Inequality*. London: Longman.

Beynon, H. and Blackburn, R.M. (1972) *Perceptions of Work: Variations Within a Factory*. Cambridge: Cambridge University Press.

Beynon, H. and Glavanis, P. (eds) (1999) *Patterns of Social Inequality*. London: Longman.

Biernacki, R. (1995) *The Fabrication of Labor: Germany and Britain, 1640–1914*. Berkeley, CA: University of California Press.

Blackburn, R.M. and Prandy, K. (1997) 'The reproduction of social inequality', *Sociology*, 31(3), 491–509.

Blau, P. and Duncan, O.D. (1967) *The American Occupational Structure*. New York: Wiley.

Bond, R. and Saunders, P. (1999) 'Routes of success: influences on the occupational attainment of young British males', *British Journal of Sociology*, 50(2), 217–50.

Booth, A.L. and Satchell, S.E. (1995) 'Apprenticeships and job tenure', *Oxford Economic Papers*, 46, 676–95.

Booth, C. (1903) *Life and Labour of the People in London*. London: Macmillan.

Boudon, R. (1982) *The Crisis in Sociology: Problems of Sociological Epistemology*. London: Macmillan.

Bourdieu, P. (1984) *Distinction*. London: Routledge.

Bourdieu, P. (1994) *The State Nobility*. Cambridge: Polity.

Bourdieu, P. and Passeron, C. (1973) *Reproduction in Education, Society and Culture*. London: Sage.

Bourdieu, P. and Wacquant, L. (1999) 'On the cunning of imperialist reason', *Theory, Culture and Society*, 16(1), 41–58.

Bourdieu, P. *et al.* (1999) *The Weight of the World*. Oxford: Blackwell.

Bourke, J. (1994) *Working Class Culture in Britain 1860–1960: Gender, Class and Ethnicity*. London: Routledge.

Boyer, R. (1990) *The Regulation School: A Critical Introduction*. New York: Columbia University Press.

Bradley, H. (1989) *Men's Work, Women's Work*. Oxford: Blackwell.

Bradley, H. (1996) *Fractured Identities: Changing Patterns of Inequality*. Cambridge: Polity.

Bradley, H. (1999) *Gender and Power in the Workplace*. Basingstoke: Macmillan.

Breen, R. and Goldthorpe, J.H. (1999) 'Class inequality and meritocracy: a critique of Saunders and an alternative analysis', *British Journal of Sociology*, 50(1), 1–27.

Breen, R. and Rotman, D.B. (1995) *Class Stratification: A Comparative Perspective*. London: Harvester Wheatsheaf.

Breiger, R. (1990) *Social Mobility and Social Structure*. Cambridge: Cambridge University Press.

Brenner, R. (1976) 'Agrarian class structure and economic development in pre-industrial Europe', *Past and Present*, 70, 30–74.

Briggs, A. (1960) 'The language of class in early nineteenth century England', in A. Briggs and J. Saville (eds) *Essays in Labour History in Memory of G.D.H. Cole*. London: Macmillan.

Brint, S. (1993) *In An Age of Experts*. Berkeley, CA: University of California Press.

Brook, L. (ed.) (1992) *British Social Attitudes, Cumulative Sourcebook: The First Six Surveys*. Aldershot: Gower.

Brown, R. (1994) 'Cultural capital and social exclusion: some observations on recent trends in education, employment and the labour market', *Work, Employment and Society*, 9(1), 29–51.

Brown, R. and Scase, D. (1994) *Higher Education and Corporate Realities: Class, Culture and the Decline of Graduate Careers*. London: UCL Press.

Brubaker, R. (1984) *The Limits of Rationality: An Essay in the Social and Moral Thoughts of Max Weber*. London: Allen & Unwin.

Bryson, B. (1996) '"Anything but heavy metal": Symbolic exclusion and musical dislikes', *American Sociological Review*, 61, 844–99.

Buckingham, A. (1999) 'Is there an underclass in Britain?', *British Journal of Sociology*, 50(1), 49–75.

Bulmer, M. (ed.) (1975) *Working Class Images of Society*. London: Routledge.

Bulmer, M., Bales, K. and Sklar, K.K. (1994a) 'The social survey in historical perspective', in M. Bulmer, K. Bales and K.K. Sklar (eds) *The Social Survey in Historical Perspective, 1880–1940*. Cambridge: Cambridge University Press.

Bulmer, M., Bales, K. and Sklar, K.K. (1994b) *The Social Survey in Historical Perspective, 1880–1940*. Cambridge: Cambridge University Press.

Burtless, G. (1995) 'International trade and the rise of earnings inequality', *Journal of Economic Literature*, 33, 800–16.

Butler, D. and Stokes, D. (1969) *Political Change in Britain*. London: Macmillan.

Butler, T. and Savage, M. (eds) (1995) *Social Change and the Middle Classes*. London: UCL Press.

Burawoy, M. (1985) *The Politics of Production*. London: Verso.

Callon, M. (ed.) (1998a) *The Law of the Markets* (*Sociological Review* Monograph). Oxford: Blackwell.

Callon, M. (1998b) 'Introduction: the embeddedness of economic markets in economics', in M. Callon (ed.) *The Laws of the Markets*. Oxford: Blackwell.

Campbell, A. (1980) *Archetypal Proletarians*. London: Routledge.

Cannadine, D. (1990) *The Decline and Fall of the British Aristocracy*. New Haven, CT: Yale University Press.

Carchedi, G. (1977) *On the Economic Identification of Social Classes*. London: Routledge.

Carling, A. (1990) *Social Division*. London: Verso.

Casey, C. (1995) *Work, Self and Identity After Industrialism*. London: Routledge.

Castells, M. (1996) *The Rise of the Network Society*. Oxford: Blackwell.

Castells, M. (1997) *The Power of Identity*. Oxford: Blackwell.

Castells, M. (1998) *The End of the Millennium*. Oxford: Blackwell.

Caygill, H. (1998) *Walter Benjamin: The Colour of Experience*. London: Routledge.

CCCS (Centre for Contemporary Cultural Studies) (Women's Studies Group) (1978) *Women Take Issue: Aspects of Women's Subordination*. London: Hutchinson.

CCCS (Centre for Contemporary Cultural Studies) (1982) *The Empire Strikes Back*. London: Hutchinson.

Chandler, A.P. (1990) *Scale and Scope: The Dynamics of Industrial Capitalism*. London: Bellknap.

Chaney, D. (1997) *Lifestyles*. London: Routledge.

Clark, J., Modgil, C. and Modgil, S. (eds) (1990) *John H. Goldthorpe: Consensus and Controversy*. London: Falmer.

Clark, T., Lipset, S.M. and Rempel, M. (1993) 'The declining political significance of social class', *International Sociology*, 8(3), 293–316.

Clegg, S. (1989) *Modern Organisation*. London: Sage.

Cockburn, C. (1983) *Brothers: Male Dominance and Technical Change*. London: Pluto.

Cockburn, C. and Ormrod, S. (1993) *Gender and Technology in the Making*. London: Sage.

Cohen, G.A. (1978) *Karl Marx's Theory of History: A Defence*. Oxford: Oxford University Press.

Cohen, G.A. (1988) *History, Labour and Freedom: Themes from Marx*. Oxford: Clarendon.

Cohen, G.A. (1995) *Self-ownership, Freedom and Equality*. Cambridge: Cambridge University Press.

Collier, A. (1994) *Critical Realism*. London: Verso.

Collins, R. (1975) *Conflict Sociology: Towards an Explanatory Science*. London: Academic Press.

Cowell, F., Jenkins, S.P. and Litchfield, J.A. (1996) 'The changing shape of the UK income distribution', in J. Hills (ed.) *New Inequalities: The Changing Distribution of Income and Wealth in the United Kingdom*. Cambridge: Cambridge University Press.

Coxon, A.P. and Jones, C.L. (1978) *The Images of Occupational Prestige*. London: Macmillan.

Coxon, A.P. and Jones, C.L. (1979) *Class and Hierarchy: The Social Meaning of Occupations*. London: Macmillan.

Crewe, I. and Sarlvik, B. (1983) *Decade of Dealignment*. Cambridge: Cambridge University Press.

Crompton, R. (1986) 'Women and the service class', in R. Crompton and M. Mann (eds) *Gender and Social Class*. Cambridge: Polity.

Crompton, R. (1995) 'Women's employment and the "middle class"', in T. Butler and M. Savage (eds) *Social Change and the Middle Classes*. London: UCL Press.

Crompton, R. (1997) *Women and Work in Modern Britain*. Oxford: Oxford University Press.

Crompton, R. (1998) *Class and Stratification*, 2nd edn. Cambridge: Polity.

Crompton, R. and Gubbay, J. (1977) *Economy and Class Structure*. London: Macmillan.

Crompton, R. and Sanderson, K. (1990) *Gendered Jobs and Social Change*. London: Unwin Hyman.

Crompton, R., Devine, F., Savage, M. and Scott, J. (eds) (2000) *Renewing Class Analysis*. (*Sociological Review* Monograph). Oxford: Blackwell.

Crouch, C. and Heath, A.F. (1992) *Social Research and Social Reform: Essays in Honour of A.H. Halsey*. Oxford: Clarendon.

Currie, R. and Hartwell, R.M. (1965) The Making of the English Working Class, *Review of Economic History*, xviii(3).

Dahrendorf, R. (1959) *Class and Class Conflict in Industrial Society*. London: Routledge & Kegan Paul.

Dale, A. and Egerton, M. (1997) *Highly Educated Women: evidence from the National Child Development Study* (research paper no. 25). London: HMSO.

Dandeker, C. (1988) *Surveillance, Power and Modernity: Bureaucracy and Discipline*. Cambridge: Polity.

Danzinger, S. and Gottschalk, P. (eds) *Uneven Tides: Rising Inequality in America*. New York: Russell Sage Foundation.

Darlington, R. (1994) *The Dynamics of Workplace Unionism: Shop Steward Organisation in Three Merseyside Plants*. London: Mansell.

Davis, K. and Moore, W.E. (1945) 'Some principles of stratification', reprinted in L.A. Coser and B. Rosenberg (eds) *Sociological Theory* (1964). London: Collier-Macmillan.

Deleuze, G. and Guttari, F. (1982) *A Thousand Plateaus: Capitalism and Schizophrenia*. London: Athloen.

Dennis, D., Henriques, F. and Slaughter, C. (1956) *Coal is Our Life*. London: Tavistock.

Devine, F. (1992a) *Affluent Workers Revisited*. Edinburgh: Edinburgh University Press.

Devine, F. (1992b) 'Social identities, class identity and political perspectives', *Sociological Review*, 40, 229–52.

Devine, F. (1998a) 'Class analysis and the stability of class relations', *Sociology*, 32(1), 23–42.

Devine, F. (1998b) *Social Class in Britain and America*. Edinburgh: Edinburgh University Press.

Devine, F. and Savage, M. (2000) 'Conclusion: renewing class analysis', in R. Crompton, F. Devine, M. Savage and J. Scott (eds) *Renewing Class Analysis* (*Sociological Review* Monograph). Oxford: Blackwell.

Dex, S. (1987) *Women's Occupational Mobility*. Basingstoke: Macmillan.

Doeringer, P.B. and Piore, M.J. (1971) *Internal Labour Markets and Manpower Analysis*. Lexington, MA: D.C. Heath.

du Gay, P. (1996) *Consumption and Identity at Work*. London: Sage.

Duncan, S. (1990) 'Do house prices rise that much? a dissenting view', *Housing Studies*, 5(3), 192–208.

Eder, K. (1993) *The New Politics of Class*. London: Sage.

Edgell, S. (1992) *Class*. London: Routledge.

Edgell, S., Hetherington, K. and Warde, A. (eds) (1996) *Consumption Matters* (*Sociological Review* Monograph). Oxford: Blackwell.

Egerton, M. and Savage, M. (2000) 'Age stratification and class formation: a longitudinal study of the social mobility of young men and women', *Work, Employment and Society*, 14(1): 23–50.

Eley, G. and Nield, K. (1995) 'Starting over: the present, the post-modern, and the moment of social history', *Social History*, 20(3), 355–64.

Elliott, R.F. and Dufus, K. (1996) 'What has been happening to pay in the public service sector of the British economy? Developments over the period 1970–1992', *British Journal of Industrial Relations*, 34(1), 51–87.

Elster, J. (1985) *Making Sense of Marx*. Cambridge: Cambridge University Press.

Erickson, B. (1996) 'Culture, class, and connections', *American Journal of Sociology*, 102(1), 217–51.

Erikson, R. (1984) 'Social class of men, women and families', *Sociology*, 18, 500–14.

Erikson, R. and Goldthorpe, J.H. (1992) *The Constant Flux*. Oxford: Clarendon.

Esping-Andersen, G. (1990) *The Three Worlds of Welfare Capitalism*. Oxford: Clarendon.

Esping-Andersen, G. (ed.) (1994) *Changing Classes*. London: Sage.

Evans, G. (1992a) 'Testing the validity of the Goldthorpe class schema', *European Sociological Review*, 8(3), 211–32.

Evans, G. (1992b) 'Is Britain a class-divided society? A re-analysis and extension of Marshall *et al.*'s study of class consciousness', *Sociology*, 26(2), 233–58.

Evans, G. (1997) 'Political ideology and popular beliefs about class and opportunity: evidence from a survey experiment', *British Journal of Sociology*, 48(2), 450–70.

Evans, G. (1999a) 'On tests of validity and social class: why Prandy and Blackburn are wrong', *Sociology*, 32(1), 189–202.

Evans, G. (ed.) (1999b) *The End of Class Politics?* Oxford: Clarendon.

Evans, G. and Mills, C. (1998) 'Identifying class structure: a latent class analysis of the criterion related and construct validity of the Goldthorpe class schema', *European Sociological Review*, 14, 87–106.

Featherstone, M. (1988) 'Lifestyle and consumer capitalism', *Theory, Culture and Society*, 4(1), 55–70.

Feinstein, C. (1996) 'The equalising of wealth in Britain since the second world war', *Oxford Review of Economic Policy*, 12(1), 96–105.

Fernie and Metcalf (1995) 'Participation, contingent pay, representation and workplace performance: evidence from Great Britain, *British Journal of Industrial Relations*, 33(3): 375–415.

Fielding, A.J. (1995) 'Migration and middle class formation in England and Wales, 1981–1991', in T. Butler and M. Savage (eds) *Social Change and the Middle Classes*. London: UCL Press.

Fischer, C.S., Hout, M., Jankowski, M.S. *et al.* (1996) *Inequality by Design: Cracking the Bell Curve Myth*. Princeton, NJ: Princeton University Press.

Fiske, J. (1987) *Understanding Popular Culture*. London: Unwin Hyman.

Fogelman, K. (1983) *Growing Up in Great Britain*. London: Macmillan.

Foucault, M. (1966) *The Order of Things*. London: Tavistock.

Foucault, M. (1977) *Discipline and Punish*. Harmondsworth: Penguin.

Fowler, B. (1996) *Pierre Bourdieu and Cultural Theory: Critical Investigations*. London: Sage.

Fox, P. (1994) *Class Fictions: Shame and Resistance in the British Working Class Novel*, Durham, NC: Duke University Press.

Gallie, D. (1983) *Social Inequality and Class Radicalism in France and Britain*. Cambridge: Cambridge University Press.

Gallie, D. (1988) *Employment in Britain*. Oxford: Blackwell.

Gallie, D., Marsh, C. and Vogler, C. (eds) (1994) *Social Change and the Experience of Unemployment*. Oxford: Clarendon.

Gallie, D., Penn, R. and Rose, M. (eds) (1996) *Trade Unionism in Recession*. Oxford: Clarendon.

Gallie, D., White, M., Cheng, Y. and Tomlinson, M. (1998) *Restructuring the Employment Relationship*. Oxford: Clarendon.

Geroski P., Gregg, P. and Desjonqueres, T. (1995) 'Did the retreat of UK trade unionism accelerate during the 1990–1993 recession?', *British Journal of Industrial Relations*, 33(1), 35–42.

Gershuny, J. (1994) 'Post-industrial career structures in Britain', in G. Esping-Andersen (ed.) *Changing Classes*. London: Sage.

Gershuny, J. (2000) 'Social position from narrative data', in R. Crompton, F. Devine, M. Savage and J. Scott (eds) *Renewing Class Analysis* (*Sociological Review* Monograph). Oxford: Blackwell.

Gerteis, J. and Savage, M. (1998) 'The salience of class in Britain and America: a comparative analysis', *British Journal of Sociology*, 49(2), 252–74.

Giddens, A. (1971) *Capitalism and Modern Social Theory*. Basingstoke: Macmillan.
Giddens, A. (1973) *The Class Structure of the Advanced Societies*. Basingstoke: Macmillan.
Giddens, A. (1984) *The Constitution of Society*. Cambridge: Polity.
Giddens, A. (1990) *The Consequences of Modernity*. Cambridge: Polity.
Giddens, A. (1991) *Modernity and Self-identity*. Cambridge: Polity.
Giddens, A. (1994) *Beyond Left and Right*. Cambridge: Polity.
Giddens, A. (1997) *Sociology*, 3rd edn. Cambridge: Polity.
Giddens, A. and Stanworth, P. (eds) (1974) *Elites and Power in British Society*. Cambridge: Cambridge University Press.
Gilloch, G. (1996) *Myth and Metropolis*. Cambridge: Polity.
Gilroy, P. (1987) *There Ain't No Black in the Union Jack: The Cultural Politics of Race and Nation*. London: Unwin Hyman.
Ginn, J., Arber, S., Brannen, J. *et al.* (1996) 'Feminist failures: a reply to Hakim on women's employment', *British Journal of Sociology*, 47(1), 167–77.
Glass, D.V. (1954) *Social Mobility in Britain*. London: Routledge.
Glucksmann, M. (1990) *Women Assemble*. London: Routledge.
Glucksmann, M. (1999) *Cottons and Casuals*, mimeo. Durham: British Sociological Association Press.
Glyn, A. and Miliband, D. (eds) *Paying for Inequality: The Economic Cost of Social Injustice*. London: Rivers Oram.
Goldthorpe, J.H. (1964) 'Social stratification in industrial societies', in P. Halmos (ed.) *The Development of Industrial Societies* (*Sociological Review* Monograph). London: Routledge.
Goldthorpe, J.H. (1982) 'On the service class: its formation and future', in A. Giddens and G. MacKenzie (eds) Social Class and the Division of Labour. Basingstoke: Macmillan.
Goldthorpe, J.H. (1983) 'Women and class analysis: in defence of the conventional view', *Sociology*, 17, 465–78.
Goldthorpe, J.H. (1988) 'The intellectuals and the working class', in D. Rose (ed.) *Social Stratification and Economic Change*. London: Hutchinson.
Goldthorpe, J.H. (1990) 'A response', in J. Clark, C. Modgil and S. Modgil (eds) *John H. Goldthorpe: Consensus and Controversy*. London: Falmer.
Goldthorpe, J.H. (1991) 'The uses of history in sociology: reflections of some recent tendencies', *British Journal of Sociology*, 42(2), 211–31.
Goldthorpe, J.H. (1995) 'The service class revisited', in T. Butler and M. Savage (eds) *Social Change and the Middle Classes*. London: UCL Press.
Goldthorpe, J.H. (1996) 'Class analysis and the reorientation of class theory: the case of persisting differentials in educational attainment', *British Journal of Sociology*, 45, 481–505.
Goldthorpe, J.H. (1998) 'Rational action theory for sociology', *British Journal of Sociology*, 49(2), 167–92.
Goldthorpe, J.H. and Erikson, R. (1992) *The Constant Flux: A Study of Class Mobility in Industrial Societies*. Oxford: Clarendon.
Goldthorpe, J.H. and Hope, K. (1974) *The Social Grading of Occupations: A New Approach and Scale*. Oxford: Clarendon.
Goldthorpe, J.H. and Lockwood, D. (1968a) *The Affluent Worker: Political Attitudes and Behaviour*. Cambridge: Cambridge University Press.
Goldthorpe, J.H. and Lockwood, G. (1968b) *The Affluent Worker: Industrial Attitudes and Behaviour*. Cambridge: Cambridge University Press.
Goldthorpe, J.H. and Lockwood, D. (1969) *The Affluent Worker in the Class Structure*. Cambridge: Cambridge University Press.

Goldthorpe, J.H. and Marshall, G. (1992) 'The promising future of class analysis', *Sociology*, 26, 381–400.

Goldthorpe, J.H., with Llewellyn, C. and Payne, C. (1980) *Social Mobility and the Class Structure in Modern Britain*. Oxford: Clarendon.

Goldthorpe, J.H., with Llewellyn, C. and Payne, C. (1987) *Social Mobility and the Class Structure in Modern Britain*, 2nd edn. Oxford: Clarendon.

Goodman, A. and Webb, S. (1994) 'For richer, for poorer: the changing distribution of income in the UK, 1961–91', *Fiscal Studies*, 15(3), 64–86.

Goodman, A., Johnson, P. and Webb, S. (1997) *Income Inequality in the UK*. Oxford: Oxford University Press.

Gordon, D., Edwards, R.C. and Reich, M. (1975) *Labour Market Segmentation*. Lexington, MA: D.C. Heath.

Gosling, A. and Meghir, C. (1994) 'What has happened to men's wages since the mid 1960s?', *Fiscal Studies*, 15(4), 63–87.

Gospel, H. (1998) 'The revival of apprenticeship training in Britain', *British Journal of Industrial Relations*, 3, 435–58.

Gregson, N. (1991) 'On the (ir)relevance of structuration theory', in D. Held and J. Thompson (eds) *Structuration Theory*. Cambridge: Polity.

Grey, C. (1994) 'Career as projection of the self and labour process discipline', *Sociology*, 28, 479–98.

Grusky D. and Sorenson, J. (1998) 'Can class analysis be salvaged?' *American Journal of Sociology*, 103(5), 1187–234.

Gubbay, J. (1997) 'A Marxist critique of Weberian class analysis', *Sociology*, 31(1), 143 52.

Habermas, J. (1984) *Towards a Theory of Communicative Action*. Boston, MA: MIT Press.

Hacking, I. (1983) *Representing and Intervening: Introductory Topics in the Philosophy of Nature*. Cambridge: Cambridge University Press.

Hakim, C. (1995) 'Five feminist myths about women's employment', *British Journal of Sociology*, 46(3), 429–55.

Halford, S. and Savage, M. (1995a) 'Restructuring organisations, changing people: gender and restructuring in banking and local government', *Work, Employment and Society*, 9(1), 97–122.

Halford, S. and Savage, M. (1995b) 'The bureaucratic career: demise or adaptation?', in T. Butler and M. Savage (eds) *Social Change and the Middle Classes*. London: UCL Press.

Halford, S. and Savage, M. (1997) 'Rethinking restructuring; agency, identity, and embodiment', in R. Lee and J. Wills (eds) *Geographies of Economies*. London: Edward Arnold.

Halford, S., Savage, M. and Witz, A. (1997) *Gender, Career and Organisations: Current Developments in Banking, Nursing and Local Government*. Basingstoke: Macmillan.

Hall, J. and Jones, D.C. (1950) 'The social grading of occupations', *British Journal of Sociology*, 1, 31–5.

Hall, S. (1980) *Culture, Media, Language: Working Papers in Cultural Studies, 1972–1979*. London: Unwin Hyman.

Hall, S. and Jacques, M. (1987) *New Times: The Changing Face of Politics in the 1990s*. London: Lawrence & Wishart.

Hall, S. and Jefferson, S. (eds) (1975) *Resistance through Rituals*. London: Hutchinson.

Halle, D. (1993) *Inside Culture: Art and Class in the American Home*. Chicago: University of Chicago Press.

Halsey, A.H., Heath, A. and Ridge, J. (1980) *Origins and Destinations*. Oxford: Clarendon.

Hamnett, C. (1995) 'Home ownership and the middle classes', in T. Butler and M. Savage (eds) *Social Change and the Middle Classes*. London: UCL Press.

Hamnett, C. and Seavers, J. (1996) Home ownership, housing wealth and wealth distribution in J. Hills (ed.) *New Inequalities: The Changing Distribution of Income and Wealth in the United Kingdom*. Cambridge: Cambridge University Press.

Hanlon, G. (1999) 'Professionalism and expertise: service class politics and the redefinition of professionalism', *Sociology*, 32(1), 43–63.

Hannah, L. (1983) *The Rise of the Corporate Economy*, 2nd edn. London: Methuen.

Harkness, S., Machin, S. and Waldfogel, J. (1996) 'Women's pay and family incomes in Britain, 1979–91', in J. Hills (ed.) *New Inequalities: The Changing Distribution of Income and Wealth in the United Kingdom*. Cambridge: Cambridge University Press.

Harrison, R. (ed.) (1978) *Independent Collier: The Coal Miner as Archetypal Proletarian Reconsidered*. New York: St Martin's Press.

Harrop, M. (1980) 'Popular conceptions of mobility', *Sociology*, 14(1), 89–98.

Harvey, D. (1989) *The Condition of Post-modernity*. Oxford: Blackwell.

Hearn, J. and Parkin, W. (1987) *'Sex' at 'Work': The Power and Paradox of Organisation Sexuality*. Brighton: Harvester.

Heath, A.F. (1981) *Social Mobility*. London: Fontana.

Heath, A.F. (2000) 'Social mobility', in A.H. Halsey (ed.) *Social Trends in British Society*. Oxford: Clarendon.

Heath, A.F. and Cheung, J. (1999) *Education and Social Mobility*, mimeo.

Heath, A.F., Jowell, R. and Cartice, J. (1985) *How Britain Votes*. Oxford: Pergamon.

Heelas, P., Lash, S. and Morris, P. (eds) (1996) *Detraditionalisation*. Oxford: Blackwell.

Hennis, W. (1988) *Max Weber: Essays in Reconstruction*. London: Allen & Unwin.

Hennock, E.P. (1976) 'Poverty and social theory: the experience of the 1880s', *Social History*, 1, 67–91.

Hennock, E.P. (1987) 'The measurement of poverty: from the metropolis to the nation, 1880–1920', *Economic History Review*, 40(2), 208–27.

Herrnstein, R.J. and Murray, C. (1993) *The Bell Curve*. New York: Free Press.

Hetherington, K. (1998) *Expressions of Identity*. London: Sage.

Hills, J. (ed.) (1996) *New Inequalities: The Changing Distribution of Income and Wealth in the United Kingdom*. Cambridge: Cambridge University Press.

Hindess, B. and Hirst, P. (1975) *Pre-capitalist Modes of Production*. London: Routledge & Kegan Paul.

Hirst, P. and Thompson, G. (1997) *Globalisation in Question: The International Economy and the Possibility of Governance*. Cambridge: Polity.

Hobsbawm, E. (1980) *The Forward March of Labour Halted*. London: Lawrence & Wishart.

Hochschild, A. (1985) *The Managed Heart: The Commercialisation of Human Feeling*. Berkeley, CA: University of California Press.

Hoggart, R. (1956) *The Uses of Literacy*. Harmondsworth: Penguin.

Hollowell, P. (1968) *The Lorry Driver*. London: Routledge.

Honneth, A. (1984) The Struggle for Recognition. Boston, MA: MIT Press.

Iganski, P. and Payne, G. (1999) 'Socio-economic restructuring and employment: the case of ethnic minority groups', *British Journal of Sociology*, 2(June), 195–216.

Imada, T. (1998) 'Class consciousness in Japan', paper presented at 'The Future of the Middle Classes' Conference, Paris.

Ingham, G. (2000) 'Financial institutions and social polarisation', in R. Crompton, F. Devine, M. Savage and J. Scott (eds) *Renewing Class Analysis* (*Sociological Review* Monograph). Oxford: Blackwell.

Ingleheart, R. (1990) *Culture Shift in Advanced Industrial Society*. Princeton, NJ: Princeton University Press.

Irwin, S. (1995) *Rights of Passage: Social Change and the Transition from Youth to Adulthood*. London: UCL Press.

Jay, M. (1973) *The Dialectical Imagination: A History of the Frankfurt School and the Institute of Social Research, 1923–1950*. Boston, MA: Little, Brown.

Jenkins, R. (1991) *Pierre Bourdieu*. London: Routledge.

Jessop, R. (1990) 'Regulation theories in retrospect and prospect', *Economy and Society*, 19(2), 153–216.

Jessop, R., Bonnet, K. and Ling, T. (1988) *Thatcherism: a Tale of Two Nations*. Cambridge: Polity.

Johnson, P. and Sears, G. (1995) 'Pensioner income inequality', *Fiscal Studies*, 16(4), 69–94.

Johnson, R. (1978) 'Thompson, Genovese and socialist-humanist history', *History Workshop Journal*, 6, 79–100.

Johnson, R. (1979) 'Introduction', in Centre for Contemporary Cultural Studies, *Unpopular Education: Schooling and Social Democracy in England Since 1944*. London: Hutchinson.

Johnson, T. (1990) 'Ideology and action in the work of John Goldthorpe', in J. Clark, C. Modgil and S. Modgil (eds) *John H. Goldthorpe: Consensus and Controversy*. London: Falmer.

Joseph Rowntree Foundation (1995a) *Inquiry into Income and Wealth*, vol. 1. York: Joseph Rowntree Foundation.

Joseph Rowntree Foundation (1995b) *Inquiry into Income and Wealth*, vol. 2. York: Joseph Rowntree Foundation.

Joyce, P. (ed.) (1987) *The Historical Meanings of Work*. Cambridge: Cambridge University Press.

Joyce, P. (1990) *Visions of the People*. Cambridge: Cambridge University Press.

Joyce, P. (1993) 'The imaginary discontents of social history: a note of response to Mayfield and Thorne, and Lawrence and Taylor', *Social History*, 18(1), 81–5.

Joyce, P. (1994) *Democratic Subjects: The Self and the Social in 19th Century England*. Cambridge: Cambridge University Press.

Joyce, P. (1995) 'The end of social history?', *Social History*, 20(1), 73–92.

Kavanagh, D. (1990) 'Ideology, sociology and the strategy of the British Labour party', in J. Clark, C. Modgil and S. Modgil (eds) *John H. Goldthorpe: Consensus and Controversy*. London: Falmer.

Kelly, W. (1998) 'Mainstream consciousness and Japanese culture', paper presented at 'The Future of the Middle Classes' Conference, Paris.

Kelsall, R.K. (1955) *Higher Civil Servants in Great Britain*. London: Routledge.

Kirk, N. (1994) 'History, language, ideas and post-modernism: a materialist view', *Social History*, 19(2), 221–40.

Klein, J. (1965) *Samples from English Culture*. London: Routledge.

Kumar, K. (1995) *From Post-industrial to Post-modern Society: New Theories of the Contemporary World*. Oxford: Blackwell.

Laclau, E. and Mouffe, C. (1985) *Hegemony and Socialist Strategy*. London: Verso.

Lamont, M. (1992) *Money, Morals and Manners: The Culture of the French and American Upper Class*. Chicago: Chicago University Press.

Lash, S. (1994) 'Reflexive modernisation', in U. Beck, A. Giddens and S. Lash (eds) *Reflexive Modernisation: Politics, Tradition and Aesthetics in the Modern Social Order*. Cambridge: Polity.

Lash, S. and Urry, J. (1987) *The End of Organised Capitalism*. Cambridge: Polity.

Lash, S. and Urry, J. (1994) *Economies of Signs and Spaces*. London: Sage.

Latour, B. (1994) *We Have Never Been Modern*. Oxford: Blackwell.

Lawrence, J. (1998) *Representing the People*. Cambridge: Cambridge University Press.

Lawrence, J. and Taylor, M. (1993) 'The poverty of protest: Gareth Stedman Jones and the politics of language – a reply', *Social History*, 18(1), 1–15.

Lee, D. and Turner, B. (eds) (1996) *Conflicts About Class: Debating Inequality in Late Industrialism*. London: Longman.

Leslie, D. and Pu, Y. (1996) 'What caused rising earning inequality in Britain? Evidence from time series, 1970–1993', *British Journal of Industrial Relations*, 34(1), 111–30.

Lipietz, A. (1987) *Mirages and Miracles: the Crises of Global Fordism*. London: Verso.

Lissenburgh, S. and Bryson, A. (1996) *The Returns of Graduation*. London: HMSO.

Littler, C. (1982) *The Development of the Labour Process in Capitalist Society: A Comparative Analysis*. London: Heinemann.

Lockwood, D. (1958) *The Blackcoated Worker: A Study in Class Consciousness*. London: Allen & Unwin.

Lockwood, D. (1964) 'System integration and social integration', in G.K. Zollschan and W. Hirsh (eds) *Explorations in Social Change*. London: Routledge and Kegan Paul.

Lockwood, D. (1966) 'Sources of variation in working class images of society', *Sociological Review*, 14, 249–63.

Lockwood, D. (1988) 'The weakest link in the chain? Some comments on the Marxist theory of action', in D. Rose (ed.) *Social Stratification and Economic Change*. London: Hutchinson.

Lockwood, D. (1992) *Solidarity and Schism: The Problem of Disorder in Durkheimian and Marxist Sociology*. Oxford: Clarendon.

Lockwood, D. (1995) 'Marking out the middle class(es)', in T. Butler and M. Savage (eds) *Social Change and the Middle Classes*. London: UCL Press.

Lockwood, D. (1996) 'Civic integration and class formation', *British Journal of Sociology*, 47(3), 531–50.

Longhurst, B.J. and Savage, M. (1996) 'Social class, consumption and the influence of Bourdieu: some critical issues', in S. Edgell, K. Hetherington and A. Warde (eds) *Consumption Matters* (*Sociological Review* Monograph). Oxford: Blackwell.

Ludtke, A. (1982) 'Dig where you stand', in R. Samuel (ed.) *People's History and Socialist Theory*. London: Routledge.

Lukes, S. (1971) *Power: A Radical View*. Basingstoke: Macmillan.

Lupton, T. (1963) *On the Shop Floor: Two Studies of Industrial Organisation and Output*. Oxford: Pergamon.

Lury, C. (1995) *Consumer Culture*. Oxford: Blackwell.

Lury, C. (1996) *Consumer Culture*, 2nd edn. Oxford: Blackwell.

Lury, C. (1998) *Prosthetic Culture*. London: Routledge.

Lyotard, J-F. (1979) *The Post-modern Condition*. Manchester: Manchester University Press.

Lyotard, J-F. (1984) *The Post-modern Condition: A Report on Knowledge*. Manchester: Manchester University Press.

McDowell, L. (1997) *Capital Culture: Gender at Work in the City*. Oxford: Blackwell.

Machin, S. (1996) 'Wage inequality in the UK', *Oxford Review of Economic Policy*, 12(1), 47–64.

McKenna, F. (1980) *The Railway Worker, 1840–1970*. London: Faber & Faber.

McKibbin, R. (1998) *Classes and Cultures: England, 1918–1951*. Oxford: Clarendon.

MacKinlay, A. and Starkey, K. (eds) (1998) *Foucault, Management and Organisation Theory*. London: Sage.

Mann, M. (1970) 'The social cohesion of liberal democracy', *American Journal of Sociology*, 35, 423–39.

Mann, M. (1973) *Consciousness and Action Amongst the Western Working Class*. Basingstoke: Macmillan.

Marcuse, H. (1964) *One Dimensional Man: Studies in the Ideology of Advanced Industrial Society*. London: Routledge & Kegan Paul.

Marsden, D. and Richardson, R. (1994) 'Performing for pay? The effects of "merit pay" on motivation in the public sector', *British Journal of Industrial Relations*, 32, 2.

Marshall, G. (1988) 'Some remarks on the study of working class consciousness', in
   D. Rose (ed.) *Social Stratification and Economic Change*. London: Hutchinson.

Marshall, G. (1997) *Repositioning Class*. London: Sage.

Marshall, G. and Firth, D. (1999) 'Social mobility and personal satisfaction', *British
   Journal of Sociology*, 50(1), 28–48.

Marshall, G., Newby, H., Rose, D. and Vogler, C. (1988) *Social Class in Modern Britain*.
   London: Hutchinson.

Marshall, G., Roberts, S. and Burgoyne, C. (1994) 'Social class and underclass in Britain
   and America', *British Journal of Sociology*, 47(1), 22–44.

Marshall, G., Swift, A. and Roberts, S. (1997) *Against the Odds? Social Class and Social
   Justice in Industrial Societies*. Oxford: Clarendon.

Marshall, T.H. (1950) *Citizenship and Social Class: and Other Essays*. Cambridge: Cambridge University Press.

Martin, B. (1994) 'Understanding class segmentation in the labour market: an empirical study of earnings determination in Australia', *Work, Employment and Society*,
   8, 357–85.

Martin, B. (1998) 'Knowledge, identity, and the middle class: from collective to individualized class formation?', *Sociological Review*, 46(4), 653–86.

Massey, D. (1994) *High-tech Fantasies: Science Parks in Society, Science and Space*. London:
   Routledge.

Massey, D. and Catalano, G. (1978) *Capital and Land: Land Ownership by Capital in
   Great Britain*. London: Edward Arnold.

Mayfield, D. and Thorne, S. (1992) 'Social history and its discontents: Gareth Stedman
   Jones and the politics of language', *Social History*, 17(2), 165–88.

Miles, A.G. (1999) *Occupational Change and Social Mobility in England, 1830–1914*.
   Basingstoke: Macmillan.

Miles, A.G. and Vincent, D. (eds) (1993) *Building European Society: Occupational Change
   and Social Mobility 1830–1914*. Manchester: Manchester University Press.

Miles, A.G., Savage, M. and Vincent, D. (1995) *Pathways and Prospects: The Development
   of the Modern Bureaucratic Career*, final report to ESRC.

Mills, C. (1995) 'Managerial and professional work histories', in T. Butler and M.
   Savage (eds) *Social Change and the Middle Classes*. London: UCL Press.

Mills, C. and Savage, M. (1998) 'Working class formation and work-life mobility in
   Britain, 1880–1950', paper presented for 2nd European Conference on History
   and Social Science, Amsterdam.

Mincer, J. (1980) 'Human capital and earnings', in A.B. Atkinson (ed.) *Wealth, Income
   and Inequality*. Oxford: Clarendon.

Modood, T., Berthoud, R., Lakey, J. *et al.* (1997) *Ethnic Minorities in Britain: Diversity
   and Disadvantage*. London: Routledge.

Moore, B. (1966) *The Social Origins of Dictatorship and Democracy*. Harmondsworth:
   Penguin.

More, C. (1980) *Skill and the English Working Class*. London: Croom Helm.

Morris, L. and Scott, J. (1994) 'The attenuation of class analysis? Some comments on
   "Social class and underclass in Britain and the USA"', *British Journal of Sociology*,
   47(1), 45–55.

Morris, T. (1996) 'Annual review article', *British Journal of Industrial Relations*, 33, 117–35.

Muller, W. (1990) 'Social mobility in industrial nations', in J. Clark, C. Modgil and
   S. Modgil (eds) *John H. Goldthorpe: Consensus and Controversy*. London: Falmer.

Munro, R. (1996) 'The consumption view of self: extension, exchange and identity', in
   S. Edgell, K. Heatherington and A. Warde (eds) *Consumption Matters* (*Sociological
   Review* Monograph). Oxford Blackwell.

Newby, H. (1975) *The Deferential Worker*. London: Penguin.

Noble, T. (1995) 'Occupational mobility and social change in Britain', *Hitotsubashi Journal of Social Studies*, 27, 65–90.

Pahl, R. (1984) *Divisions of Labour*. Oxford: Blackwell.

Pahl, R. (1989) 'Is the emperor naked?', *International Journal of Urban and Regional Research*, 13, 711–20.

Pahl, R. (1993) 'Does class analysis without class theory have a future?', *Sociology*, 27, 253–8.

Pakulski, J. and Waters, M. (1996) *The Death of Class*. London: Sage.

Pateman, C. (1988) *The Sexual Contract*. Cambridge: Polity.

Pawson, R. (1989) *A Measure for Measures*. London: Routledge.

Pawson, R. (1993) 'Social mobility', in D.J.H. Morgan and L. Stanley (eds) *Debates in British Sociology*. Manchester: Manchester University Press.

Payne, G. (1987a) *Mobility and Change in Modern Societies*. London: Macmillan.

Payne, G. (1987b) *Employment and Opportunity*. Basingstoke: Macmillan.

Payne, G. (1990) 'Social mobility in Britain: a contrary view', in J. Clark, C. Modgil and S. Modgil (eds) *John H. Goldthorpe: Consensus and Controversy*. London: Falmer.

Payne, G. (1992) 'Competing views of contemporary social mobility and social divisions', in R. Burrows and C. Marsh (eds) *Consumption and Class: Divisions and Change*. Basingstoke: Macmillan.

Penn, R. (1981) *Skilled Manual Workers in the Class Structure*. Cambridge: Cambridge University Press.

Perkin, H. (1968) *The Origins of Modern English Society, 1780–1980*. London: Routledge.

Petersen, R. and Kern, R. (1996) 'Changing highbrow taste: from snob to omnivore', *American Sociological Review*, 61, 900–07.

Phillips, B. and Taylor, A. (1980) 'Sex and skill', *Feminist Review*, 6, 79–83.

Polanyi, K. (1957) *The Great Transformation*. Boston, MA: Beacon.

Poovey, M. (1995) *Making a Social Body*. Boston, MA: Harvard University Press.

Postone, M. (1993) *Time, Labour and Social Domination: A Reinterpretation of Marx's Critical Theory*. Cambridge: Cambridge University Press.

Poulantzas, N. (1975) *Classes in Contemporary Capitalism*. London: Verso.

Prandy, K. (1997) 'Class and continuity in social reproduction: an empirical investigation', *British Journal of Sociology*, 46(2), 340–64.

Prandy, K., Stewart, A. and Blackburn, R.M. (1980) *Social Stratification and Occupations*. London: Macmillan.

Price, R. (1997) 'Postmodernism as theory and history', in J. Belchem and N. Kirk (eds) *Languages of Labour*. Aldershot: Ashgate.

Ray, L. and Reed, M. (1993) *Organising Modernity: New Weberian Perspectives on Work, Organisation and Society*. London: Routledge.

Read, D. (1998) *The Power of News: A History of Reuters*. Oxford: Clarendon.

Reay, D. (1998) 'Rethinking social class: qualitative perspectives on class and gender', *Sociology*, 32(2), 259–75.

Reid, I. (1989) *Class in Britain*. Cambridge: Polity.

Reid, I. (1998) *Class in Britain*, 2nd edn. Cambridge: Polity.

Renner, K. (1978) 'The service class', in T. Bottomore and P. Goode (eds) *Austro-Marxism*. Oxford: Oxford University Press.

Rex, J. (1968) *Key Problems of Sociological Theory*. London: Routledge

Rex, J. and Moore, R. (1967) *Race, Community and Conflict: A Study of Sparkbrook*. Oxford: Oxford University Press.

Roberts, E. (1984) *A Woman's Place*. Oxford: Blackwell.

Roemer, J. (1982) *A General Theory of Exploitation and Class*. Cambridge, MA: Harvard University Press.

Rose, D. (ed.) (1988) *Social Stratification and Economic Change*. London: Hutchinson.

Rose, D. (1997) *Constructing Classes: Towards a New Social Classification for the UK*. Swindon: ESRC.

Rose, M. (1996) 'Still life in Swindon: case studies of union survival and employer policy in a "Sunrise" labour market', in D. Gallie, R. Penn and M. Rose (eds) *Trade Unionism in Recession*. Oxford: Clarendon.

Rose, N. (1989) *Governing the Soul: The Shaping of the Private Self*. London: Routledge.

Rose, N. (1993) 'Government, authority and expertise in advanced liberalism', *Economy and Society*, 22(3), 283–99.

Rowntree, B.S. (1902) *Poverty: A Study of Town Life*, 2nd edn. London: Macmillan.

Rubinstein, W.D. (1981) *Men of Property*. London: Croom Helm.

Runciman, W.G. (1966) *Relative Deprivation and Social Justice*. Harmondsworth: Penguin.

Runciman, W.G. (1997) *A Treatise on Social Theory (Volume 3): Applied Social Theory*. Cambridge: Cambridge University Press.

Said, E. (1998) *Orientalism*. Harmondsworth: Penguin.

Saunders, P. (1989) 'Left write in sociology', *Network*, 44, 3–4.

Saunders, P. (1990a) *Social Class and Stratification*. London: Routledge.

Saunders, P. (1990b) *A Nation of Homeowners*. London: Allen & Unwin.

Saunders, P. (1995) 'Might Britain be a meritocracy?' *Sociology*, 29, 23–41.

Saunders, P. (1997) 'Social mobility in Britain', *Sociology*, 31(2), 261–88.

Saunders, P. and Harris, C. (1994) *Privatisation and Popular Capitalism*. Buckingham: Open University Press.

Savage, M. (1987) *The Dynamics of Working Class Politics: The Labour Movement in Preston, 1880–1940*. Cambridge: Cambridge University Press.

Savage, M. (1993) 'Career mobility and class formation: British banking workers and the lower middle classes', in A.G. Miles and D. Vincent (eds) *Building European Society: Occupational Change and Social Mobility 1830–1914*. Manchester: Manchester University Press.

Savage, M. (1994) 'Class analysis and its futures', *Sociological Review*, 42(3), 531–48.

Savage, M. (1996a) 'Space, networks, and class formation', in N. Kirk (ed.) *Social Class and Marxism: Challenges and Defences*. Aldershot: Scholar.

Savage, M. (1996b) 'Social mobility and the survey method: a critical analysis', in D. Bertaux and P. Thompson (eds) *Pathways to Social Class: Qualitative Approaches to Social Mobility*. Oxford: Clarendon.

Savage, M. (1998) 'Discipline, surveillance and the "career": employment on the Great Western Railway, 1833–1914', in A. MacKinlay and K. Starkey (eds) *Foucault, Management and Organization*.

Savage, M. (2000) 'Class and manual work cultures, 1945–1979', in J. McIlroy and N. Fishman (eds) *Trade Unionism in Britain, 1945–1979*. Aldershot: Scholar.

Savage, M. and Butler, T. (1995) 'Assets and the middle classes in contemporary Britain', in T. Butler and M. Savage (eds) *Social Change and the Middle Classes*. London: UCL Press.

Savage, M. and Egerton, M. (1998) 'Social mobility, individual ability and the inheritance of class inequality', *Sociology*, 31(4), 645–72.

Savage, M. and Miles, A. (1994) *The Remaking of the British Working Class, 1840–1940*. London: Routledge.

Savage, M. and Witz, A. (eds) (1992) *Gender and Bureaucracy* (*Sociological Review* Monograph). Oxford: Blackwell.

Savage, M., Barlow, J., Dickens, P. and Fielding, A.J. (1992) *Property, Bureaucracy and Culture: Middle Class Formation in Contemporary Britain*. London: Routledge.

Savage, M., Bearman, P. and Stovel, K. (forthcoming) 'Class formation and spatial networks: British bank workers 1880–1960', *International Journal of Urban and Regional Research*.

Savage, M., Bagnall, G. and Longhurst, B. (forthcoming) 'Ordinary, ambivalent and defensive: class identities in the north-west of England', *Sociology*.

Scase, D. (1992) *Class*. Buckingham: Open University Press.

Scott, J. (1982) *The Upper Class: Property and Privilege in Britain*. London: Macmillan.

Scott, J. (1991) *Who Rules Britain?* Cambridge: Polity.

Scott, J. (1996) *Stratification and Power: Structures of Class, Status and Command*. Cambridge: Polity.

Scott, J. (1997) *Corporate Business and Capitalist Elites*. Oxford: Oxford University Press.

Sennett, R. and Cobb, J. (1971) *The Hidden Injuries of Class*. London: Fontana.

Sennett, R. and Cobb, J. (1993) *The Hidden Injuries of Class*, 2nd edn. London: Fontana.

Shields, R. (1992) *Places on the Margin*. London: Routledge.

Skeggs, B. (1997) *Formations of Class and Gender*. London: Sage.

Small, S. (1994) *Racialised Barriers: The Black Experience in the US and England*. London: Routledge.

Smart, B. (1990) *Modern Conditions, Post-modern Controversies*. London: Routledge.

Smelser, N. (1962) *Social Change in the Industrial Revolution*. Aldershot: Gregg revivals.

Social Trends (1996) *Social Trends*, J. Church (ed.). London: HMSO.

Somers, M. (1992) 'Narrativity, narrative identity and social action: rethinking English working class formation', *Social Science History*, 16, 600–19.

Sorensen, A. (1986) 'Theory and methodology in social stratification', in U. Himmelstrand (ed.) *Sociology from Crisis to Science?* London: Sage.

Sorensen, A. (2000) 'Employment relations and class structure', in R. Crompton, F. Devine, M. Savage and J. Scott (eds) *Renewing Class Analysis (Sociological Review Monograph)*. Oxford: Blackwell.

Spencer, P. (1996) 'Reactions to a flexible labour market', in R. Jowell, J. Curtice, A. Park, L. Brook and K. Thomson (eds) *British Social Attitudes: The 13th Report*. Aldershot: Dartmouth and SCPR.

Stedman Jones, G. (1974) 'Working class culture and working class politics in London 1870–1900: notes on the remaking of a working class', *Journal of Social History*, 7, 460–507.

Stedman Jones, G. (1984) *Languages of Class*. Cambridge: Cambridge University Press.

Steiberg, M.W. (1997) 'A way of struggle: a reformulation and affirmation of E.P. Thompson's class analysis in the light of post-modern theories of language', *British Journal of Sociology*, 48(3), 471–92.

Stovel, K., Savage, M. and Bearman, P. (1996) 'Ascription into achievement: career systems in Lloyds Bank 1880–1940', *American Journal of Sociology*, 102, 358–99.

Strathern, M. (1991) *Partial Connections*. Savage, MD: Rowman & Littlefield.

Szreter, S. (1996) *Fertility, Class and Gender in Britain, 1860–1914*. Cambridge: Cambridge University Press.

Theodossiou, I. (1996) 'Promotions, job seniority, and product demand effects on earnings', *Oxford Economic Papers*, 48, 456–72.

Thompson, E.P. (1963) *The Making of the English Working Class*. London: Gollancz.

Thompson, E.P. (1965) 'The peculiarities of the English', *Socialist Register*, 2.

Thompson, E.P. (1978) *The Poverty of Theory*. London: Merlin.

Thompson, E.P. (1995) *Customs in Common*. Harmondsworth: Penguin.

Thornton, S. (1995) *Club Cultures: Music, Media and Sub-cultural Capital*. Cambridge: Polity.

Tilly, C. (1998) *Durable Inequalities*, Cambridge, MA: Harvard University Press.

Tolliday, S. and Zeitlin, J. (1987) *Shop Floor Bargaining and the State: Historical and Comparative Perspectives*. Cambridge: Cambridge University Press.

Tropp, A. (1957) *The Schoolteachers: The Growth of the Teaching Profession in England and Wales*. London: Heinemann.

Tunstall, J. (1962) *The Fishermen*. London: MacGibbon & Kee.

Turner, B. (1988) *Status*. Milton Keynes: Open University Press.

Turner, B. (1989) 'Ageing, politics and sociological theory', *British Journal of Sociology*, 40(4), 588–606.

Vanneman, R. and Canon, L.W. (1987) *The American Perception of Class*. Philadelphia, PA: Temple University Press.

Vernon, J. (1993) *Politics and the People: A Study of English Political Culture, c. 1815–1867*. Cambridge: Cambridge University Press.

Vernon, J. (1994) 'Who's afraid of the "linguistic turn"? The politics of social history and its discontents', *Social History*, 19(1), 81–98.

Vincent, D. (1990) *Poor Citizens: Poverty and the State in 20th Century Britain*. London: Longman.

Vincent, D. (1993) 'Mobility, bureaucracy and careers in early twentieth century Britain', in A.G. Miles and D. Vincent (eds) *Building European Society: Occupational Change and Social Mobility 1830–1914*. Manchester: Manchester University Press.

Wahrman, D. (1994) *Imagining the Middle Class: The Political Representation of Class in Britain*. Cambridge: Cambridge University Press.

Wajcman, J. (1998) *Managing Like a Man*. Cambridge: Polity.

Walby, S. (1986) *Patriarchy at Work*. Cambridge: Polity.

Warde, A. (1994) 'Consumers, identity and belonging: reflections on some theses of Zygmunt Bauman', in N. Abercrombie, R. Keat and N. Whiteley (eds) *The Authority of the Consumer*. London: Routledge.

Warde, A. (1997) *Consumption, Food and Taste: Culinary Antinomies and Commodity Culture*. London: Sage.

Warde, A., Martens, L. and Olsen, W. (1999) 'Consumption and the problem of variety: cultural omnivorousness, social distinction and eating out', *Sociology*, 33(1), 105–28.

Webb, P. and Farrell, D.M. (1999) 'Party members and ideological change', in G. Evans and P. Norris (eds) *Critical Elections: British Parties and Voters in Long-term Perspective*. London: Sage.

Weber, M. (1905) The protestant ethic and the spirit of capitalism, *Archiv fur Sozialwissenschaft und Sozialpolitik*, 20, 1–54.

Weber, M. (1947) *From Max Weber* (H. Gerth and C.W. Mills, eds). London: K. Paul Trench, Trubner & Co.

Weber, M. (1948) 'Science as a vocation', in H. Gerth and C. Wright Mills (eds) *From Max Weber*. London: Routledge.

Westergaard, J. (1970) 'The rediscovery of the cash nexus', in R. Miliband and J. Saville (eds) *The Socialist Register*. London: Merlin.

Westergaard, J. (1990) 'Social Mobility in Britain', in J. Clark, C. Modgil and S. Modgil (eds) *John H. Goldthorpe: Consensus and Controversy*. London: Falmer.

Westergaard, J. (1995) *Who Gets What? The Hardening of Class Inequality in the Late Twentieth Century*. Cambridge: Polity.

Westergaard, J. and Resler, H. (1975) *Class in a Capitalist Society*. Harmondsworth: Penguin.

White, J. (1983) *Campbell Bunk*. London: Routledge.

Whyte, W.H. (1957) *Organisation Man*. London: Cape.

Wiggershaus, R. (1994) *The Frankfurt School: Its History, Theories and Political Significance*. Cambridge: Polity.

Williams, R. (1956) *Culture and Society*. Harmondsworth: Penguin.

Williams, R. (1958) *The Long Revolution*. Harmondsworth: Penguin.

Williams, R. (1975) *Keywords*. London: Fontana.

Willis, P. (1975) *Learning to Labour: How Working Class Kids Get Working Class Jobs*. Farnborough: Saxon House.

Witz, A. (1992) *Patriarchy and Professions*. London: Routledge.

Witz, A. (1995) 'Gender and service class formation', in T. Butler and M. Savage (eds) *Social Change and the Middle Classes*. London: UCL Press.

Witz, A. and Savage, M. (1992) 'The gender of organizations', in M. Savage and A. Witz (eds) *Gender and Bureaucracy* (*Sociological Review* Monograph). Oxford: Blackwell.

Wood, E.M. (1986) *The Retreat from Class*. London: Verso.

Wright, E.O. (1978) *Class, Crisis and the State*. London: Verso.

Wright, E.O. (1985) *Classes*. London: Verso.

Wright, E.O. (ed.) (1989) *The Debate on Classes*. London: Verso.

Wright, E.O. (1996) *Class Counts*. Oxford: Oxford University Press.

Wright Mills, C. (1951) *White Collar*. New York: Oxford University Press.

Yeo, E. (1996) *The Contest for Social Science: Relations and Representations of Gender and Class*. London: Rivers Oram.

Young, K. (1992) 'Class, race and opportunity', in SCPR, *British Social Attitudes: The 9th report*. Aldershot: Dartmouth.

Young, M. and Willmott, P. (1956) 'The Hall-Jones Scale', *British Journal of Sociology*, 1, 317–45.

Zeitlin, M. (1974) 'Corporate ownership and control: the large corporation and the capitalist class', *American Journal of Sociology*, 79(5), 1073–119.

Zimmeck, M. (1988) 'The new women and the machinery of government: a spanner in the works', in R. McLeod, (ed.) *Government and Expertise: Specialists, Administrators and Professionals, 1860–1919*. Cambridge: Cambridge University Press.

Zweig, F. (1961) *The Worker in an Affluent Society: Family Life and Industry*. London: Heinemann.

Index